EMPIRICAL JUSTIFICATION

A PALLAS PAPERBACK

PAUL K. MOSER

Department of Philosophy, Loyola University of Chicago

EMPIRICAL
JUSTIFICATION

D. REIDEL PUBLISHING COMPANY

A MEMBER OF THE KLUWER ACADEMIC PUBLISHERS GROUP

DORDRECHT / BOSTON / LANCASTER / TOKYO

Library of Congress Cataloging in Publication Data

Moser, Paul K., 1957–
    Empirical justification.

    (Philosophical studies series in philosophy ; v. 34)
    Bibliography: p.
    Includes index.
    1.   Justification (Theory of knowledge)   2.   Empiricism.
3.   Epistemics.   4.   Rationalism.   I.   Title.   II.   Series.
BD212.M67   1985   121   85–24436
ISBN 90–277–2041–X
ISBN 90–277–2042–8 (pbk.)|

Published by D. Reidel Publishing Company,
P.O. Box 17, 3300 AA Dordrecht, Holland.

Sold and distributed in the U.S.A. and Canada
by Kluwer Boston Inc.,
190 Old Derby Street, Hingham, MA 02043, U.S.A.

In all other countries, sold and distributed
by Kluwer Academic Publishers Group,
P.O. Box 322, 3300 AH Dordrecht, Holland.

D. Reidel Publishing Company is a member of the Kluwer Group.

Also published in 1985 in hardbound edition by Reidel
in the Series Philosophical Studies Series in Philosophy, Volume 34

For Denise and Anna

TABLE OF CONTENTS

PREFACE

Broadly speaking, this is a book about truth and the criteria thereof. Thus it is, in a sense, a book about justification and rationality. But it does not purport to be about *the* notion of justification or *the* notion of rationality. For the assumption that there is just one notion of justification, or just one notion of rationality, is, as the book explains, very misleading. Justification and rationality come in various kinds. And to that extent, at least, we should recognize a variety of notions of justification and rationality. This, at any rate, is one of the morals of Chapter VI.

This book, in Chapters I—V, is mainly concerned with the kind of justification and rationality characteristic of a truth-seeker, specifically a seeker of truth about the world impinging upon the senses: the so-called empirical world. Hence the book's title. But since the prominent contemporary approaches to empirical justification are many and varied, so also are the epistemological issues taken up in the following chapters. For instance, there will be questions about so-called coherence and its role, if any, in empirical justification. And there will be questions about social consensus (whatever it is) and its significance, or the lack thereof, to empirical justification. Furthermore, the perennial question of whether, and if so how, empirical knowledge has so-called foundations will be given special attention. But in disagreement with the growing majority of contemporary philosophers, I argue for the indispensability of foundations, of a certain sort, in empirical knowledge. My argument constitutes Chapters I—V of what follows.

This book has been several years in the making, and owes much to many colleagues, critics, and friends. Often the colleagues and critics were also friends, and so much of the critical input was constructive and friendly. Of such input I want to emphasize that there is none more beneficial than which an author can receive. My sustained research on theories of justification began several years ago with my doctoral dissertation written at Vanderbilt University. At Vanderbilt my work on justification benefited immensely from numerous discussions with Jeffrey Tlumak, John Post, John Compton, Michael Hodges, Clement

Dore, and Lee Rowen. Jeffrey Tlumak deserves special thanks for his consistent willingness to provide meticulous written comments on my earlier essays on justified belief. His comments have had a favorable, if sometimes indirect, influence on many arguments in the present book. I am also grateful to the Vanderbilt University Special Awards Committee for a full-time research grant extending from June 1982 to June 1983. With this support I was able, unencumbered by the cares of the world, to conceive, and to begin to carry out, the program of this book. Since 1983 my work on justification has benefited considerably from numerous discussions with colleagues and graduate students at Loyola University of Chicago, and from interaction with the participants in Robert Audi's 1984 NEH Institute on Action Theory. (It was during Audi's Institute that I drafted a version of Chapter VI of this book.) In this connection I especially thank my Loyola colleagues, Harry Gensler and Arnold Vandernat, and the NEH Institute contributors Robert Audi, Alfred Mele, and Hector-Neri Castañeda. My philosophical discussions with these philosophers have been consistently enjoyable and profitable. I want also to thank Peter Klein and Robert Audi for extensive written comments on the penultimate version of this book. Their thoughtful comments prompted corrections, clarifications, and improvements of other sorts at many points.

Finally, and perhaps most of all, I am grateful to my wife, Denise, for providing daily encouragement and support during the difficult period of research and writing. I would also thank my daughter, Anna, but being only a few months old, she is not quite ready yet to appreciate the joys of epistemology. Nonetheless, I dedicate this book to Denise and Anna.

A few sections of the book derive from material in the following articles: 'Two Paradoxes of Rational Acceptance', *Erkenntnis* 23 (1985), 127–41; 'Whither Infinite Regresses of Justification?', *The Southern Journal of Philosophy* 23 (1985), 65–74; 'Justified Doubt Without Certainty', *The Pacific Philosophical Quarterly* 65 (1984), 97–104; and 'On Negative Coherentism and Subjective Justification', *The Southern Journal of Philosophy* 22 (1984), 83–90. I thank the editors for permission to use parts of these articles.

CHAPTER I

JUSTIFICATION AND THE REGRESS PROBLEM

Belief without any justification is blind, or at least unreasonable. One major value of justification is that it relates belief to some relevant end in view. When the end is truth, and truth alone, *epistemic* justification is all-important. But epistemic justification is not the only kind of justification. Consider prudential justification, for instance. Many of our beliefs are prudentially justified because they are likely to have prudential consequences, that is, because they probably play an important role in bringing about what is in our best prudential interest. But many prudentially justified beliefs are obviously unlikely to be true. Consider, for instance, the case of a person washed asea some 200 miles from the nearest shore. This person, we may plausibly assume, has overwhelming evidence indicating that he cannot swim to safety. But since it is probably in this person's best prudential interest to believe that he can swim to safety — for given that belief, he will continue to swim and might be rescued — he is, presumably, prudentially justified in believing that he can swim to safety. Clearly, if he had no such belief, he would probably drown immediately, without even trying to reach safety. Thus, although this person's overwhelming evidence indicates it is false that he can swim to safety, he may nonetheless be prudentially justified in believing that he can, because it is probably in his best prudential interest to believe this.

Epistemic justification is significantly different from prudential justification. In one sense, epistemic justification is disinterested justification. For the epistemic justification of a belief does not depend on a person's desiring that belief to be true. And a belief's being in one's best prudential interest is never a sufficient condition for that belief's being epistemically justified. Furthermore, one is not epistemically justified in believing a proposition that is unlikely to be true on one's evidence. Epistemic justification, by definition, is the kind of justification appropriate to knowledge. That is, it is the kind of justification characterizing true beliefs which qualify as knowledge. (But I do not intend to suggest here that justified true belief is sufficient for knowledge.) Let us, then, avoid any confusion of prudential and epistemic justification.[1]

Although epistemic justification may apply to nonempirical as well as empirical beliefs, I shall be concerned throughout this book mainly with the epistemic justification of a certain species of empirical belief. Empirical beliefs, roughly speaking, are those beliefs whose epistemic justification requires some experiential evidence. In Chapter V, I shall clarify the relevant notion of experiential evidence. I shall be primarily concerned, in what follows, with the epistemic justification of *particular observation beliefs*, that is, beliefs involving particular (as opposed to universal) propositions whose nonlogical constants are, or are definable by, terms true of external perceptual objects and their properties. More specifically, I aim to determine whether, and if so under what conditions, anyone is epistemically justified in holding any particular observation belief. Accordingly, I shall frequently speak of a person's being *justified in holding some belief*, or being *justified in believing some proposition*. With such talk I intend to suggest that justification applies basically to certain persons with respect to their having beliefs. But it is convenient as well as natural to speak of the justification of *beliefs*, so long as we understand that such justification is always relative to some person. Thus I shall also frequently speak of a person justifiably believing something, or believing something with justification, though of course there is an obvious difference between justified belief and merely justifiable belief.

My talk of *belief*, however, is obviously ambiguous between an act or state of believing and an object of belief. I believe that attention to the context of my remarks will usually remove this ambiguity. An object of a belief that such-and-such is the case is, in my terminology, a *proposition*. Thus, with respect to the claim that a person believes that *p*, I take '*p*' to refer to some proposition. But if this talk of propositions somehow offends, one can safely replace it with talk of statements. As for a belief-state, it may be either dispositional or occurrent. Roughly speaking, a belief-state is just a conviction or a readiness to affirm what is believed. Thus, a sufficient condition of a sincere person's believing that *p* is his conviction to affirm that *p* if he is asked whether *p* is the case and if he wants to give a sincere answer. But I shall not assume that belief is purely behavioral in the sense that necessarily there is some behavioral sign or evidence of every belief. Furthermore, I shall often use the term 'accept' as synonymous with 'believe'. And when I say that a person "accepts" or "believes" some proposition, I do not mean, as do some pragmatist philosophers of science, that he is simply assuming this proposition to be useful for future theoretical investigations. Rather, I intend to suggest that he accepts or believes this proposition to be *true*. I shall clarify the relevant notion of truth in the next section.

I shall observe the familiar distinction between *doxastic* and *propositional* justification, that is, between a person's being justified in believing some proposition and some proposition's being justified for a person. Consider, for instance, the empirical proposition that at present there is a blue book on my desk. I believe this proposition at present, and I suspect that most nonskeptics who examined my present situation would grant that I am justified in believing this proposition at present. Further, if I am justified in believing this proposition at present, then I do believe this proposition at present. Notice, however, that this proposition could be justified for me even if I were not justified in believing it. For all my evidence might indicate that there is a blue book on my desk, but I still might not believe that there is a blue book on my desk. Or, alternatively, I might have such optimal evidence, but believe only for the wrong reasons that there is a blue book on my desk. In either case, the proposition in question would be justified for me even if I were not justified in believing it. Clearly, then, a person can have propositional justification for some proposition even though he lacks doxastic justification for it.[2]

Propositional justification is basic to doxastic justification in the sense that it is a necessary condition of doxastic justification. Thus, if a person is justified in believing a proposition, then that proposition is justified for him. Doxastic justification, roughly speaking, depends on the manner in which a person's beliefs are related to the conditions for propositional justification. Thus, if a proposition, p, is justified for a person because of evidence, e, then that person is justified in believing that p if and only if his belief that p is appropriately related to e. In short, it seems that to be doxastically justified the belief that p must somehow be *based on e*. And we might propose, for instance, that the relevant basing relation is actually a causal relation. In any case, I shall be concerned in the following chapters to determine the necessary and sufficient conditions for the propositional and doxastic epistemic justification of a certain species of empirical proposition.

Already I have relied on the notions of *evidence* and *good reasons*, and these notions obviously will play a major role in the following arguments and discussions. At present I offer only a rough characterization of these notions. Good reasons for the truth of a particular belief are just justifying reasons for that belief. Good reasons for the truth of a

belief ordinarily consist of other beliefs or propositions, but I do not
want to restrict reasons to beliefs. For in Chapter V, I shall argue that
certain events of experiencing or sensing can function as justifying
reasons for beliefs of a certain kind. This view, of course, agrees in spirit
with those traditional empiricist theories of knowledge that countenance
the importance of experiential evidence to the epistemic justification of
empirical beliefs. Evidence, roughly speaking, is the epistemic support
for a belief; that is, it is just the epistemic reasons supporting the truth of
a belief. Epistemic reasons for observation beliefs are disinterested
reasons, insofar as they do not logically depend on anyone's desires or
interests. Since evidence consists of epistemic reasons, it is similarly
disinterested. (Hereafter, my talk of reasons, evidence, and justification
will always concern disinterested, epistemic reasons, evidence, and justification unless I explicitly indicate otherwise; but I shall not always use
the modifiers 'epistemic' and 'disinterested'.) The evidence for a belief
may or may not be justifying. It is justifying if and only if it consists of
good reasons. And just what constitutes good reasons for empirical
beliefs will be the main subject of dispute throughout the following
chapters. Yet we should recognize from the start that all good reasons
may be *prima facie* reasons. That is, they may be defeasible in the sense
that they can lose their justificational efficacy once one acquires certain
additional reasons. But I shall not take a final stand on this issue until
Chapter V.

The importance of reasons in epistemic justification supports, I
believe, a normative conception of epistemic justification. On one such
conception, epistemic justification is essentially related to the so-called
cognitive goal of truth, insofar as an individual belief is epistemically
justified only if it is appropriately directed toward the goal of truth.
More specifically, on the present conception, one is epistemically justified in believing a proposition only if one has good reason to believe
it is true. To accept a proposition in the absence of good reason is to
neglect the cognitive goal of truth. Such acceptance, according to the
present normative conception of justification, is epistemically irresponsible. On this conception, one has an epistemic responsibility to believe
only those propositions which are likely to be true on one's evidence;
and thus one has an epistemic responsibility to believe only those propositions one has good reason to believe are true. (Here I assume that
one's evidence making a proposition likely to be true provides a good
reason for the belief that that proposition is true.) Apart from con-

formity to such an epistemic responsibility, it is unclear how one could make a conscious effort to avoid false beliefs. Let us thus say that if one believes a proposition without any good reason for it, then one is epistemically irresponsible. But, given the present normative conception of justification, one is not epistemically justified in believing any proposition that one is epistemically irresponsible in believing. Consequently, on this conception of justification, one is epistemically justified in believing a proposition only if one has some good reason to believe it to be true. In Chapter IV, I shall contrast this normative conception of justification with a prominent alternative conception, and argue that this normative conception is preferable. However, I find it useful at present to contrast epistemic justification with what it clearly is not.

1. JUSTIFICATION AND TRUTH

I have suggested that epistemic justification is essentially related to the cognitive goal of truth. But what is this goal, and what is truth? According to a somewhat oversimplified characterization, the quest for truth has two major components: We aim both to avoid as much error as we can and to obtain as much truth as we can. If we relinquish either component the quest becomes a cinch. For simply to avoid error we only have to refrain from believing anything, and simply to obtain truth we only have to believe everything. But our quest, unfortunately, is not quite so simple. Its components often push us in opposite directions, driving us to risk error for the sake of comprehensive truth and to sacrifice comprehensive truth for the sake of avoiding error.

Further, it is somewhat implausible to hold that an epistemic agent should aim just to obtain as much truth and avoid as much error as possible. For it is plausible to suppose that some truths are epistemically more important than others, perhaps because of their explanatory value. Ideally, it seems an epistemic agent should aim to acquire not just any truths, but the epistemically important truths. Apart from such a requirement one could achieve the forementioned epistemic goal by having a belief-set of the following sort: I call this object '1'; I call that object '2'; I call this third object '3'; and so on. But it is quite implausible to suppose that the quest for truth can be satisfied so easily. We need to assume, then, that the quest for truth aims at epistemically important truths. And, for present purposes, it is helpful, even if somewhat vague, to hold that an epistemically important proposition has explanatory value.

Later, in Chapter V, I shall argue that some particular observation beliefs are epistemically justified because of their explanatory value. (For more on epistemic objectives, see the following section and Chapter VI.)

As for a definition of *truth* itself, it is hard to improve upon the classical Aristotelian conception of truth expressed by the following dictum of Aristotle's: "To say of what is that it is not, or of what is not that it is, is false, while to say of what is that it is, or of what is not that it is not, is true."

The familiar absolute conception of truth is actually no more than a summary statement of this Aristotelian conception of truth; it states simply:

It is true that *p* if and only if *p*.

Thus, for instance, it is true that the sky is blue if and only if the sky is blue. On this conception, a true proposition is simply a proposition stating how things are. Alfred Tarski has argued persuasively that the absolute conception of truth provides us with a material adequacy condition that any acceptable definition of truth should entail.[3] Tarski's adequacy condition is simply:

S is true if and only if *p*,

where '*p*' stands for any sentence of the language for which truth is being defined, and '*S*' stands for a name of the sentence that replaces '*p*'. A simple instance of Tarski's adequacy condition is:

'The sky is blue' is true if and only if the sky is blue.

As Tarski notes, we may think of each instance of his adequacy condition as a *partial* definition of truth, since each instance will state the truth-conditions of some specific sentence. But when a truth-bearer is a proposition rather than a sentence, we will have to replace Tarski's adequacy condition with the above principle I called 'the absolute conception of truth'. Hereafter, however, when I refer to the absolute conception of truth, I shall be referring either to that principle or to Tarski's adequacy condition. When appropriate, the context will indicate which condition of the absolute conception of truth is directly relevant.

A likely objection to the absolute conception of truth is that it is useless because it fails to provide a criterion by means of which we can tell whether a particular proposition or sentence is true or false. But such an objection, I suspect, stems from a confusion of the *definition* and the *criteria* of truth.[4] The absolute conception of truth is definitional, and not criterial, as it purports simply to give some sense to the term 'true'. That is, the absolute conception of truth aims only to fix the sense of 'true' when this term applies to individual propositions and sentences. Thus that conception of truth does not purport to provide us with the criteria of truth.

But typically a theory of empirical justification does purport to provide us with criteria of truth for empirical propositions, at least in one sense of 'criteria of truth'. We must distinguish, in this connection, between warranting and guaranteeing criteria of truth. A guaranteeing criterion of truth is an infallible criterion of truth. That is, if C is a guaranteeing criterion of truth, then necessarily if a proposition, p, satisfies C, then p is true. A warranting criterion of truth, in contrast, is fallible. It is not necessarily the case that if p satisfies a warranting criterion, then p is true. But obviously our warranting criteria for truth should be such that if a proposition satisfies them, then it will be likely to be true. In the following section I shall try to explain just how likely such a proposition's truth must be. I believe warranting criteria for truth are highly desirable primarily because it is ordinarily much easier for us to determine whether a proposition satisfies warranting criteria than to determine whether it satisfies guaranteeing criteria.[5]

Some philosophers, however, would reject any suggestion that a theory of epistemic justification involves warranting rather than guaranteeing criteria for truth. These philosophers hold that epistemic justification *entails* truth in the sense that necessarily if a proposition is epistemically justified, then it is true.[6] But this view is very implausible, since it rules out the justification of all false propositions, regardless of how much evidence they enjoy. This view implies, for instance, that astronomers working in the Ptolemaic tradition before Copernicus were not, and in fact could not be, justified in believing the distinctive false propositions of their theory. And this implication seems especially implausible when we consider the fact that the Copernican theory was based on the same kind of evidence as was the Ptolemaic theory: the recorded positions of the sun, the moon, and the planets on the celestial sphere at different times. Thus, I find it implausible to regard the Ptolemaic theory as unjustified and unjustifiable just because it is false. Of course we can justifiably regard the Ptolemaic theory as unjustified at

present, but this is only because of evidential considerations. At present
we, of course, have a competing theory that enjoys better evidence in its
favor than does the Ptolemaic theory. But before Copernicus there was
no such competitor, and the Ptolemaic theory qualified as the superior
explanatory account. Thus, even though the Ptolemaic theory is false,
one may plausibly argue that it was justifiable for certain theorists
before Copernicus. More generally, then, it seems implausible to hold
that justification entails truth.

It seems even more implausible to hold that justification and truth are
one and the same thing. Many proponents of the thesis that truth is
"warranted assertibility" apparently hold that there is no difference
between justification and truth. These theorists apparently identify truth
with justification. But at present it seems very implausible to collapse the
distinction between justification and truth. For justification is perspectival in a way that truth is not. This is illustrated by the fact that a proposition, such as that there is a blue book on my desk, may be justified
for me but not for you. Such a difference, it seems, is often due to differ-
ing input from our environment. However, given the forementioned
absolute conception of truth, we cannot assume that it is true for me that
there is a blue book on my desk but false for you. For on that conception
of truth, truth is free of the kind of relativity that characterizes justification. Thus, I shall not assume that justification and truth are one and the
same thing.

Although it is implausible to hold either that justification and truth
are identical or that justification entails truth, there may still be a positive relation between justification and truth. A natural proposal relating
the two is that a person is epistemically justified in believing a proposition if and only if he is justified in believing that it is *true*. This is a proposal not so much about epistemic justification as about believing as
believing-true. Note that we can plausibly say with respect to prudential
justification also that a person is prudentially justified in believing that p
if and only if he is prudentially justified in believing that p is true. This
suggests that the present proposal to relate epistemic justification and
truth is inadequate. A better proposal is that a proposition is epistemically justified for a person if and only it is likely to be true on that
person's evidence. But such a proposal requires us to examine the relation between epistemic justification and probability.

2. JUSTIFICATION AND PROBABILITY

In attempts to relate justification to probability it is customary to refer to justified belief as "rational acceptance." I sometimes follow this custom in the present section.

Many philosophers assume that (1) if a person, S, is rational, then (a) S will accept all the recognized logical consequences of every proposition he accepts; (b) S will accept the recognized conjunction of any propositions he accepts; and (c) S will not accept any proposition he recognizes to be inconsistent. Another assumption of long standing is that S can rationally accept an empirical proposition, p, even if p is not certain in any probability sense. That is, for p to be rationally acceptable, the probability of p need not equal 1; it need only be sufficiently high. Given the latter assumption, we might propose the following as a plausible principle:

(2)   S can rationally accept p if and only if p has a probability n such that $0.5 < n \leqslant 1$.

(2) and (1), however, give rise to the lottery paradox first noticed by Henry Kyburg.[7] As (2) implies that some specifiable probability greater than 0.5 is sufficient for rational acceptance, we have:

(2S)   S can rationally accept p if p has a probability n such that $0.5 < n$.

The value of 'n' in (2S), let us assume, is 0.9. Let us also assume that S is certain, in some probability sense, that just one ticket will win the fair one-hundred ticket lottery in which he is participating. On the present evidence, the probability that any ticket, t_i, in the set of tickets (t_1, t_2, . . . , t_{100}) will win is .01; and thus the probability that t_i will lose is .99. Consequently, given (2S) and the assumption that $n = 0.9$, S can rationally accept with regard to each ticket t_i that it will lose. But this latter proposition, in conjunction with the rationally acceptable proposition that some ticket or other will win, entails a contradiction. And if S recognizes this, then by (1a) S can rationally accept a contradiction. But this, of course, is to contradict (1c). Something, then, has gone away.

To determine exactly where the problem lies, I shall retrace the steps leading to the paradox. But this time I shall speak of justification instead of rational acceptance. Modifying (2S) slightly, we have this principle:

(2S1)   If Prob $(p) > 0.5$, and if S believes that p in light of the relevant evidence (*i.e.*, the evidence making p probable), then S
is justified in believing that p.

Our initial assumption was that S is certain that the lottery is fair and
that just one ticket will win. Thus, if we let 'p_i' abbreviate 'ticket i will
win,' the following is true:.

(3)   Prob $(p_1 \lor p_2 \lor \ldots \lor p_{100}) = 1$.

Given that S recognizes the evidence for this probability, and believes in
light of this evidence that one ticket will win, (3), in conjunction with
(2S1), implies:

(4)   S is justified in believing that $(p_1 \lor p_2 \lor \ldots \lor p_{100})$.

Furthermore, given (2S1) and the relevant evidence, which S recognizes,
that makes it probable that each ticket, t_i, will lose, we may infer:

(5)   S is justified in believing that $-p_1$, and S is justified in believing that $-p_2$, and ..., and S is justified in believing that
$-p_{100}$.

But given (1b), or the Conjunctivity of Justification Principle:

(1b1)   If S is justified in believing that h_1, and S is justified in believing that h_2, and ..., and S is justified in believing that h_n,
then S is justified in believing that $(h_1 \& h_2 \& \ldots \& h_n)$,

(5) implies:

(6)   S is justified in believing that $(-p_1 \& -p_2 \& \ldots \& -p_{100})$.

And on the basis of an epistemic analogue to De Morgan's Law, (6) is
equivalent to:

(7)   S is justified in believing that $-(p_1 \lor p_2 \lor \ldots \lor p_{100})$.

(7) and (4), however, imply that S is justified in believing a contradiction. If we assume that S recognizes the contradiction, this implication
runs afoul of (1c).

    We have at least four possible ways to avoid the paradox under
scrutiny: (i) We can reject any probabilistic rule of rational acceptance;
(ii) We can give up all talk of rational acceptance and settle for partial
belief; (iii) We can reject any purely probabilistic rule of acceptance like

(2S1) and talk of rational acceptance only of propositions more probable than any competing propositions relative to a particular evidence
base; or (iv) We can dispense with the Conjunctivity of Justification
Principle, that is, (1b1). In what follows I shall resolve the lottery paradox by relying on what may be viewed as a variant on strategies (iii) and
(iv). In any case, my effort will show that strategies (i) and (ii) are too
extreme as reactions to the lottery paradox.

As a replacement of the purely probabilistic principle (2S1), consider
the following principle:

(2S2)   If Prob (p) > Prob (−p), and Prob (p) > the probability of
any other proposition, q, competing with p, and if S believes
that p in light of the relevant evidence, then S is justified in
believing that p, and S is not justified in believing that −p or
any other proposition, q, competing with p.

Of course for maximum precision we should relativize the probabilities
in (2S2) to a particular time and to S, but for simplicity I shall suppress
such qualifications here. To qualify as a competitor of p, a proposition,
q, need not be a direct contradictory of p, having the form '−p'; it is sufficient that q be logically contrary to p. Thus, two propositions are
competitors if and only if they are such that they cannot both be true.[8]
For instance, the proposition displayed in (6) above (i.e., (−p_1 & −p_2 &
. . . & −p_{100})) competes with the proposition displayed in (3) (i.e., (p_1 ∨
p_2 ∨ . . . ∨ p_{100})), even though these propositions are not direct con-
tradictories in the forementioned sense. One might object, however, that
on this notion of competition (2S2) is somewhat redundant, since whenever Prob (p) > Prob (−p), then Prob (p) > the probability of any
other proposition, q, logically contrary to p. Given an epistemic interpretation of probability, such an objection evidently will rely on the
following principle: Whatever disconfirms a proposition, p, for S, also
disconfirms for S any proposition, q, entailing p. But one problem facing
this principle is that S may be quite unaware of, or even have reason
to reject, the entailment relation between q and p. It is doubtful that
under such conditions q would be actually disconfirmed for S.[9] Note
also in this connection that the way we relativize competition to what S
is aware of will determine the stringency of the notion of competition.
For instance, if we stipulate that all propositions logically contrary to S's
belief that p are competitors of p for S, then the set of competitors
against S's belief that p will be exceedingly large. A more moderate, and

apparently preferable, proposal is that the competitors of p for S are just those contraries to p of which S is actually aware.

The following considerations indicate that (2S2) does not give rise to the lottery paradox. Notice first that the following equation is true:

(8) $\text{Prob}-(p_1 \lor p_2 \lor \ldots \lor p_{100}) = \text{Prob}(-p_1 \ \& \ -p_2 \ \& \ \ldots \ \& \ -p_{100})$.

And given the Special Multiplication Rule from the probability calculus:

(SMR) $\text{Prob}(p \ \& \ q/e) = \text{Prob}(p/e) \times \text{Prob}(q/e)$ (where p and q are stochastically independent),

we may infer:

(9) $\text{Prob}(-p_1 \ \& \ -p_2 \ \& \ \ldots \ \& \ -p_{100}) =$
         $\text{Prob}(-p_1) \times \text{Prob}(-p_2) \times \ldots \times \text{Prob}(-p_{100})$.

By a simple mathematical probability calculation, we know that, where $0 < i \leqslant 100$, $\text{Prob}(-p_i) < 1$; and thus we may infer that $\text{Prob}(-p_1 \ \& \ -p_2 \ \& \ \ldots \ \& \ -p_{100}) < 1$. We may infer this even if we reject (SMR), for with respect to each conjunct c_i of $(-p_1 \ \& \ -p_2 \ \& \ \ldots \ \& \ -p_{100})$, $\text{Prob}(c_i) < 1$. Thus, given (8), we have:

(10) $\text{Prob}-(p_1 \lor p_2 \lor \ldots \lor p_{100}) < 1$.

And given (3) we may infer that $\text{Prob}(p_1 \lor p_2 \lor \ldots \lor p_{100}) > \text{Prob}-(p_1 \lor p_2 \lor \ldots \lor p_{100})$. Hence, assuming that $(p_1 \lor p_2 \lor \ldots \lor p_{100})$ is more probable than any other competitor, we may also infer, via (2S2), that (4) is true and (7) is not. (2S2), then, has not given rise to the lottery paradox.

The paradox, I believe, has a natural explanation: The truth of (7) and the truth of (4) are determined by contrasting bases for the assignment of probabilities. (7), via (6), is based on (5), which arises from a simple mathematical probability calculation regarding the chances that each ticket t_i will win. (4), in contrast, is based on (3), which does not depend on any such calculation. It should come as no surprise that two contrasting bases for the assignment of probabilities can support two competing propositions both of which enjoy a degree of probability greater than 0.5. The competing propositions in the present case are, of course, $(p_1 \lor p_2 \lor \ldots \lor p_{100})$ and $-(p_1 \lor p_2 \lor \ldots \lor p_{100})$. Once we notice that the former proposition enjoys a higher probability than the latter, on the total evidence, we may infer, given (2S2) and the natural assumption that there are not any more probable competitors, that the former proposition is rationally acceptable, or justified, for S while the latter is not. Thus, any trace of paradox has now vanished.

There are, however, several likely objections I should anticipate. The first stems from the writings of Gilbert Harman. Harman rejects probabilistic rules of rational acceptance, because he finds them to be incompatible with what he takes to be the natural explanation of Gettier examples.[10] One such example is:

1.   Jones knows he has seen his officemate Mr. Nogot driving a Ford.
2.   Jones knows he has heard Nogot, who has always been honest, claim to own a Ford.
3.   Jones knows he has seen an auto registration made out in Nogot's name.
4.   Jones infers (the intermediate conclusion m): His officemate Nogot owns a Ford.
5.   Jones infers (the final conclusion n): Someone in his office owns a Ford.

It turns out, however, that although 1−3 and the final conclusion n are true, the intermediate conclusion m is false. Thus, even though Jones has a justified belief that n, he does not know that n. Harman explains such a Gettier example by appealing to the following principle:

P.   Reasoning that essentially involves false conclusions, intermediate or final, cannot give one knowledge.

Probabilistic rules of acceptance, Harman claims, do not permit such an explanation of Gettier examples, for given that the probability of n is just as high as that of m, such rules license the direct acceptance of n without any appeal to m.

But in reply to Harman, we should note, first, that his principle P is inadequate as a general explanation of Gettier examples. There are examples very much like Gettier's original examples which do not involve false intermediate conclusions.[11] One such example would proceed directly from 1−3, in the above example, to the true existential generalization of the propositions said to be known in 1−3, and then to the final conclusion n. The second point of reply is that no one, to my knowledge, has ever intended probabilistic rules of acceptance to explain the possession of knowledge or the lack thereof in various construals of Gettier examples, or in any examples for that matter. Rather, such rules are concerned solely with rationally acceptable, or justified, belief, which we should not confuse with knowledge. Thus, to discredit probabilistic rules of acceptance, Harman needs to show, in the present case for instance, that n cannot be *justified* without an intermediate conclusion like m, and not that such rules conflict with P or that knowledge of n requires a true intermediate conclusion m.

Another likely objection is that the above solution to the lottery paradox is too costly insofar as it turns on a rejection of the Conjunctivity of Justification Principle (1b1). After all, (2S2) implies that (7) is false while (5) is true. And in rejecting the Conjunctivity of Justification Principle, we invalidate reductio arguments which derive (the acceptability of) a contradiction from the conjunction of a group of propositions each of which a person accepts.[12] But I submit that this objection derives its force from a *non sequitur*. Admittedly, (2S2) can override (1b1) in special circumstances, such as those in which a competing proposition is more probable than the relevant instantiation of the matrix in the consequent of (1b1). But it does not thereby follow that the reductio procedure is itself threatened. For that procedure can still generally rely on (1b1) in cases where (2S2) does not override.

A third likely objection is that principle (2S2) was able to avoid the lottery paradox only because we assumed that $\text{Prob}(p_1 \lor p_2 \lor \ldots \lor p_{100}) = 1$ while $\text{Prob}-(p_1 \lor p_2 \lor \ldots \lor p_{100}) < 1$. The paradox is ineliminable, so the objection goes, if we assume that $\text{Prob}(p_1 \lor p_2 \lor \ldots \lor p_{100}) = \text{Prob}-(p_1 \lor p_2 \lor \ldots \lor p_{100}) < 1$. But it seems clear that (2S2) is untouched by such an objection, for (2S2) says nothing about the rational acceptability of equally probable competing propositions. Admittedly, if (2S2) implied that when $\text{Prob}(p) = \text{Prob}(-p)$ both p and $-p$ are rationally acceptable, the paradox would persist. But (2S2) is perfectly compatible with the stricture that under such a stalemated condition it is rational to withhold acceptance or to accept either p or $-p$ but not both. The present objection raises, in effect, the question of the *necessary* conditions of rational acceptance, and thus I must now face this issue squarely.

It is common to assume, in accordance with (2), that a sufficiently high degree of probability is necessary for rational acceptance, or justified belief. Thus, the following is a widely accepted principle:

(2N) S is justified in believing that p only if p has a probability n such that $0.5 < n$.

But in conjunction with the strictures set by (1) above, (2N) gives rise to an epistemic version of the paradox of the preface. Let us assume that S is a historian of philosophy who has just finished proof-reading and reaffirming his acceptance of each sentence in his just-completed history of 20th-century Anglo-American philosophy. S recognizes, let us suppose, that due to his fallibility and the length of his manuscript, it is highly probable that his book is incorrect in some detail or other. So S, being rational, refrains from accepting the conjunction of the sentences in his book. But since S accepts each sentence in his book, he also accepts, given (1b1), the conjunction of those sentences. Obviously, however, this implication contradicts the preceding supposition.

On the face of it, the present paradox derives mainly from the following assumption:

A.   S's fallibility and the length of his book make it highly probable that at least one of the book's sentences is false.

Assumption A, we have assumed, implies that the probability of the conjunction of the sentences in S's book is less than 0.5, or:

(11) $\text{Prob}(s_1 \mathbin{\&} s_2 \mathbin{\&} \ldots \mathbin{\&} s_n) < 0.5$.

Given (11) and (2N), we may infer that:

(12)   S is not justified in believing that $(s_1 \mathbin{\&} s_2 \mathbin{\&} \ldots \mathbin{\&} s_n)$.

But we have already assumed that S rationally accepts each of the sentences in his book, or:

(13)   S is justified in believing that s_1, and S is justified in believing that s_2, and . . . , and S is justified in believing that s_n.

Given (1b1), we may infer from (13) that:

(14)   S is justified in believing that $(s_1 \mathbin{\&} s_2 \mathbin{\&} \ldots \mathbin{\&} s_n)$,

which of course contradicts (12). Something, then, has obviously gone wrong.

Some philosophers take the present paradox to show that probabilistic rules of acceptance are unacceptable.[13] But it seems at first blush that the easiest way out of the paradox is to reject assumption A. The underlying assumption of this strategy would be that A is false under the envisaged circumstances because our historian S has subjected his work to prolonged scrutiny and has found each sentence contained therein to be rationally acceptable. In light of such effort and the resulting verdict, we might propose, it is *not* probable that at least one of the sentences in S's book is false. Thus the gist of this strategy, apparently, is that (13) falsifies, or overrides, A.

Let us ask, then, whether in light of S's fallibility and the length of his book, it can be highly probable that at least one of the book's sentences is false even though S is justified in believing each sentence found in it. Consider, in this connection, the natural possibility that the factors of fallibility and length have figured in the occurrence of errors in each of S's previous few books. If this is true of S's past experience, there would be a high probability that S's present book, which by hypothesis is as lengthy as and written under conditions similar to the previous books, is erroneous in some detail or other. And this probability could be very high even if we introduce assumption (13) that S is justified in believing each sentence in his present book. For the evidence supporting (13) does not in any way conflict with, and thus does not discredit, the evidence based on S's past experience that supports A and thus (11). As in the case of the lottery paradox, we have here contrasting evidence bases which, on the basis of certain epistemic principles, provide us with conflicting justificatory claims. The epistemic principles in this case are (1b1), once again, and (2N). If these principles are unexceptionable, we are faced again with paradox in the theory of rational acceptance.

Although someone might still contest the claim that (13) and A are compatible, let us grant their compatibility now for the sake of argument. A, we may assume, implies that:

(15) $\text{Prob}(-s_1 \lor -s_2 \lor \ldots \lor -s_n) > 0.5.$

And by a variant of De Morgan's Law we obtain:

(16) $\text{Prob} - (s_1 \& s_2 \& \ldots \& s_n) > 0.5,$

which implies (11), or:

(17) $\text{Prob} - (s_1 \& s_2 \& \ldots \& s_n) > \text{Prob}(s_1 \& s_2 \& \ldots \& s_n).$

In light of (2S2) it seems that our historian S is justified in believing that $-(s_1 \& s_2 \& \ldots \& s_n)$. Further, if, as it is natural to assume, the antecedent of (2S2) expresses a necessary as well as a sufficient condition of rational acceptance, then we can avoid the paradox at hand. The necessary condition of rational acceptance, which I hinted at in the consequent of (2S2), is simply:

(2N1)   If S is justified in believing that p, then $\text{Prob}(p) > \text{Prob}(-p)$, and Prob $(p) >$ the probability of any other proposition, q, competing with p.

The thrust of (2N1) is simply that if p is rationally acceptable, then p is more probable than all of its competitors. Maximum precision requires once again that we relativize the probabilities in (2N1) to a particular time and to S, but for simplicity I shall continue to suppress such qualifications here. (2N1) seems to be stricter than (2N), as (2N1) demands that a rationally acceptable proposition, p, be more probable than not only $-p$ but also any other proposition competing with p. In light of (2N1) and the assumption that A and thus (11) are true, we may infer that (14) is false. Accordingly, (1b1) has been overridden once again by a general epistemic principle, in this case by (2N1). And since (2N1) invalidates the move from (13) to (14) under the present circumstances in which (11) is true, the epistemic variant of the paradox of the preface loses its force. For we are now without a proposition such as (14) to contradict (12).

(2N1), however, is not the only principle that can fill the order for a necessary condition of rational acceptance. A slightly more liberal principle is:

(2N2)   If S is justified in believing that p, then $\text{Prob}(p) \geqslant \text{Prob}(-p)$ and $\text{Prob}(p) \geqslant$ the probability of any other proposition q competing with p.

(2N2) requires that a rationally acceptable proposition be either more probable than or as probable as any competing proposition. One might also regard the necessary condition stated by (2N2) as sufficient for rational acceptance. I shall not defend (2N2) as stating a necessary and sufficient condition, but I believe that if one defends it as such, then one must add, given (1c), that only one, and not both, of equally probable contradictory propositions is rationally acceptable at a time. The important point, however, is that we can bring (2N) into conformity with (2S2) in at least two ways, via either (2N1) or (2N2). Hence, more than one probabilistic rule of acceptance can successfully avoid the above paradoxes.

Combining principles (2S2) and (2N1), we arrive at the following probabilistic analysis of epistemic justification:

PJ.   A person, S, is justified in believing that p at a time t if and
        only if at t, p is more probable on S's total evidence than any
        of p's competitors, including $-p$, and S believes that p in light
        of the relevant evidence.

As PJ is concerned with epistemic justification, we may construe its talk
of probability in accordance with Carnap's epistemic interpretation of
probability.[14] Thus, we may construe 'Prob(p) $=$ n' as 'the degree of
confirmation of p equals n.' This kind of probability is, of course, relative to a person and a time, but it is not subjective, since it does not entail anything about a subjective belief-state of a person. PJ, I have
argued, can provide us with an easy way out of the lottery paradox and
the epistemic version of the paradox of the preface, but one might
object to PJ on the ground that it permits us to believe with justification
certain propositions we recognize to be inconsistent. In connection with
the lottery paradox, PJ grants justification to each and every member of
the following set of propositions:

(18) $\{(p_1 \lor p_2 \lor \ldots \lor p_{100}), -p_1, -p_2, \ldots -p_{100}\}$.

This set is logically inconsistent in the sense that it is logically impossible
for all of its members to be true. And since PJ permits that a person can
be justified in believing each and every member of (18), PJ also permits
that a person can be justified in believing an inconsistent set of propositions, even when this person recognizes the inconsistency. Thus, given
PJ, we can be justified in believing something that guarantees error on
our part. One might be inclined, therefore, to dispense with PJ on the
ground that it conflicts with the epistemic goal of believing all and only
true propositions.[15]

    This objection, I concede, is well-taken, but it loses its force if we
modify the epistemic goal it assumes. This goal is equivalent to what
Keith Lehrer has called "the maxiverific ideal." The maxiverific ideal,
roughly speaking, is to be a person of such great epistemic perfection
that whenever a proposition is true one accepts it, in accordance with
some rational methodology, and whenever a proposition is false one
does not accept it. But this ideal clearly is not equivalent to the epistemic objective of maximizing true belief and minimizing false belief.
The latter objective, unlike the former, is not a goal of epistemic perfection. For it permits that a person may sacrifice epistemic perfection in
order to maximize true belief. The latter, nonperfectionist objective

does, of course, place a premium on minimizing false belief, but not on avoiding it at any cost. The distinctive feature of the nonperfectionist objective, then, is that it permits us to maximize true belief even when we are certain that in doing so some false beliefs will result.

The choice between the two objectives in question, as Lehrer observes, brings us to the bottom rock of epistemic preferences. But I believe we can say something in favor of the weaker, nonperfectionist objective. This objective is clearly in accordance with the common willingness of persons to maximize true belief when mistakes are highly probable but not highly consequential. But we cannot say the same of the perfectionist objective, given its opposition to our losing epistemic perfection. Of course, I am not suggesting that people are generally opposed to epistemic perfection; rather, I am claiming that ordinarily a person is willing to lose his epistemic perfection if in doing so he can considerably increase his true beliefs. However, I doubt that this consideration counts much against the perfectionist objective. Yet such a consideration does suggest that the nonperfectionist epistemic objective is not obviously irrational. Note also, in this connection, that the present nonperfectionist objective may be plausibly construed as requiring mainly that one maximize *the difference*, or even *the ratio*, between one's set of true beliefs and one's set of false beliefs.

Clearly, we can invoke Lehrer's maxiverific ideal to deny that we are justified in believing any proposition we know to be self-contradictory. But can we say the same of the nonperfectionist objective? I believe so. By definition, any single proposition we know to be self-contradictory must be false. Thus, in believing such a proposition we would increase not our true beliefs, but only our false beliefs. Hence, if our epistemic objective is to maximize true beliefs and minimize false beliefs, we are not justified in believing any single proposition we know to be self-contradictory. But this consideration does not preclude our being justified in believing all the members of a set of propositions we know to be logically inconsistent. We have seen in connection with the lottery paradox that we can be justified in believing each and every member of the inconsistent set (18). In the context of a fair lottery, it will not be unusual for us to be justified in believing each member of (18). And given the certainty of the proposition that $(p_1 \lor p_2 \lor \ldots \lor p_{100})$, we will have excellent reason to believe that at least one member of the subset $\{-p_1, -p_2, \ldots -p_{100}\}$ is false. But, of course, we will lack any way to determine just *which* member is false. And we cannot reasonably expect to increase our true beliefs by rejecting any of the subset's members at random. Further, we would be imprudently skeptical to reject all of the subset's members. For in doing so, we would lose the chance to increase our true beliefs by 99 propositions. Hence, we should concede that there can be logically inconsistent sets all of whose members we can justifiably believe, even when we recognize the inconsistency.

Does it also follow, then, that we may reinstate the Conjunctivity of Justification Principle (1b1) and assume that one can be justified in believing that $(-p_1 \,\&\, -p_2 \,\&\, \ldots \,\&\, -p_{100})$ as well as that $(p_1 \,\vee\, p_2 \,\vee\, \ldots \,\vee\, p_{100})$? This might seem to follow, since the primary aim of my permitting (2S2) and (2N1) to override the Conjunctivity of Justification Principle was to avoid an inconsistency. But now that I have tolerated inconsistency among our justified beliefs, so the anticipated objection goes, there is no good reason to qualify or to override the Conjunctivity of Justification Principle.[16]

Several reasons have been offered for qualifying the Conjunctivity Principle which are logically independent of my proposed solution to the lottery paradox.[17] But in connection with the present discussion, recall the earlier suggestion that some inconsistencies are acceptable while others are not. Obviously a proposition we know to be inconsistent is unacceptable, from an epistemic point of view, if our acceptance of it increases only our false beliefs. Accordingly, I have claimed that we cannot rationally accept a single proposition we know to be self-contradictory. But this leaves open the natural question about the acceptability of a couple of pairwise inconsistent propositions. In connection with the lottery paradox, for instance, we confronted the two inconsistent propositions that no ticket will win the lottery and that some ticket or other will win. I introduced principle (2S2) mainly to preclude our being justified in believing both of those propositions at the same time. And given the nonperfectionist epistemic objective, we can resist the rational acceptance of those two propositions on the ground that it would not really be conducive to maximizing true beliefs and minimizing false beliefs. In accepting such pairwise inconsistent propositions, we acquire one more true belief only by acquiring another false one. Hence, in that case we do not really make any mileage on the road to accomplishing the nonperfectionist epistemic objective.

We have seen, then, that in some cases the Conjunctivity of Justification Principle should be overridden by a principle like PJ. But of course we should not assume that PJ can provide us with anything like a full account of justification. For PJ is actually neutral as regards the major competing accounts of epistemic justification. It says nothing, for instance, about just what constitutes good evidence for empirical beliefs, or about what provides the best solution to the most difficult problem facing a theory of justification, namely, the epistemic regress problem. Before turning to the regress problem, however, I shall comment briefly on the relation of justification to knowledge.

3. JUSTIFICATION AND KNOWLEDGE

Justification derives much of its importance as a key component of most, if not all, empirical knowledge. Of course, in light of Gettier examples we cannot assume without argument that justified true belief is sufficient for empirical knowledge. But we may assume that in most, if not all, cases if one knows that p, then one is justified in believing that p. Some philosophers have constructed cases which purportedly show that some empirical knowledge does not require justified belief. Many of these cases involve the so-called knowledge possessed by unusual predictors and oracles, but I find it less than obvious that these cases actually involve knowledge. Further, such cases should probably lead us to recognize that philosophers often rely on fundamentally different notions of knowledge. In any case, Alvin Goldman has appealed to different, less unusual cases to deny that empirical knowledge requires justified belief.[18] Goldman's general aim in discussing these cases is to develop a causal theory of knowing. Thus some philosophers have been led to assume that if we accept a causal theory of knowing, then we should deny that knowledge requires justification. But it should be emphasized that Goldman's apparent rejection of the justification condition clearly comes with a significant qualification. Goldman's actual claim here is simply that one can know that p even if p is neither self-warranting nor supported by self-warranting propositions. Thus, in developing his causal theory, Goldman is not really denying the justification condition for knowledge; rather, he is rejecting only a particular type of foundationalist approach to justification. Incidentally, Goldman, among others, has come also to reject any so-called "internalist" account of justification that requires that one be aware, in some way, of one's reasons for one's justified beliefs. And this rejection commits Goldman to a version of so-called "epistemic externalism". I shall define and critically assess such externalism in Chapter IV.

The view that empirical knowledge requires *justified* belief receives some support from the fact that empirical knowledge is not just true belief. We can acquire true belief in any number of fortuitous and unreasonable ways, and so true belief is insufficient for empirical knowledge. But what more is needed if a true belief is to qualify as knowledge? Although there is not uniform agreement on this issue, philosophers generally agree that a true belief qualifies as knowledge only if it is not accidentally, or coincidentally, true. The general agreement here is on the fact that the true belief qualifying as knowledge must satisfy the truth condition for knowledge *in an appropriate way*. Precisely what constitutes such an appropriate way is, of course, a matter of much controversy. But few, if any, would deny that knowledge requires that its belief condition be appropriately related to its truth condition. For instance, the belief condition cannot be coincidentally related to the truth condition.

Now it is plausible to hold that what is needed to provide the appropriate relation between the belief condition and the truth condition is a justification condition. According to this view, we should regard as involving a justification condition any condition for knowledge that supplements, and purportedly appropriately relates, the belief and truth conditions. Thus, on the present view, any reliability or causal condition for knowledge involves a justification condition, even if it is held that a knower need not be aware of the satisfaction of this third condition. More generally, then, in proposing that empirical knowledge requires justification, I am proposing simply that the belief and the truth conditions must be appropriately related by a further condition involving a justification condition. Of course it might be objected that a fourth condition, rather than the justification condition, for knowledge can appropriately relate the belief and truth conditions. But such an objection is ineffective at best, since any plausible fourth condition for knowledge involves the justification condition insofar as it is mainly a qualification on that condition. This is true, at any rate, of the prominent so-called defeasibility conditions for knowledge. In sum, then, since the belief and truth conditions of knowledge must be appropriately related, it is quite plausible to suppose that empirical knowledge requires a justification condition of some sort. Precisely what is involved in this justification condition is the main subject of the following chapters.

Although knowledge requires a justification condition, I shall not assume that necessarily if one knows that *p*, then one is able to set forth a justification of one's belief that *p*. For it is implausible to assume that one's being justified in believing that *p* requires that one be able to *set forth* a justification of one's belief that *p*. Note that to be able to set forth a justification of a belief, one must be linguistically proficient to a certain extent. But it is not at all clear that linguistic proficiency is a prerequisite of one's having a justified belief. For a similar reason, furthermore, I shall not assume that one's *having* a justification for a particular empirical belief is the same as one's *showing* that this belief is (likely to be) true, or that one has good evidence for it.

In summary, then, the present and preceding sections support this important moral: We should not confuse the concept of epistemic justification with the related concepts of truth, probability, knowledge, and showing evidence. With this in mind, let us turn now to the epistemic regress problem, which will set the course for the rest of this book.

4. THE EPISTEMIC REGRESS PROBLEM

A simple example will help to clarify the regress problem. While jogging along the shore of the Pacific, Sally thinks how refreshing a swim in the ocean would be, but decides against it because she believes that swimming is dangerous today. Her belief that swimming is dangerous today, let us assume, is justified by her beliefs that there will be a lightning storm today, and that swimming during a lightning storm is dangerous. Furthermore, her belief that there will be a lightning storm today is justified by her beliefs that cumulonimbus clouds are visible in the sky, that she hears thunder in the distance, and that the weatherman has predicted a lightning storm for today. Thus, we may assume that Sally's belief that swimming is dangerous today is inferentially justified by these other beliefs of hers. For these other beliefs can serve as premises in a simple argument whose conclusion is the belief that swimming is dangerous today. And Sally might construct such an argument to show that her belief that swimming is dangerous today is justified. But at present I am concerned not so much with the *showing* or *giving* of justification as with the *having* of it. My concern, more specifically, is with the necessary and sufficient conditions of the inferential justification of empirical beliefs. Thus, an immediately relevant question is: Can the beliefs justifying Sally's belief about the danger of swimming today extend infinitely, with each of these beliefs being itself inferentially justified by some other belief? Or must Sally's inferentially justified belief be justified ultimately by some belief that is not inferentially justified, but immediately justified? There are some other options we must consider, but before mentioning them I shall state the regress problem more formally in terms of evidence chains.

An evidence chain for a person's belief that e_0 is just a series of beliefs (or sets of beliefs) $e_1, e_2, e_3, \ldots$, such that e_1 justifies the belief that e_0, and for any e_i in this series e_i justifies e_{i-1}. Let us assume, then, that a person, S, is justified in believing a proposition, e_0, because S is justified in believing that another proposition, e_1, is true and that e_1 entails e_0. Under these conditions, S is inferentially justified in believing that e_0. Let us assume also that S is inferentially justified in believing that e_1 on the basis of another proposition, e_2, and that S is similarly inferentially justified in believing that e_2. Under these conditions, the evidence chain for e_0 extends at least to e_2. But this chain may or may not terminate with e_2 or some other proposition in the series. It might continue infinitely or it might form a circle. In either case, the evidence chain for e_0 would not terminate. However, this evidence chain might terminate either in some unjustified belief of S's or in some immediately justified belief of S's. We have, then, at least four possible accounts of inferential justification: inferential justification via infinite regresses, via justificatory circles of some sort, via the unjustified, and via immediate justification. Although proponents of infinite justificatory regresses are uncommon, the other three accounts enjoy considerable representation among contemporary philosophers. In accordance with custom, I shall call the proponents of circles of justification "coherentists"; and the proponents of justification via the unjustified "contextualists"; and the proponents of justification via immediate justification "foundationalists".

Given the four possible accounts of inferential justification, foundationalists typically have invoked a simple argument from elimination for the existence of immediately justified foundations of justification. A familiar version of the argument runs as follows. The evidence chain for e_0 cannot extend infinitely if e_0 is to be justified for S, since no matter how far back in such an infinite regress we go, we always find a proposition that is only inferentially justified in the sense that it is justified if and only if its successor is. Also, the evidence chain for e_0 cannot form a circle if e_0 is to be justified for S. For a circular evidence chain is equivalent to the claim that e_0 is justified by e_1, e_1 is justified by $e_2, \ldots, e_{n-1}$ is justified by e_n, and e_n is justified by e_0. Since the latter claim, in conjunction with the assumption that epistemic justification is transitive, implies that e_0 justifies e_0, circular evidence chains are unacceptable. Furthermore, the evidence chain for e_0 cannot terminate with an unjustified belief, if e_0 is to be justified for S. For if the terminus of an evidence chain is unjustified, it can hardly justify any other link in the chain; most importantly, it cannot justify e_0. Hence, we are left with the fourth and final option, the situation in which the evidence chain for e_0 terminates with an immediately justified belief. On this option, the terminus of the evidence chain for e_0 is itself justified, and therefore it can transfer justification along the chain to e_0. The foundationalist concludes, accordingly, that all inferential justification depends on immediately justified, foundational beliefs, and that since some beliefs are inferentially justified, there are foundations of justification. Hereafter, I shall refer to the foregoing argument as *the traditional regress argument*, and to the problem giving rise to it as *the regress problem*.

Despite the venerable heritage of the traditional regress argument, this argument leaves much to be desired. One questionable point in the argument is the claim that an evidence chain extending infinitely is inadequate for inferential justification since no matter how far back in such a chain we go we always find a proposition that is only inferentially justified. In making this claim, the foundationalist apparently is assuming that an evidence chain is adequate for inferential justification only if this chain includes some proposition that is immediately justified. But since this assumption is the very point at issue in the debate between the foundationalist and the proponent of infinite justificatory regresses, we should question the present step of the argument. Another dubious step in the traditional regress argument is the assumption that the coherentist's circles of justification are literal circles involving transitivity. Although this assumption may be true of some traditional coherentists, the prominent contemporary coherentists explain inferential justification in terms of non-literal circles, that is, "circles" of mutual justification characterized by *non*transitive justificatory relations. Thus, the traditional regress argument falters at a second point. And still another weakness in the traditional argument is its neglect of a fifth option, namely, the skeptical option. Once the foundationalist eliminates the first three competing accounts of inferential justification, he typically concludes immediately that his account of inferential justification via immediately justified beliefs is acceptable. But this conclusion clearly is illicit prior to an examination of the relevant skeptical arguments purporting to show |that no beliefs are immediately justified or inferentially justified. That is, the foundationalist can invoke the regress argument in support of foundationalism only after he has successfully defended his account of immediate justification and of inferential justification via immediate justification against the relevant skeptical objections. In sum, then, the traditional regress argument fails on at least three major counts.

However, in the following chapters I shall develop an extended eliminative regress argument for foundationalism that overcomes the weaknesses of the traditional argument. My strategy is quite straightforward. In Chapter II, I shall argue that the leading contextualist accounts of inferential justification are unacceptable and unpromising as solutions to the regress problem. And in Chapter III, I shall argue that the leading coherentist accounts of inferential justification are similarly unacceptable and unpromising. But this will not be the end of the argument. For in Chapter IV, I shall argue not only that the relevant kind of infinite justificatory regresses is conceptually impossible, but also that the leading contemporary versions of foundationalism are also unacceptable and unpromising as solutions to the epistemic regress problem. Thus, at the end of Chapter IV it will seem that the regress argument actually supports a version of epistemological skepticism rather than foundationalism. But in Chapter V, I shall develop a version of epistemic foundationalism that avoids the serious problems facing the theories I oppose in the earlier chapters. In doing so, I shall also meet the relevant skeptical objections and solve the epistemic regress problem as it applies to observation beliefs about what we currently perceive. Overall, then, I intend to show that a certain version of foundationalism, namely epistemic intuitionism, provides the best available explanation of the inferential justification of such observation beliefs, and thus provides the best available solution to the epistemic regress problem regarding such observation beliefs. Furthermore, in the concluding chapter I shall argue that an account of epistemic justification cannot by itself provide a full explanation of rational belief.

NOTES

[1] I shall characterize some other kinds of justification in Chapter VI, and provide a rational means of resolving conflicts of various kinds of justification.
[2] For more on the distinction between propositional and doxastic justification see

Roderick Firth, 'Are Epistemic Concepts Reducible to Ethical Concepts?' in *Values and Morals: Essays in Honor of William Frankena, Charles Stevenson, and Richard Brandt*, A. I. Goldman and J. Kim (eds.) (D. Reidel, Dordrecht, 1978), p. 218.

[3] See Tarski, 'The Semantic Conception of Truth', *Philosophy and Phenomenological Research* **4** (1944), 341–375. For a useful summary of Tarski's account of truth see Susan Haack, *Philosophy of Logics* (Cambridge University Press, Cambridge, 1978), pp. 99–110. Haack points out some of the noteworthy limitations of Tarski's account. On the absolute conception of truth in general, see John L. Mackie, *Truth, Probability, and Paradox* (Clarendon Press, Oxford, 1973), Chapter 2.

[4] Incidentally, Keith Lehrer has suggested that the familiar correspondence and coherence notions of truth stem from a confusion of the definition and the criterion of truth. He argues plausibly that once we strip them of their criterial features they reduce to the absolute conception of truth. See Lehrer, *Knowledge* (Clarendon Press, Oxford, 1974), pp. 42–47.

[5] For further discussion of the distinction between guaranteeing and warranting criteria of truth see Nicholas Rescher, *The Coherence Theory of Truth* (Clarendon Press, Oxford, 1973), pp. 12–22.

[6] See, for example, Panayot Butchvarov, *The Concept of Knowledge* (Northwestern University Press, Evanston, 1970), pp. 47–51, and Robert F. Almeder, 'Truth and Evidence', *Philosophical Quarterly* **24** (1974), 365–368.

[7] See Kyburg, *Probability and the Logic of Rational Belief* (Wesleyan University Press, Middletown, CT, 1961), p. 197, and *idem, Probability and Inductive Logic* (Macmillan, New York, 1970), Chapter 13. Cf. Risto Hilpinen, 'Rules of Acceptance and Inductive Logic', *Acta Philosophica Fennica* **22** (1968), 39–49.

[8] This notion of competition, incidentally, differs from Keith Lehrer's most recent notion of competition. On Lehrer's notion, a proposition p competes with a proposition q if p diminishes the probability of q when conjoined with q. See Lehrer, 'Coherence and the Racehorse Paradox', in P. French *et al*, (eds.), *Midwest Studies in Philosophy, Vol. V: Studies In Epistemology*, (University of Minnesota Press, Minneapolis, 1980), p. 188. A similar notion of competition is espoused by Marshall Swain, *Reasons and Knowledge* (Cornell University Press, Ithaca, 1981), pp. 129–133. One serious problem with this more liberal notion of competition is that, if used in a principle like (2S2), it entails that the proposition that we sometimes have nonveridical perceptions, such as during hallucination or daydreaming, undermines the justification of many ordinary observation beliefs we typically assume to be justified. I shall return to this notion of competition in Chapter III.

[9] I should stress, however, that even if some variant of the objection at hand were to go through, the most it would show is that (2S2) is somewhat redundant.

[10] See Harman, *Thought* (Princeton University Press, Princeton, 1973), pp. 120–124, and *idem*, 'Induction', in M. Swain (ed.), *Induction, Acceptance, and Rational Belief* (D. Reidel, Dordrecht, 1970), pp. 85–86.

[11] Such examples have been set forth, for instance, by Richard Feldman, 'An Alleged Defect in Gettier Counter-Examples', *Australasian Journal of Philosophy* **52** (1974), 68–69, and Keith Lehrer, 'The Gettier Problem and the Analysis of Knowledge', in G. S. Pappas (ed.), *Justification and Knowledge*, (D. Reidel, Dordrecht, 1979), p. 75. For a useful discussion of such examples, see Robert Shope, *The Analysis of Knowing* (Princeton University Press, Princeton, 1983), Chapter 1.

[12] Thus Mark Kaplan, 'Rational Acceptance', *Philosophical Studies* **40** (1981), 132—133, and *idem*, 'A Bayesian Theory of Rational Acceptance', *Journal of Philosophy* **78** (1981), 309.

[13] See, for example, Marsha Hanen, 'Confirmation, Explanation, and Acceptance', in K. Lehrer (ed.), *Analysis and Metaphysics: Essays in Honor of R. M. Chisholm*, (D. Reidel, Dordrecht, 1975), pp. 118—123.

[14] See Rudolf Carnap, 'Inductive Logic and Rational Decisions', in R. Carnap and R. Jeffrey (eds.), *Studies in Inductive Logic and Probability*, (University of California Press, Berkeley, 1972), p. 25. Cf. R. G. Swinburne, *Introduction to Confirmation Theory* (Methuen, London, 1973), Chapter 1, and especially Henry Kyburg, 'Epistemological Probability', in *Epistemology and Inference* (University of Minnesota Press, Minneapolis, 1983), pp. 204—216.

[15] Lehrer has supported the consistency requirement on this ground in *Knowledge*, pp. 202—206, in 'Reason and Consistency', in *Analysis and Metaphysics*, pp. 66—71, and in 'Self-Profile', in R. J. Bogdan (ed.), *Keith Lehrer*, (D. Reidel, Dordrecht, 1981), pp. 47—48. A useful discussion of Lehrer's consistency requirement can be found in Richmond Campbell, 'Can Inconsistency Be Reasonable?', *Canadian Journal of Philosophy* **11** (1981), 245—270.

[16] This is the thrust of an argument of Lehrer's in his 'Reply to Pappas', in *Keith Lehrer*, pp. 226—227.

[17] See, for example, Henry Kyburg, 'Conjunctivitis', in M. Swain (ed.), *Induction, Acceptance, and Rational Belief*, pp. 55—82. A reason I *reject* rests on the assumption that justified belief in conjunctive propositions with logically independent conjuncts is governed by the multiplicative axiom of the probability calculus — that the probability that any two conjuncts are true equals the prior probability of the first multiplied by the conditional probability of the second given the first. Given this axiom, if we have even a modestly large set of contingent propositions whose individual probabilities are very high yet less than 1.0, the probability of the conjunction of the propositions will be very low, failing to satisfy even liberal probability requirements on justified belief. The decline in probability of conjunctive beliefs which the axiom entails is too precipitous to make it plausible to suppose that justified belief behaves in accordance with it.

[18] See Goldman, 'A Causal Theory of Knowing', *Journal of Philosophy* **64** (1967), 370—371, and *idem*, 'Discrimination and Perceptual Knowledge', *Journal of Philosophy* **73** (1976), 790—791. For a discussion of, as well as a response to, several other philosophers who deny that knowledge requires justified belief see Marshall Swain, *Reasons and Knowledge* (Cornell University Press, Ithaca, 1981), pp. 40—44. Swain discusses some of the unusual cases mentioned above.

CHAPTER II

EPISTEMIC CONTEXTUALISM:
JUSTIFICATION VIA THE UNJUSTIFIED

Wittgenstein sets forth a central tenet of epistemic contextualism when he claims that "at the foundation of well-founded belief lies belief that is not founded".[1] If we construe Wittgenstein's claim as stating that at the foundation of *justified* beliefs lie beliefs that are *un*justified, then we have the first purported solution to the epistemic regress problem. The contextualist solution, like the foundationalist solution, proposes that evidence chains terminate, but unlike the foundationalist solution, it ordinarily proposes that the foundations of justification are themselves unjustified. Perhaps, then, we should state the minimal thesis of epistemic contextualism as follows:

CE1. A belief is inferentially justified if and only if it has an evidence chain that terminates in some belief that is unjustified.

But this is obviously an unacceptable thesis. It permits that an evidence chain for an inferentially justified belief can terminate in *any* unjustified belief. But we surely do not want to hold that a belief can be inferentially justified for us by a belief we know to be false. Thus the foundations of justification cannot be just any unjustified beliefs.

Contextualists generally hold that the foundations of justification are those beliefs that a certain community of believers takes for granted, or accepts without any reasons. Let us then revise CE1 as follows:

CE2. A person's (S's) belief that *p* is inferentially justified if and only if it has an evidence chain that terminates in some unjustified belief that S's fellow-believers generally accept without any reasons.

Clearly, CE2 is not very helpful in its present form. For it fails to specify who the relevant fellow-believers are and how many of them must accept the unjustified foundational belief in question. Furthermore, CE2 says nothing about S's awareness of the consensus of his fellow-believers. Presumably, S must be justified in believing that most of his fellow-believers accept the foundational belief in question.

Otherwise, it will be possible for S himself to have no reason whatsoever to believe that *p* is true. But how can S be justified in believing
anything about his fellow-believers' beliefs and agreements? Obviously
CE2 provides no answer to this important question.

Perhaps we can remove some of the major shortcomings of CE2 by
examining the leading versions of epistemic contextualism. Many
prominent contextualists have appealed to contextualism in some form
to explain the justification of scientific theories, whereas others have
invoked contextualism to explain the justification of ordinary observation beliefs. Two leading members of the former group are Thomas
Kuhn and Harold Brown, and some representative members of the
latter group are Wittgenstein, David Annis, and Michael Williams. I
turn first to an examination of contextualist efforts to explain the justification of scientific theories, or, for short, "scientific justification". In
doing so, I intend to illustrate how contextualism characterizes justification as an intrinsically social phenomenon.

1. CONTEXTUALISM AND SCIENTIFIC JUSTIFICATION

Proponents of the contextualist theory of scientific justification claim
that scientific justification is always relative to some conceptual
perspective or framework that determines what scientific questions are
worthy of investigation and what kinds of answers to scientific problems are justifiable. More specifically, Harold Brown has argued that
scientific presuppositions are basic to the justification of any scientific
theory. He designates those propositions that express scientific presuppositions as 'paradigmatic propositions'.[2] Two familiar examples of
such propositions are 'all celestial motions are circular' and 'physical
space is Euclidean'. Kuhn has also stressed the importance of presuppositions in the justification of scientific theories. Scientific presuppositions, according to Kuhn, form the basis of a "paradigm" or a
"disciplinary matrix". A disciplinary matrix is basically the complex of
shared beliefs that accounts for general agreement among the scientists
in any given scientific community. It consists, in part, of shared beliefs
in particular explanatory and heuristic models, in certain scientific
values for theory-choice, and in certain "exemplars", or concrete
problem solutions.[3] Thus the acceptance of a particular disciplinary
matrix is really the acceptance of the basic presuppositions of a
particular world-view. According to Kuhn, scientists ordinarily come

to accept a disciplinary matrix by means of a scientific education, and they rely on the matrix in the justification of any scientific theory. In sum, then, Kuhn and Brown hold that scientific presuppositions are basic to all scientific justification, and that these presuppositions are not themselves empirically justified.

A central tenet of Kuhn and Brown's contextualism is that scientific presuppositions are not permanent, but that they change along with fundamental changes in the structure of scientific research. Kuhn holds that a change from one set of scientific presuppositions to another, i.e., a "paradigm-change", is a transition between "incommensurable" views. Kuhn's doctrine of the incommensurability of competing scientific paradigms includes three main theses. First, the proponents of different scientific paradigms practice science in different worlds in the sense that, due to diverse scientific presuppositions, they see different things when they look from the same place in the same direction. For example, upon looking toward the east at dawn Kepler and Galileo saw a static sun, whereas Tycho Brahe saw a mobile sun. Second, the proponents of different paradigms disagree about what problems an acceptable scientific theory must solve. Newtonian and Aristotelian physicists, for example, disagreed about whether a theory of motion must explain the cause of the attractive forces between bodies. Third, within a new paradigm old terms take on new meanings. Consider, for instance, the different senses of 'fall' in Aristotelian and Newtonian physics. In the former, fall is simply motion to a body's natural place, but in the latter it is motion due to gravitation. The usual result of such change in meaning is misunderstanding between the proponents of different paradigms.

Kuhn has argued that because a paradigm-change is a transition between incommensurable views it cannot be brought about by an appeal to logic and observation. Nor can one make the transition one step at a time. Like a gestalt switch, the transition occurs all at once or not at all. The choice of a new paradigm is thus unlike the choice of a particular theory within a paradigm, since paradigm-choice, according to Kuhn, is not ordinarily guided by the evaluative procedures of normal, nonrevolutionary science. Kuhn claims:

The man who embraces a new paradigm at an early stage must often do so in defiance of the evidence provided by problem-solving. He must, that is, have faith that the new paradigm will succeed with the many large problems that confront it, knowing only that the older paradigm has failed with a few. A decision of that kind can only be made on faith.[4]

In light of this claim, Kuhn's critics have frequently objected that Kuhn depicts scientific change as basically irrational. And it is clear that such an objection is not totally without warrant. However, Kuhn has come to oppose any suggestion that a scientific community's choice of a new paradigm is made without good reasons. He now claims simply that scientists often choose a new paradigm without *conclusive* reasons to believe that it will ultimately succeed as an adequate basis for the solution of important scientific problems. Thus, Kuhn now maintains that the intention of the previous quote is simply to deny that the reasons in favor of a new paradigm are proofs and that the reasons against an old paradigm are disproofs.

As for the justification of a scientific theory within a particular paradigm, Kuhn and Brown hold that there is no epistemic standard higher than the consensus of the scientific community. Kuhn is especially clear on this point. He holds that the best way to decide whether one scientific theory is more reasonable to believe than another is as follows:

Take a *group* of the ablest people with the most appropriate motivation; train them in some science and in the specialties relevant to the choice at hand; imbue them with the value system, the ideology current in their discipline (and to a great extent in other scientific fields as well); and, finally, let them make the choice.[5]

Thus, Kuhn's account of scientific justification is intrinsically social. It implies that we can explain the justification of scientific theories not by an appeal to unambiguous ahistorical epistemic rules or standards, but only by an examination of the relevant scientific community, particularly its shared values, likes, and dislikes.

The shared values of a scientific community, according to Kuhn, provide the best guidance in the community's decision whether one theory is more reasonable to believe than another.[6] Among these values we usually find: (1) accuracy, or agreement of a theory with the results of previously accepted experiments and observations; (2) consistency, *i.e.*, a theory should be internally consistent and consistent with other currently accepted theories; (3) broad scope, *i.e.*, the consequences of a theory should extend beyond the particular observations it was designed to explain; (4) simplicity, *i.e.*, a theory should bring order to otherwise unordered phenomena; and (5) fruitfulness, *i.e.*, a theory should reveal new phenomena and new relations among phenomena. Each of these values is somewhat vague, and consequently scientists often disagree about how they should apply a particular value to a particular decision. For example, one scientist may construe simplicity as quantitative simplicity, whereas another scientist may construe it as qualitative simplicity. Furthermore, scientific values often conflict with each other when one applies them together. It might be the case, for instance, that simplicity or fruitfulness guides the scientist to choose one theory, whereas accuracy guides him to choose another. And unfortunately we cannot reconcile all value-conflicts simply by positing accuracy as the most decisive value. For often one of two competing theories is very accurate in one area of experience, whereas the other theory is very accurate in another area. The oxygen theory, for example, could explain weight relations in chemical reactions better than the phlogiston theory, but the phlogiston theory could better explain the metals' being much more alike than the ores from which they came. Consequently, Kuhn emphasizes that the scientific community must decide in which area accuracy is more important.[7] And the consensus of the scientific community is important in the application of the other scientific values also, since those values provide only a rough guide for the community's choice of the most reasonable theory. In fact, according to contextualists such as Kuhn and Brown, the consensus of the current scientific community is the highest court of appeals concerning the justification of any scientific theory.

One might wonder just how Kuhn's emphasis on the significance of scientific values to scientific justification relates to his emphasis on the significance of community consensus to scientific justification. A natural question, in this connection, is whether the scientific values in question can have any epistemic significance independently of the actual decision of the scientific community to countenance those values. The thoroughgoing contextualist would oppose an affirmative answer to this question. Richard Rorty, for instance, says the following about the scientific values emphasized by Kuhn:

We would do well to abandon the notion of certain values floating free of the educational and institutional patterns of the day. We can just say that Galileo was *creating* the notion of 'scientific values' as he went along, that it was a splendid thing that he did so, and that the question of whether he was 'rational' in doing so is out of place.[8]

(The present quote is, of course, directly concerned with the creation of the *notion* of scientific values, yet it seems clear that Rorty would also ascribe the creation and significance of the values themselves to the members of a scientific community.) Although I doubt that Kuhn and Brown would accept the claim that *Galileo* was the creator of the notion of scientific values, I believe they would have no objection to the suggestion that the epistemic significance of the scientific values derives wholly from a consensus of the scientific community. That is, according to contextualism, scientists do not countenance certain scientific values because it is rational or conducive to truth to do so; rather, it is rational to countenance certain scientific values because the community of scientists does so. Thus, the consensus of the scientific community, rather than the set of scientific values, is epistemically fundamental. It is true that once a scientific community agrees on the epistemic significance of certain scientific values, those values will influence the subsequent cognitive decisions of the members of that community, but we should not infer from this that those values have any epistemic significance independently of the community consensus. For social consensus, according to the contextualist, is fundamental to all epistemic assessment.

I want to raise several major objections to the foregoing contextualist model of scientific justification, but before turning to objections, I need to set forth a concise statement of the contextualist's basic epistemic principle. I propose the following:

> CE3.   A person, S, is inferentially justified in believing that *p* (where *p* is some empirical proposition) at a time, *t*, if and only if at *t* almost all members of a scientific community, C, relevant to S agree that *p* explains, in accordance with certain scientific values accepted by C, certain (unjustified) starter propositions, which according to the members of C need explaining, better than any available competing propositions.

CE3, I believe, provides a plausible summary statement of the notion of scientific justification espoused by Kuhn and Brown. Notice that according to CE3 the consensus of the scientific community plays a decisive role at three levels. First, a community consensus gives rise to a set of scientific values that provides the community with a number of general epistemic principles. Our current scientific values, according to Kuhn, state that an acceptable theory should be accurate, consistent, comprehensive, simple, and fruitful. Second, a consensus of the scientific community determines, in light of its disciplinary matrix, what propositions an acceptable theory needs to explain, and what scientific problems an acceptable theory needs to solve. This consensus will provide a set of unjustified starter propositions in relation to which other propositions can be justified. Third, a consensus of the scientific community determines what propositions are inferentially justified by their providing the best explanatory account, in accordance with the scientific values accepted by the community, of the relevant starter propositions. Clearly, then, on the contextualist account, a community consensus is basic to the inferential justification of any scientific theory.

A natural objection to the contextualist account of scientific justification is that it confuses descriptive and normative matters. Epistemic justification, we might propose, is a normative notion, and hence we should not define it in terms of something factual, such as the conduct and consensus of the current scientific community. Obviously, the scientific community can reach a consensus in many ways, and it is doubtful that all of these ways are epistemically significant. Consider, for instance, the Lysenko affair that occurred in the scientific community of the Soviet Union in the late 1920s. The politically forced consensus of the Lysenkoites resulted in widespread rejection of modern genetics in the Soviet Union, and this consensus held sway over Soviet biology well into the 1960s. In light of the real possibility of such political demogoguery, it seems absurd to define scientific justification in terms of the consensus of the current scientific community.

The contextualist might reply that the Lysenko affair does not provide a *reductio ad absurdum* of his theory because his theory relies on the consensus of the *world-wide* scientific community. The world-wide scientific community, of course, did not accept Lysenkoism, and thus the contextualist might conclude that he can easily avoid the objection at hand. But this reply is obviously too facile. For the crucial objection is that it is quite possible to have a politically forced consensus of the world-wide scientific community, but that such a consensus would not be epistemically significant.

A natural counter-reply is that the contextualist does not permit just anyone to participate in forming an epistemically significant consensus; only trained scientists can bring about the relevant consensus.[9] But this reply does not take the contextualist very far. For it is quite possible that trained scientists will begin to choose their theories solely, or at least primarily, from personal financial motives; in fact, some neo-marxist theorists have suggested that this is more than a mere possibility at present. But it is difficult to see how financial motives can underlie a consensus with epistemic significance.

At this point the contextualist might reply that what is "scientific" is defined by certain values that are not necessarily exemplified in the cognitive decisions of the current so-called "scientific" community. That is, he might claim that these values are necessary ingredients of any genuine scientific community. Each scientific community may rank and apply these values in its own special way, but once a community neglects or renounces these values it ceases to be scientific. This seems to be the best reply available to the contextualist, as it apparently enables him to preserve the normative character of scientific justification. That is, this reply will enable the contextualist to deny that just *any* community consensus is sufficient to provide epistemic justification, and to hold that a community consensus is epistemically significant only if it conforms to a certain set of scientific values.

I believe that contextualists such as Kuhn and Brown would have little objection to the foregoing reply. But Brown complicates matters when he claims that we can derive the norms of scientific justification from an examination of the practices of the scientific community.[10] He holds that we can look back over the history of science and discover just what has advanced the development of science and what has hindered it. On the basis of this discovery, Brown claims, we can make general recommendations about scientific procedure. We might recommend, for example, that contemporary scientists make theory choices in accordance with the set of scientific values emphasized by Kuhn. In any case, Brown claims that we can derive "ought" from "is"; that we can determine how scientists ought to make epistemic assessments of theories from an examination of how scientists have in fact made such assessments.

I have two problems with Brown's proposal to derive "ought" from "is". First, he must face the difficult problem of determining which communities, whether past or present, qualify as genuine scientific communities. Presumably, he needs to have at hand a list of necessary and sufficient conditions of a scientific community, such as a list of shared scientific values, before he can search history for the scientific groups providing us with the desired scientific values. But if this is so, it then seems that Brown must presuppose that certain values are scientific before he can examine the relevant scientific communities from which he intends to derive those values. Brown apparently believes that this kind of circularity is not vicious but virtuous because all historical inquiry requires presuppositions. But I find it clear that the circularity here is less than virtuous. For if Brown must presuppose that the very values he intends to derive are scientific, and thus epistemically significant, his purported derivation will be useless.

My second problem with Brown's proposal is that the history of science is highly diversified in such a way that the various so-called scientific communities do not share a uniform system of scientific values. Some scientific communities show little, if any, recognition of the five scientific values I listed above. The ancient Babylonian astronomers, for example, were not concerned, so far as we know, with theoretical simplicity and generality in the way that most speculative astronomers are. Rather, they apparently were concerned almost exclusively with practical achievements in celestial forecasting. And without much difficulty one can multiply examples of cases in which some group of scientists consistently neglects some of the scientific values in question.[11] Consequently, we should reject any suggestion that all of the scientific values in question are exemplified in every scientific community, or that the recognition of each of those values is a necessary condition of a scientific community. At most the recognition of only some of those values is a necessary condition of a scientific community. Of course, a contextualist might propose that, due to the prominence of the five scientific values in modern science, each of those values has become a necessary ingredient of a scientific community. And this proposal is somewhat plausible. Further, I grant that if the contextualist construes scientific values as necessary ingredients of a scientific community, he can countenance the normative character of scientific justification and prevent contextualism from collapsing into an extreme version of epistemic historicism that defines scientific justification in terms of the actual conduct and consensus of the current so-called scientific community. But, unfortunately, this is not the end of problems confronting contextualism.

One major problem facing the contextualist arises from the fact that a person will be justified in believing that p on the basis of a scientific community's consensus only if he is aware of the existence of the relevant consensus supporting the belief that p. Call this consensus 'C', for short. A natural question concerns the nature of the required awareness of C. Must the awareness involve justified belief that C exists? It would seem so. For if C alone is to provide a person with good reasons, or justification, for his belief that p, and if this person is not justified in believing that C exists, then this person will himself have no good reason, or justification, for his belief that p. In such a case, we might be inclined to say that there *is* justification for the belief that p, if C exists; but it would be quite gratuitous to say that the person in question *has* this justification for his belief that p. For from this person's own epistemic perspective, which does not include justified belief that C exists, the belief that p will be at best coincidentally true, and thus, despite the existence of C, this person will not be justified in believing that p. Consequently, to be justified in believing that p, this person must be justified in believing something about the views of the epistemically significant scientific community. For instance, he must be able to determine just what the relevant scientific community agrees on. But given contextualist epistemic principles, how can he do this?

Note that according to contextualist principles like CE3 a person is inferentially justified in believing that p so long as the belief that p is supported by a consensus of the relevant scientific community. But the above considerations suggest that a person must first acquire a justified belief about what the relevant scientific community agrees on. And, of course, one can ordinarily do this only by reading the writings of the relevant scientists and considering whether their views are widely agreed upon and likely to be true given one's evidence. But this means that one's justified beliefs about whether something is supported by a scientific consensus must somehow be based ultimately on one's own experiential evidence, and not on an external scientific consensus. For the only way one can acquire good reasons to believe anything about such a consensus is by means of one's own experience. But the contextualist principle CE3 conflicts with this fact, and hence should be rejected. (I shall be able to develop this argument further in Chapter V, after some additional distinctions have been made; at that point I shall also clarify the notion of experiential evidence.)

Even if the contextualist can provide an adequate account of how a person can be justified in believing that the relevant scientific community agrees on something, there is still the crucial question whether a scientific consensus formed in accordance with the five forementioned scientific values is *epistemically* significant, *i.e.*, whether it can provide one with a good reason to believe something to be *true*. It should be emphasized that contextualists such as Kuhn and Brown would definitely reject any suggestion that a scientific consensus about the rational acceptability of a theory enables one to conclude that this theory is more likely to be true than not in the absolute sense of truth mentioned in the previous chapter.[12] Most contextualists are quite unwilling to argue that there is any necessary connection between a theory's being in accordance with certain scientific values and its likelihood of being *true*. In claiming that a theory is rationally accept-able or justified, contextualists such as Kuhn and Brown seem to be claiming not that the theory is likely to be true, but rather that the theory promises to advance scientific investigation by solving certain scientific problems. Thus, according to these contextualists, scientific justification is to be defined not in terms of a theory's likelihood of being true, but rather in terms of a theory's ability to solve certain scientific problems the current scientific community deems important. This approach to scientific justification is developed most explicitly in the writings of Larry Laudan. Laudan explicitly defines the justifica-tion of a scientific theory in terms of the theory's problem-solving capability.[13]

But for purposes of developing an account of epistemic justification, there are two noteworthy shortcomings of the contextualist's problem-solving approach. First, since the notion of an acceptable problem-solution presupposes the notion of a theory's having satisfied certain standards or norms of justification, it is unclear how we can rely, without circularity, on the notion of an acceptable problem-solution to elucidate the notion of epistemic justification. Second, given the emphasis that Kuhn, Brown, and Laudan place on problem-solving as opposed to likely truth, and given their failure to relate scientific values to such truth, it is questionable whether their contextualism is even relevant to epistemic justification of the sort characterized in Chapter I. At most, it seems, their contextualism provides an account of some kind of rational acceptability that does not entail a high probability of truth. But, of course, this is not to say that problem-solving approaches to scientific rationality are worthless; nor is this to assume that some empirical beliefs are in fact epistemically justified in the relevant sense. Rather, the main point here is that the contextualism of Kuhn, Brown, and Laudan appears not to be directly relevant to the question of whether, and if so how, some empirical beliefs are epistemically justified.

I have two final objections to a contextualist principle such as CE3. First, the proponents of such a principle need to provide a clear account of the necessary and sufficient conditions of a scientific community. Otherwise, we will be unable to tell *whose* consensus constitutes the basis of all scientific justification. But, as the previous discussion indicates, this is by no means an easy task for the contextualist to accomplish. Second, the contextualist needs to explain just what constitutes a *consensus* of the scientific community. Must there be a unanimous decision in favor of the acceptability of a theory? Or is a simple majority decision sufficient? Further, what if the scientific community has a split decision about the acceptability of a particular theory? Should we then say that both the theory *and* its denial are rationally acceptable? In any case, there is rarely, if ever, complete agreement among the members of a scientific community, and even if there were such agreement, it would be very difficult to verify. But, as I have argued, one's verifying that there is some sort of consensus among the members of the relevant scientific community is centrally important to the contextualist account of scientific justification. And until the contextualist can explain how one can be justified in believing anything about the relevant scientific community, contextualism remains seriously incomplete.

Let us turn, then, to the contextualism of Wittgenstein, Annis, and Williams to determine whether the foregoing kinds of problems are eliminable.

2. CONTEXTUALISM WITHOUT A SCIENTIFIC COMMUNITY

It is clear that the contextualist accounts of justification outlined by Wittgenstein, Annis, and Williams do not agree at all points. In fact, it is arguable that Wittgenstein's account of justification in *On Certainty* is itself internally inconsistent. Wittgenstein's already quoted remark that "at the foundation of well-founded belief lies belief that is not founded" suggests that certain unjustified *beliefs* provide the foundations of justification, but Wittgenstein frequently claims that although giving grounds or evidence comes to an end, the end is not an ungrounded presupposition, but an ungrounded way of *acting*.[14] I am unsure about what Wittgenstein means by 'presupposition,' but I believe that a plausible way to reconcile his apparently conflicting claims is to construe the unjustified foundational beliefs in question as beliefs solely about certain ungrounded ways of acting. Given this construal, we could permit Wittgenstein to shift from talk of certain unjustified foundational beliefs to talk of certain ungrounded ways of acting, especially if the latter is simply elliptical for the former. In any case, some of Wittgenstein's remarks in *On Certainty* clearly endorse the contextualist thesis that all inferential justification terminates with certain unjustified foundational beliefs, and in the present section I shall be primarily concerned with the plausibility of these and related remarks. The related remarks occur in recent essays by Michael Williams and David Annis, who recognize that they are actually elaborating on several basic theses of Wittgenstein's contextualism.[15]

As Williams construes contextualism, it is the view that justification always takes place in a context of inquiry in which the inquirers take some things for granted. *De facto* acceptance is basic to all justification, but such acceptance does not require that some beliefs be intrinsically acceptable or immediately justified as the traditional foundationalists hold. It requires only that in any context of inquiry we have some beliefs we do not consider open to doubt. And the set of beliefs not open to doubt can change from context to context, and from time to time. This kind of contextualism entails a contextualization of all justification, that is, a relativizing of all justification to some concrete epistemic situation in which inquirers simply accept certain claims. And since justification can vary from context to context, Williams stresses that justification has no essence. But we can nonetheless make the general claim, on the contextualist account, that justification always requires that someone simply accept certain beliefs which are themselves unjustified but which nonetheless can somehow provide justification for certain other beliefs.

Fortunately we can look to Annis to find some of the details required to flesh out the contextualist account. Annis' contextualism involves the notion of an "issue-context" and an appropriate "objector-group". The issue-context regarding a particular belief is simply the specific issue someone raises about that belief. And the appropriate objector-group is just the group of people qualified to raise objections about a particular belief. On Annis' account, a belief is *contextually basic* for a person, S, relative to a particular appropriate objector-group at a time, t, if and only if at t the appropriate objector-group in question does not require S to have reasons for the belief to be justified in holding it. Suppose, for instance, a person with normal vision and the requisite perceptual concepts pointed to a red chair in front of him and said 'This is a red chair'. Ordinarily an objector-group consisting of normal perceivers will raise no objections to such a claim. And if at a particular time the members of an appropriate objector-group do not raise any objections, then the statement in question will be contextually basic relative to that objector-group at that time. But of course some member of the appropriate objector-group might object to the statement in question on the ground that there is a red light shining on the chair. And such an objection will call for an appropriate response, which will serve as a reason for the statement in question. But given such a reason, that statement will no longer be contextually basic for the person making it.

Perhaps the simplest way for us to characterize a contextually basic belief is as a belief that one's peers permit one to hold without any reasons. But, in accordance with the previous paragraph, contextualists typically emphasize that what is basic for a person in one context may be nonbasic in another, due, for instance, to a change in the appropriate objector-group. For example, my friends innocent of epistemology would permit me to claim without argument that there is a red chair before me, but my fellow epistemologists would ordinarily demand reasons for such a claim. Relative to the former group, then, my belief is basic, but relative to the latter group it will ordinarily be nonbasic. Because of the significance of actual objector-groups to epistemic justification, Annis claims that we should naturalize justification; that is, he claims that we should define epistemic justification in terms of the actual social practices and norms of various objector-groups.[16] And this, as we have seen, is a proposal typical of the contextualists.

But what is not typical about Annis' account is its claim that contextually basic beliefs are actually justified. Most contextualists follow Wittgenstein in holding that basic beliefs are *un*justified starter beliefs on the basis of which all other beliefs are justified. But I doubt that Annis' departure from the crowd here is really more than terminological. For Annis clearly holds that social agreement is basic to the justification of any belief. Certain beliefs are contextually basic, according to Annis' contextualism, just because the members of an appropriate objector-group agree that those beliefs are justified without any reasons. And certain other beliefs are inferentially justified just because the members of an appropriate objector-group agree that the reasons supporting those beliefs are adequate. On Annis' account, then, no beliefs are justified without the general agreement of the members of some appropriate objector-group.

Contrary to the contextualism of Kuhn, Brown, and Laudan, however, Annis holds that the social practices and norms relative to which justification is defined are epistemic in the sense that they have as their goals truth and the avoidance of error. And he claims that we can criticize these practices and norms insofar as they fail to achieve their goals. But I find it unclear how the contextualist can justify any such criticism. On the contextualist model, the only access one has to truth is via the social practices and epistemic norms countenanced by the members of some appropriate objector-group, i.e., by one's peers. Thus, ultimately a social consensus provides whatever criteria for truth one might have. There are, on the contextualist model, no epistemic norms or criteria for truth independent of those arising from a social consensus. But if this is so, how can one criticize certain social practices and norms for failing to provide one with truth? Annis' reply, I suspect, would include the claim that one social consensus and the epistemic norms arising from it can be more conducive to truth than another social consensus and the epistemic norms arising from it. But clearly his reply must also include the claim that we can have access to certain criteria enabling us to tell whether one social consensus is more truth-conducive than another. But how can the contextualist gain access to such criteria? Does a social consensus provide the answer once again? If so, on what ground can we hold that one social consensus is superior to another as regards epistemic import? It seems that at this point the contextualist must invoke epistemically significant factors other than a social consensus to defend his theory. Otherwise, he will be unable to maintain that one social consensus can be superior to another as regards epistemic import. But the appeal to epistemic factors independent of social consensus would constitute a departure from contextualism. For the central thesis of contextualism is that a social consensus of some sort is a sufficient as well as a necessary condition, or a fundamental determinant, of any epistemc justification.

I find it clear, however, that a social consensus cannot be a suffi-

cient condition of the epistemic justification of any belief. A sufficient
condition for the epistemic justification of a belief provides a good
reason for one's taking that belief to be true. But a social consensus
by itself is always insufficient to provide such a reason. A social
consensus about the rational acceptability or the truth of a particular
belief enables one to hold simply that *many people agree* that this
belief is rationally acceptable or true. But clearly such agreement is
insufficient by itself to give one a good reason to believe that this
belief *is* rationally acceptable or true. Note that if a social consensus
were sufficient for justification, then every belief, including contradic-
tions, could be justified, since we can have a social consensus about
every belief. But surely not every belief can be justified. Admittedly, if
the people participating in the consensus almost always have true
beliefs, then this consensus may have some epistemic significance. But
this epistemic significance will be due not to the consensus itself, but
rather to the reliability of the beliefs of those participating in the
consensus. And such reliability cannot arise from a social consensus,
nor can a social consensus by itself provide good reason for one to
believe that the beliefs in question are reliable. Such a belief about
reliability will find epistemic support, or good reasons, only in certain
sound epistemically significant arguments, *i.e.*, arguments that can
provide one with good reasons for taking something to be true. In
sum, then, a social consensus enables us to say merely what certain
people happen to believe. But what certain people happen to believe
is irrelevant, from an epistemic point of view, to what there is
good reason for one to believe true. Hence, given their reliance
on social consensus, the contextualist accounts I have been discussing
are irrelevant to an effort to provide an account of epistemic
justification.[17]

A related problem with the contextualism of Wittgenstein, Williams,
and Annis is that it has very little, if anything, to say to the skeptic
claiming that everything the members of a particular community agree
on may be unjustified. Williams claims that this possibility stressed by
the radical skeptic is really impossible. And he advises that we should
not take such a skeptic seriously because in doing so we end up
with a pointless debate and an indefensible theory of knowledge.[18]
Unfortunately Williams does not explain just how our taking the
radical skeptic seriously leads to an untenable epistemology. But he
does repeat with approval Wittgenstein's dictum that to doubt anything

we must always have some beliefs that are not open to doubt. Wittgenstein's dictum takes the following form at paragraph 115 of *On Certainty*:

If you tried to doubt everything you would not get as far as doubting anything. The game of doubt itself presupposes certainty.

Some of Wittgenstein's remarks suggest that certainty is indubitability.[19] But a belief can be indubitable in a psychological sense or in an epistemic sense. A belief is indubitable for a person in a psychological sense if he is psychologically incapable of refraining from holding it. And a belief is indubitable for a person in an epistemic sense if he can not have (good) grounds for refraining from holding it. Some of Wittgenstein's remarks suggest that he is concerned with a psychological sense of certainty, whereas others suggest a nonpsychological sense of certainty. But I believe that Wittgenstein's dictum at paragraph 115 is wrong on either interpretation of certainty. Thus, in the following section, I shall construct an argument which, without presupposing anything whatsoever to be certain in either sense, shows that at least one proposition can be uncertain on the basis of specific grounds for doubt.[20]

3. CONTEXTUALISM AND SKEPTICISM

One of the most powerful skeptical arguments employs the Cartesian Evil Demon Hypothesis (EDH), which states that due to a deceiving demon whatever proposition, p, is evidently true for a person, S, is actually false. The argument also uses this notion of epistemic possibility: p is epistemically possible for S at time t if and only if S is not certain of $-p$ at t. A familiar version of the argument is:

(I) 1. The following proposition is epistemically possible for S: '2 + 3 = 5' is evidently true for S, and the EDH is true.
   2. If p entails q, and p is epistemically possible for S, then q is epistemically possible for S.
   3. ('2 + 3 = 5' is evidently true for S, and the EDH is true) entails ('2 + 3 = 5' is false).
   4. Hence: ('2 + 3 = 5' is false) is epistemically possible for S.
   5. Hence: S is not certain that '2 + 3 = 5' is true.

The major problem with argument (I) is that premise 2 is false. We can instantiate the contradictory of 2 as follows: Consider a state of affairs in which S is entertaining a proposition, q, which is a remote inconsistent theorem of a certain interpreted axiomatic system. S has reflected carefully on q and therefore is certain that q is inconsistent. Hence, q is not epistemically possible for S. But S, we may assume, has not considered the theorem, p, which entails q, nor does S know that p entails q. On that assumption, p is epistemically possible for S, even though p is itself an inconsistent theorem. There is, therefore, at least one state of affairs in which p entails q and S is uncertain that $-p$ while it is false that S is uncertain that $-q$; and thus 2 is false.

Given the falsity of 2, one might jump to the conclusion that the skeptic must be certain that p entails q in premise 2 in order to wield the EDH. I grant that we can derive 4 and 5 by replacing 2 and 3 with the following premises:

2B.   If S is certain that p entails q and S is uncertain that $-p$, then S is uncertain that $-q$.

3B.   S is certain that ('2 + 3 = 5' is evidently true for S, and the EDH is true) entails the falsity of '2 + 3 = 5'.

2B appears to be an unobjectionable premise, but it requires 3B as a consequent adjustment in 3 in order to preserve validity. 3B is of course troublesome for the skeptic because it makes a claim to certainty on S's part and thus conflicts with thoroughgoing skepticism. We need then to consider some alternative candidates for the second premise of the skeptical argument.

One proposal is that we can derive the desired conclusion on the basis of the following substitutes for 2 and 3:

2C.   If S is uncertain that it is false that p entails q, and if S is uncertain that $-p$, then S is uncertain that $-q$.

3C.   S is uncertain that it is false that ('2 + 3 = 5' is evidently true for S, and the EDH is true) entails the falsity of '2 + 3 = 5'.

But, unfortunately for the skeptic, 2C is false. We can instantiate its negation with the same example I used to falsify 2. In that example, I did not assume that S is certain that p does not entail q, and thus I permitted that the proposition that p entails q may be epistemically possible for S. But the counterexample to 2 shows that if the epistemic possibility of (p entails q) and of p is due to S's unfamiliarity with those propositions, then q may be epistemically *im*possible for S while the former propositions are epistemically possible for S. Consequently, 2C fails to provide the skeptic with a viable second premise.

It seems clear, then, that the needed substitute for premise 2 must employ some epistemic notion stronger than mere epistemic possibility. On the face of it, the following principle appears to be a plausible candidate:

2D.   If S is justified in believing that p entails q, and if S is uncertain that $-p$, then S is uncertain that $-q$.

2D is impervious to the above counterexample to 2 and 2C, because, by stating that S believes that p entails q, 2D precludes that we can instantiate its negation by assuming S's unfamiliarity with (p entails q) and p. Moreover, on the assumption that S has at least an elementary understanding of entailment, S's recognition of the epistemic impossibility of q will entail, given S's justified belief that p entails q, a disclaimer regarding the epistemic possibility of p.

Endorsement of 2D, however, would be premature. For considerations of what S would *disclaim* are not directly relevant to the defense of 2D. Since S's disclaimer regarding his uncertainty that $-p$ does not entail that S is certain that $-p$, it cannot lend support to the truth of 2D. In addition, 2D is logically equivalent to the following false principle:[21]

2D1.   If S is justified in believing that p entails q, and if S is certain that p, then S is certain that q.

2D1 implies that certainty about an axiom is transmitted to a theorem even if the entailment relation between the axiom and the theorem is less than certain. But since a justificatory chain is only as strong as its weakest link, we should reject 2D1 as well as 2D.

Since the following principle avoids the problems raised by principles 2−2D, it is a promising candidate for the second premise:

2E.   If S is justified in believing that p entails q, and if S is not justified in believing that $-p$, then S is uncertain that $-q$.

2E is logically equivalent to:

2E1.   If S is justified in believing that p entails q, and if S is certain that $-q$, then S is justified in believing that $-p$.

As it is based on an epistemic analogue to modus tollens, 2E1 appears
to be unobjectionable. We can make the analogy to modus tollens
more explicit by substituting the following principles for 2E and 2E1
respectively:

2F.   If S is justified in believing that p entails q, and if S is not
        justified in believing that $-p$, then S is not justified in
        believing that $-q$.

2F1.   If S is justified in believing that p entails q, and if S is
        justified in believing that $-q$, then S is justified in believing
        that $-p$.

2F can fill the role of 2E because if S is not justified in believing that
$-q$, then S cannot be certain that $-q$. And for present purposes 2F is
preferable to 2E, since 2F focuses more clearly on the key assumption
that justification is transmissible through justified entailments. The
following steps show that 2F is equivalent to this assumption. By
substituting '$-p$' for 'p' and '$-q$' for 'q' in 2F, and by contraposing its
initial entailment and substituting in accordance with the law of double
negation, we obtain:

2F2.   If S is justified in believing that q entails p, and if S is
        not justified in believing that p, then S is not justified in
        believing that q.

Then by exportation and contraposition of the final conditional of
2F2, we arrive at:

2F3.   If S is justified in believing that q entails p, and if S is
        justified in believing that q, then S is justified in believing
        that p.

Notice that 2F3 is not equivlent to the less qualified and more
controversial transmissibility principle:

2G.   If q entails p, and if S is justified in believing that q, then S
        is justified in believing that p.

Unlike 2G, 2F3 does not apply to circumstances in which S lacks
good reason to believe that q entails p. A natural objection to 2G is
that there may be certain evidence that justifies q for S but fails to
justify p for S even though q entails p. And one might be inclined to
raise a similar objection against 2F3. But such an objection, as applied

to 2F3, is inconclusive at best, for it does not show that S is not justified in believing that p. To show the latter, one needs to show, in this case, that there is no other justifying evidence for p available to S.

But given the antecedent of 2F3, I find it clear that there is justifying evidence for p available to S. The evidence, of course, is q and (q entails p). For since S is justified in believing both that q and that q entails p, those propositions can serve S as good reasons for additional beliefs, such as the belief that p. Indeed, it is hard to see how S could have much better evidence for p. But to allay any remaining doubts about 2F3, particularly those arising from lottery-style paradoxes, let us stipulate that p and q are single noncontradictory propositions rather than sets of propositions, and assume that S believes the consequent of the relevant conditional in light of its antecedent.[22] Given these qualifications, 2F3 appears to be an unobjectionable principle. And since 2F is equivalent to 2F3, we can justifiably employ 2F as the second premise of the skeptical argument.

The next task is to instantiate the second conjunct in the antecedent of 2F, specifically as it concerns the first premise about the EDH. What we need are circumstances in which S is not justified in believing it is false that ('2 + 3 = 5' is evidently true for S, and the EDH is true). The conjunct "'2 + 3 = 5' is evidently true for S" does not raise any problems. For it is natural to assume first that most of S's evidence supports the proposition that 2 + 3 = 5, and secondly that S justifiably believes that '2 + 3 = 5' is evidently true for him. Under such circumstances S would not be justified in believing that the first conjunct is false.

But what about the second conjunct in the key clause from premise 1? Can we assume, without begging any relevant questions, that S is not justified in believing that the EDH is false? I believe so. Notice that such an assumption does not entail either that the EDH is true or that S is justified in believing that the EDH is true. For, generally, S's lack of justification with respect to $-p$ does not entail that p is true or justified. Consider, however, a possible case in which the probability of the EDH, on S's total evidence, is just as high as the probability of the denial of the EDH and of any other propositions competing with, or contrary to, the EDH. The relatively high degree of probability enjoyed by the EDH may be due in part, for instance, to the fact that almost all of the propositions which S was justified in believing in the past have turned out to be unjustified or false at present. Under such circumstances we can imagine S using an inductive inference to conclude that all of the propositions he is justified in believing are actually false. And under such circumstances it seems that S would not be justified in believing that a skeptical hypothesis such as the EDH is false.

But I do not want to suggest that all or even most of us are unjustified in denying the EDH.[23] For justification, unlike truth, is perspectival, and therefore S might not be justified in believing a proposition most of us justifiably believe. That is, any justification we might have for denying the EDH will not necessarily provide S with similar justification, for our evidence base may be significantly different from that of S. Although most of us may not have the kind of evidence base I have attributed to S, there is no inconsistency in supposing that S lacks sufficient evidence to deny the EDH. And given that supposition, S is not justified in believing that the EDH is false.

We may now reformulate the initial skeptical argument as follows:

(II) 1. S is not justified in believing it is false that ('$2 + 3 = 5$' is evidently true for S, and the EDH is true).
2. If S is justified in believing that p entails q, and if S is not justified in believing that $-p$, then S is not justified in believing that $-q$.
3. S is justified in believing that ('$2 + 3 = 5$' is evidently true for S, and the EDH is true) entails the falsity of '$2 + 3 = 5$'.
4. Hence: S is not justified in believing that $2 + 3 = 5$.
5. If S is not justified in believing that p, then S is not certain that p.
6. Hence: S is not certain that $2 + 3 = 5$.

Here we have an argument showing that a person, S, can be uncertain of one thing without being certain of anything else. Neither the logical relation between grounds for doubt and the dubitandum nor the grounds themselves are assumed to be certain in this argument. The epistemic attitude of S toward that logical relation and the grounds for doubt is at most justified belief. Furthermore, the derivation of 6 does not require that S be certain that lines 1–5 are true. It is sufficient that those lines be merely true. Hence, if lines 1–5 are merely true, then S is not certain that $2 + 3 = 5$. The skeptic, accordingly, can be uncertain of one proposition, due to the EDH, without presupposing the certainty of anything whatsoever or the justification of anything other than an entailment relation. But if this is so, it then seems that the objection of Wittgenstein and others to thoroughgoing skepticism is weaker than many have supposed.

A likely straightforward objection to my use of argument (II) is that (II) does *not* actually show that one can be uncertain of one proposition, on the basis of specific grounds for doubt, while not being certain of anything. At most (II) shows — so the objection goes — that necessarily if premises 1—5 are true of a person, then that person will be uncertain of at least one thing (on the basis of grounds for doubt). Although 1—5 do not *explicitly* assign certainty to some belief, the objection continues, (II) unfortunately leaves open the key question whether those premises logically presuppose, or require, the certainty of some belief.

The value of this objection, as I see it, is just its demand for a straightforward explanation of how the truth of premises 1—5 is logically sufficient for S's being uncertain of one proposition, on the basis of specific grounds, without being certain of any proposition. I believe 1—5 can be seen to be sufficient for such uncertainty once we recognize that the relevant sort of certainty being denied of S is *epistemic* certainty, the sort of certainty requiring epistemic indubitability (and perhaps incorrigibility also). Premises 1—5 are clearly sufficient for S's being uncertain of at least one proposition. But if this is true, then nothing in addition to the truth of 1—5 is required for S's being uncertain of at least one proposition. (This, of course, follows from the meaning of 'logically sufficient'.) The main question, then, is whether the truth of 1—5 requires certainty on S's part, *i.e.*, epistemic certainty. And upon inspection of 1—5 a negative answer will, I believe, be obvious.

Only premise 3 attributes a propositional attitude to S, viz., justified belief that a specific entailment relation holds. Thus, the main question at hand can be recast as the question whether S's justified belief (that the relevant entailment relation holds) requires S's being epistemically certain that some proposition is true. But justified belief, quite clearly, does not logically require epistemic certainty; merely justified belief is significantly weaker, from an epistemic point of view, than epistemically certain belief. For whereas epistemically certain belief logically requires at least epistemic indubitability (and perhaps incorrigibility also), merely justified belief does not. And none of the proponents of

Wittgenstein's anti-skeptical dictum has provided good reason to deny this. Thus, given familiar notions of epistemically justified and certain belief, I submit that (II) does show that a person can be uncertain of one proposition, on the basis of specific grounds, without being certain of any proposition whatsoever.

I should also anticipate a somewhat less likely objection to my use of (II) based on the following sort of familiar Cartesian argument:

(III) 1. Necessarily, if premises 1−5 of (II) are true, then S is justified in believing that an entailment relation holds.

2. But necessarily if S is justified in believing that an entailment relation holds, then S is a conscious being.

3. And necessarily if S is a conscious being, then S is epistemically certain that he exists.

4. Hence, necessarily if premises 1−5 of (II) are true, then S is epistemically certain of at least one proposition.

The main problem with this argument is that premise 3 is evidently false. Given 3, a person will be conscious only if he has a concept of existence and of himself, since certainty that one exists entails a belief that one exists, which of course requires the concepts of existence and oneself. Moreover, given 3, a person will be conscious only if he has a belief that he exists and this belief is appropriately related to his relevant evidence supporting this belief. For one's being epistemically certain that *p* entails one's being epistemically justified in believing that *p*, which requires the appropriate relation of one's belief to one's relevant justifying evidence. But both of these implications of 3 seem gratuitous at best and probably false.

Anticipating further, I suspect that some proponents of Wittgenstein's dictum would object to premise 5 of argument (II). For 5 assumes that the relevant notion of certainty is *epistemic.* One might propose, however, that Wittgenstein's claim that doubt presupposes certainty involves a *non*epistemic notion of certainty. But in that case we need to know first what the nonepistemic notion of certainty is and secondly what kind of doubt Wittgenstein is speaking of. Let us suppose that the nonepistemic notion of certainty is psychological and that the kind of doubt involved is also psychological. On this assumption Wittgenstein's claim is simply that one's refraining from believing anything requires that one have a very high degree of confidence in something. But this claim is clearly false, for some of us with skeptical proclivities refrain from believing many things but have a high degree of confidence in nothing. Perhaps, then, the kind of doubt Wittgenstein has in mind is epistemic. If so, his claim might be that one's having grounds for doubting anything requires that one have a very high degree of confidence in something. But I find this claim to fare no better than the previous one. For, as argument (II) shows, one's having grounds for doubt requires only that one be justified in believing something. But I see no reason to believe that the requisite justified belief must involve a very high degree of confidence.

Perhaps, then, Wittgenstein's notion of certainty is not psychological after all. But if it is neither epistemic nor psychological, what is it? Or, to put the question more explicitly, what kind of certainty must one possess in order to have grounds for doubting something? It is very doubtful that Wittgenstein uniformly construes certainty as entailing justified belief, for at one point he characterizes certainty as "something that lies beyond being justified or unjustified."[24] And it is similarly doubtful that certainty is mere belief, for on that construal Wittgenstein's claim at paragraph 115 seems to be the trivial claim that for one to believe that one has grounds for doubting anything one must believe something. But I can find no other plausible epistemically relevant construal of the notion of certainty in Wittgenstein's denunciation of the skeptic. Consequently, I doubt that Wittgenstein and like-minded opponents of epistemological skepticism have justifiably eliminated the possibilty of skepticism regarding empirical beliefs. Until they set forth better anti-skeptical arguments, we have good reason to conclude that they have failed to challenge the skeptic.

4. THE INADEQUACY OF CONTEXTUALISM

In light of the foregoing examination of the leading contextualist theories of epistemic justification, I find epistemic contextualism to be inadequate as a solution to the epistemic regress problem on at least four grounds.

First, contextualist justification is irrelevant to the epistemic justification of a belief. A belief is epistemically justified for a person only if he has a good reason to believe it is true. But a social consensus by itself, whether of certain scientists or of a certain nonscientific objector-group, is insufficient to provide one with a good reason to

believe anything to be true. For a social consensus will enable one to
say only what certain people merely believe, and mere belief is never
good reason for the truth of something. Unfortunately the contextualist
cannot avoid the problem at hand simply by adding that the social
consensus he invokes is arrived at in accordance with certain scientific
values the community has agreed to recognize. For such values are
epistemically insignificant if they are not related to truth in such a way
that a proposition satisfying them is likely to be true. But almost all
proponents of contextualism regarding scientific justification explicitly
deny that scientific values are so related to truth, and no contextualist,
to my knowledge, has argued that they are so related to truth. Hence, I
find no reason to believe that contextualist justification based on social
consensus is relevant to the solution of the epistemic regress problem.

Second, I find the contextualists' appeals to social consensus to be
invariably laden with vagueness. Since the notion of social consensus is
centrally important to the contextualist account of justification, one
would expect to find some careful treatments of this notion in the
contextualists' writings. But this expectation is not fulfilled. The leading
contextualists have very little to say about just whose consensus is
epistemically significant and about what kind of consensus constitutes
an epistemically significant consensus. But obviously contextualism is
seriously incomplete without a careful account of social consensus and
its relevance to epistemic considerations.

Another serious gap in the leading versions of contextualism is their
failure to relate an individual's epistemic perspective to the relevant
epistemically significant social consensus. We need to know just how
an individual can come to be justified in believing that the consensus
of the relevant group favors one view rather than another. Otherwise,
it will seem that the epistemically significant consensus is really
epistemically irrelevant to what the individual believes. But contextualists are preoccupied with social groups and communities to such
an extent that they almost invariably ignore the individual's epistemic
perspective. Typically, contextualists start and finish with the epistemic
significance of certain social groups, without ever getting around to an
account of how an individual comes to be justified in believing
something about the relevant social group. But it is arguable that this
is a reversal of the proper epistemological strategy. For a social
consensus will be epistemically relevant to an individual's beliefs only
if this individual can be justified in believing something about the

consensus. But an individual's access to information arising from a
social consensus is only by means of his own experience. The individual will have to read the writings of those involved in the relevant consensus, or get information from them in some other way. And he will
have to assess, from his own epistemic perspective, the reliability of
their reports. He will have to ask, for instance, whether it is likely that
these reports really represent the consensus of the relevant social
group, and whether it is likely that these reports are true. And surely
the individual will have to answer these questions on the basis of his
personal experience. How else could he arrive at reasonable answers?
But the contextualists typically neglect the importance of an individual's personal experience. And in doing so, they have left their account
of justification in a seriously incomplete form.

Of course some contextualists will object that their contextualism
cleanly escapes the foregoing objections insofar as it analyzes epistemic justification in terms of social *practice* rather than social consensus. According to these contextualists, some empirical beliefs are
epistemically justified by their conforming to, if not their constituting,
a social practice. Now, it is clear that many proponents of contextualism do emphasize the epistemic significance of social practice, but
I find that the role of social practice in epistemic justification is just as
dubious as the role of social consensus. My central worries concerning
the epistemic significance of social consensus apply, with the necessary
changes, to the epistemic significance of social practice. For instance,
under what conditions does a social practice make an empirical belief
likely to be true? Or, how must an individual's empirical beliefs be
related to a social practice if those beliefs are to be epistemically
justified? Obviously, not every social practice is epistemically significant; and, therefore, the contextualist owes us an account of the
conditions making a social practice epistemically significant. To my
knowledge, no contextualist has accomplished this crucial task.

My final objection to contextualism is that it has nothing to offer as
a defense against the thoroughgoing skeptic who argues that every
empirical belief we agree upon and hold to be true is unjustified and
perhaps false. Many contextualists, by way of response, faithfully
repeat Wittgenstein's claim that thoroughgoing skepticism is impossible
because all doubt requires certainty. But in the previous section I have
examined the key premise of Wittgenstein's claim and have found it to
be either false or irrelevant. Thus, until the contextualist can provide

us with a better reply to the skeptic, we may conclude that the contextualist has unjustifiably ignored the skeptic.

In light of these objections, I find it reasonable to conclude that the leading versions of epistemic contextualism not only are seriously incomplete, but also are unpromising as a solution to the epistemic regress problem.

NOTES

[1] See Ludwig Wittgenstein, in G. E. M. Anscombe and G. H. von Wright (eds.), *On Certainty* (Basil Blackwell, Oxford, 1969), paragraph 253. Cf. paragraphs 166, 136, 670.

[2] See Brown, 'Paradigmatic Propositions', *American Philosophical Quarterly* **12** (1975), 85–90, and *idem, Perception, Theory, and Commitment: The New Philosophy of Science* (University of Chicago Press, Chicago, 1977), pp. 105–106.

[3] See Thomas Kuhn, *The Structure of Scientific Revolutions, 2d ed.* (University of Chicago Press, Chicago, 1970), pp. 182–187, and *idem,* 'Second Thoughts on Paradigms', in *idem, The Essential Tension* (University of Chicago Press, Chicago, 1977), pp. 293–319. For a critical examination of Kuhn's notion of a disciplinary matrix see Frederick Suppe, 'Exemplars, Theories, and Disciplinary Matrixes', in *The Structure of Scientific Theories, 2d ed.,* F. Suppe (ed.) (University of Illinois Press, Urbana, 1977), pp. 483–499.

[4] See Kuhn, *The Structure of Scientific Revolutions, 2d ed.,* p. 158. But compare *idem,* 'Reflections on My Critics', in I. Lakatos and A. Musgrave (eds.), *Criticism and the Growth of Knowledge* (Cambridge University Press, Cambridge, 1970), p. 261.

[5] Kuhn, 'Reflections on My Critics', in *Criticism and the Growth of Knowledge,* p. 237. Cf. *idem, The Structure of Scientific Revolutions, 2d ed.,* pp. 94, 170, 200, and Brown, *Perception, Theory and Commitment,* p. 150.

[6] See Kuhn, 'Objectivity, Value Judgment, and Theory Choice', in *The Essential Tension,* pp. 320–339, and *idem, The Structure of Scientific Revolutions, 2d ed.,* pp. 184–186, 199.

[7] See Kuhn, 'Objectivity, Value Judgment, and Theory Choice', in *The Essential Tension,* p. 323. Cf. Stephen Toulmin, *Human Understanding* (Princeton University Press, Princeton, 1972), I, pp. 227–242.

[8] Rorty, *Philosophy and the Mirror of Nature* (Princeton University Press, Princeton, 1979), p. 331. Cf. *idem,* 'From Epistemology to Hermeneutics', in I. Niiniluoto and R. Tuomela (eds.), *Acta Philosophica Fennica, Vol. 30: The Logic and Epistemology of Scientific Change* (North-Holland Publishing Co., Amsterdam, 1978), p. 20.

[9] This is Brown's claim, for instance, in *Perception, Theory, and Commitment,* p. 160. Cf. Kuhn, 'Reflections on My Critics', in *Criticism and the Growth of Knowledge,* p. 263.

[10] See Brown, *Perception, Theory, and Commitment,* p. 157.

[11] On the ancient Babylonian astronomers see Stephen Toulmin and June Goodfield, *The Fabric of the Heavens* (Harper and Row, New York, 1961), pp. 23–48. Additional evidence for the variability of scientific values is provided by Toulmin,

Human Understanding, I, Chapter 4, and Larry Laudan, *Progress and Its Problems* (University of California Press, Berkeley, 1977), Chapter 4.

[12] See Kuhn, 'Reflections on My Critics', in *Criticism and the Growth of Knowledge*, p. 265; *idem, The Structure of Scientific Revolutions*, 2d ed., pp. 206–207, 170–171; and Brown, *Perception, Theory, and Commitment*, pp. 152–154.

[13] See Laudan, *Progress and Its Problems*, Chapter 4, and *idem*, 'Two Dogmas of Methodology', *Philosophy of Science* **43** (1976), 585–597, especially pp. 592–593. There is a useful discussion of problem-solving approaches to rationality in Alvin Goldman, 'Epistemology and the Theory of Problem-Solving', *Synthese* **55** (1983), 21–48.

[14] The foregoing quote is from *On Certainty*, paragraph 253. For Wittgenstein's remarks that apparently conflict with the quote see *On Certainty*, paragraphs 110, 148, 204, 342, and Wittgenstein's *Philosophical Investigations* (Basil Blackwell, Oxford, 1953), paragraphs 211, 217. See also Roger Shiner, 'Wittgenstein and the Foundations of Knowledge', *Proceedings of the Aristotelian Society* **78** (1977–78), 103–124, especially pp. 105–112.

[15] See Williams, 'Coherence, Justification, and Truth', *Review of Metaphysics* **34** (1980), 243–272, and Annis, 'A Contextualist Theory of Epistemic Justification', *American Philosophical Quarterly* **15** (1978), 213–219.

[16] See Annis, 'A Contextualist Theory of Epistemic Justification', *American Philosophical Quarterly* **15** (1978), 215. Cf. Annis, 'Epistemology Naturalized', *Metaphilosophy* **13** (1982), 201–8. Some of my criticisms of Annis' contextualism can be found in my article 'A Defense of Epistemic Intuitionism', *Metaphilosophy* **15** (1984), 196–209.

[17] Notice that a similar argument will count against the efforts to merge epistemology and psychology in W. V. Quine, 'Epistemology Naturalized', in *idem, Ontological Relativity and Other Essays* (Columbia University Press, New York, 1969), pp. 69–90, especially pp. 75–76, 78, and in Susan Haack, 'The Relevance of Psychology to Epistemology', *Metaphilosophy* **6** (1975), 161–176. See on this point Harvey Siegel, 'Justification, Discovery, and the Naturalizing of Epistemology', *Philosophy of Science* **47** (1980), 314–320.

[18] See Williams, 'Coherence, Justification, and Truth', *Review of Metaphysics* **34** (1980), 253–254, 261–262, 272.

[19] See Wittgenstein, *On Certainty*, paragraphs 337, 341–343, 454. Cf. *idem, Philosophical Investigations*, p. 224.

[20] In doing so, I shall also be opposing some anti-skeptical remarks of H. A. Prichard, *Knowledge and Perception* (Clarendon Press, Oxford, 1950), pp. 78–79, 86; Norman Malcolm, *Knowledge and Certainty* (Cornell University Press, Ithaca, 1963), pp. 68–69; James Van Cleve, 'Foundationalism, Epistemic Principles, and the Cartesian Circle', *The Philosophical Review* **88** (1979), 63–66; and Michael Williams, 'Coherence, Justification, and Truth', *Review of Metaphysics* **34** (1980), 253–254. Prichard and Malcolm suggest that grounds for doubt must be certain, whereas Van Cleve claims that the skeptic must be certain about the logical relation in which the grounds stand to the dubitandum. Williams is less clear on where certainty is required. I shall begin below with the sort of argument discussed by Van Cleve and others.

[21] To see this, consider the steps taken in the following paragraph in the move from 2F to 2F3.

58   CHAPTER II

²² This metaphorical talk of believing "in light of" shoud be analyzed, at least in part, in terms of a subjunctive conditional. Thus, if S believes that *p* in light of *q*, then S would appeal to *q* if he were to try to justify his belief that *p*. For more on this, see George S. Pappas, 'Basing Relations', in *Justification and Knowledge*, G. S. Pappas (ed.) (D. Reidel, Dordrecht, 1979), pp. 51—63.

²³ In fact, some of us evidently have a reason to hold that the EDH is false. Suppose, for instance, I justifiably believe that some physical objects are transparent, but that my body is not transparent. Given the EDH, I can infer from the foregoing assumption that (i) no physical objects are transparent, and that (ii) my body is transparent. But (i) of course implies that my body is not transparent, thus contradicting (ii). The EDH, then, can evidently be rejected by some of us on the ground that it implies a contradiction. On some other problems facing the skeptic's use of the EDH, see Peter Klein, *Certainty: A Refutation of Scepticism* (University of Minnesota Press, Minneapolis, 1981), Chapter 2.

²⁴ See *On Certainty*, paragraphs 358—359.

CHAPTER III

EPISTEMIC COHERENTISM: "CIRCLES" OF JUSTIFICATION

Epistemic coherentism provides a solution to the regress problem that is most popular among contemporary philosophers. But talk of *the* coherence theory of justification can be misleading. For 'coherentism' is actually an imprecise catchword referring to several very different theories of justification. Yet these different coherence theories do have at least one feature in common: the denial that justification requires foundations. By clarifying this metaphorical talk of foundations, we can get at the heart, or at least at one of the hearts, of epistemic coherentism. For present purposes we may regard a foundation of justification as a belief that is justified independently of any justificatory relations to other beliefs and somehow supports other justified beliefs that are not foundations. Coherentism excludes such foundations by affirming that all justified beliefs are justified in virtue of their relations to other beliefs. Thus, on the coherentist solution to the regress problem no evidence chains terminate in immediately justified, foundational beliefs. In a sense, all justification is inferential. Accordingly, we might conclude that coherentism explains inferential justification in terms of the following kind of regress:

$$e_n \text{ justifies } e_{n-1}, \ldots, e_1 \text{ justifies } e_0,$$

in which e_0 justifies e_n. And given the transitivity of justification, we might infer that e_0 justifies e_0, charge this kind of regress with literal circularity, and conclude that so far as this kind of regress is concerned, it is undecided whether e_0 is justified. But, as I suggested in Chapter I, we cannot eliminate the coherentist solution to the regress problem quite so easily. For there are several distinctive variations on the coherentist theme, and the leading versions of coherentism explain inferential justification in terms of nonliteral circles, that is, "circles" of mutual justification characterized by *non*transitive justificatory relations. In this chapter, however, I shall argue against the leading versions of epistemic coherentism. I shall show that they are unpromising as solutions to the epistemic regress problem.

It is useful to draw a distinction between negative and positive epistemic coherentism. Negative coherentism asserts that a person justifiably believes a proposition so long as he does not have a reason to refrain from believing it. Thus, on this view reasons function only in a negative manner; they serve not to justify any beliefs, but rather to disqualify candidates for justification. Positive coherentism, in contrast, assigns a positive function to reasons. Reasons, on this view, are required to provide positive support for justified beliefs. It is not enough that there is no reason to withhold a belief; a justified belief must also be positively supported by reasons. Positive coherentism has enjoyed the long-standing consensus among traditional coherentists, but I shall turn first to an examination of negative coherentism.

1. NEGATIVE COHERENTISM

John Pollock has recently defended a version of negative coherentism.[1] Pollock claims that since in deciding what to believe we have only our own beliefs to rely on, we would be irrational to withhold any of our beliefs unless we believe we should (p. 106). According to Pollock, if a person, S, believes a proposition, p, then S is justified in believing that p unless S's other beliefs support the withholding of p.[2] And S's other beliefs support the withholding of p, on Pollock's theory, if and only if S believes that he should withhold p (p. 108). Thus, we may initially state negative coherentism as follows:

NC.   S is justified in believing that p if and only if S believes that p, and S does not believe that he should withhold p.[3]

Given NC, one can be justified in believing a proposition even if one has no positive support for the truth of that proposition.

But even if we provisionally grant that only our own beliefs support the withholding of our beliefs, I still find NC to be unacceptable. Note, first, that it is actually somewhat misleading to designate such a view as 'coherentism'. NC apparently requires at most that our justified beliefs be logically consistent, but the coherence relation in its standard dress is much stronger than mere logical consistency. However, I shall not make much of this departure from the standard usage of 'coherence.' But what is objectionable is the fact that NC states neither a necessary nor a sufficient condition of epistemically justified belief.

Contrary to NC, it is doubtful that a person is justified in believing a proposition only if he does not believe he should withhold it.

Suppose a person, S, is justified in believing that p and that p entails q, and, on the basis of these beliefs, S is also justified in believing that q. But S also believes that he should withhold q, even though this belief conflicts with many of S's justified beliefs and is unjustified. Being unjustified, the belief that S should withhold q surely does not eliminate the justification of S's belief that q. S's belief that q, by hypothesis, enjoys more epistemic strength than S's unjustified belief that he should withhold q. The latter belief, being considerably weaker from an epistemic point of view, should give way to the justified belief that q, rather than conversely. For, generally, a proposition, p, cannot eliminate the justification of another proposition, q, when p is itself unjustified. But since a person can be justified in believing a proposition even if he believes he should withhold it, NC does not state a necessary condition of epistemically justified belief.

Furthermore, NC does not fare any better on its sufficient condition of justified belief. The issue, in brief, is whether a person is justified in believing a proposition when he believes the proposition and does not believe he should withhold it. Suppose a person, S, believes that a proposition, p, is true merely on the basis of groundless hearsay evidence, but also believes that p is false on the basis of evidence much better than the evidence for the truth of p.[4] Let us also assume that S does not believe that he should withhold p. This assumption is acceptable at present, since the belief that a proposition, p, is false does not entail the belief that p should be withheld. According to NC, S is justified in believing that p in the envisaged situation. But this, I find, is clearly wrong. For the evidence for the falsity of p is much better than the mere hearsay evidence for the truth of p. Thus, I submit that NC does not state a sufficient condition of justified belief.

The following example provides further evidence against NC's sufficient condition of justified belief. Suppose a person, S, believes a proposition, p, solely by way of a groundless conjecture. S has no reason to believe that p is true, nor does he presume to have such a reason. Further, S does not believe he should withhold p. But, contrary to NC, it is erroneous to assume that S is justified in believing that p in these circumstances. For such an assumption, in effect, obscures the fundamental distinction between *justified* belief and *mere* belief. *Epistemically justified* belief is necessarily related to the forementioned cognitive goal of truth, *i.e.*, the goal of believing only what is true, or at least what is likely to be true. An act of believing, in other words, is epistemically justified only insofar as it conforms to this goal of truth. But since NC allows groundless conjectures to be epistemically justified, and thus obscures the basic distinction between mere belief and justified belief, NC divorces epistemically justified belief from the cognitive goal of truth. Consequently, NC is unacceptable.

Given the foregoing objections, then, I find that we should reject NC as a principle of objective epistemic justification.

Pollock, however, may try to avoid the foregoing kinds of problems by appealing to a major restriction he places on NC. This restriction is based on an apparent difference between the objective and the subjective sense of 'should believe'. The objective sense concerns what a person should believe given his genuinely good reasons to believe something, whereas the subjective sense concerns what a person should believe given his possibly mistaken beliefs about reasons. NC, according to Pollock (p. 110), is a correct principle about subjective justification, and thus we may restate it as follows:

> NC*.   S is subjectively justified in believing a proposition p if and only if S believes that p, and S does not believe that he objectively should withhold p.

As NC* states conditions only for *subjective* justification, it apparently is compatible with any account of objective epistemic justification.

However, I doubt that the distinction between subjective and objective justification actually protects NC* from all of the above kinds of objections. My major qualms concern the sufficient condition of subjective justification stated by NC*. Suppose a person, S, believes that a proposition, p, is true solely on the basis of the slightest evidence, but also believes that p is false on the basis of evidence much better than the slight evidence for the truth of p. Let us assume also that S recognizes the strength of his evidence for p and for $-p$, but he does not believe that he objectively should withhold p. According to NC*, S is subjectively justified in believing that p in this situation. But this implication of NC* is clearly false. For in the envisaged situation S assumes that the evidence for the falsity of p is much better than the evidence for the truth of p. Thus, in the envisaged situation, S is not subjectively justified in believing that p. Hence, I doubt that NC* states a sufficient condition of subjectively justified belief. Note also that we could support a similar doubt with a less controversial example. Simply imagine a case where S believes that p on the basis of the slightest evidence, while S is aware that there is very strong evidence supporting $-p$, even though S does not believe that he objectively should withhold p. Insofar as this is a possible case, it clearly counts against NC*.

Furthermore, we can invoke a version of the earlier objection involving groundless conjecture to confirm my doubt about NC*'s sufficient condition. Suppose S believes that p solely by way of a groundless conjecture. S has no reason to believe that p is true, nor does he presume to have such a reason. But, contrary to NC*, S is not subjectively justified in believing that p in such circumstances. For S has at most *mere* belief, and not subjectively justified belief, that p is true. To preserve the relation of subjective epistemic justification to the cognitive goal of truth, and also the basic distinction between mere belief and subjectively justified belief, we need to hold that subjective epistemic justification is always based on one's beliefs about one's good reasons, and never on groundless conjecture. Consequently, we should reject NC*.

But even though NC* is unacceptable, we should hesitate to reject the general distinction between objective and subjective justification. Pollock (p. 106) invokes the following kind of case to support his notion of subjective justification: Suppose that a proposition, p, is a logical reason for a person, S, to believe that q; that is, it is logically possible that S justifiably believes that q while p is S's only reason for believing that q. Suppose also that although S believes that p, he does not believe that p is a good, *i.e.* justifying, reason for q. We may also assume, then, that S does not believe that q. Furthermore, let us suppose that a proposition, h, is not a good reason for S to believe that $-q$, even though S believes it is and believes that $-q$ on that basis. Pollock claims that given S's beliefs about reasons S would be irrational to believe that q or to refrain from believing that $-q$. He claims also that under the envisaged circumstances S could not be justified in believing that q on the basis of p, but is justified in believing that $-q$ on the basis of h. The moral of such an example, according to Pollock (p. 107), is that we should countenance a kind of subjective justification founded neither on logical reasons nor on any other intersubjective basis. If this moral is correct, we should distinguish between what a person objectively should believe given what are genuinely good reasons and what a person subjectively should believe given his beliefs about reasons.

However, once we introduce such a distinction between objective and subjective justification, it is doubtful, I have argued, that NC* provides us with an acceptable account of subjective justification. Given the above problem cases for NC and NC*, I propose the following analysis of subjective justification:

> SJ.   S is subjectively justified in believing a proposition p if and only if: (i) S believes he has a good reason to believe that p, and believes that p on the basis of this supposed good reason: (ii) if S believes that p is false, then S's belief that p is based on reasons assumed by S to be either just as good as or better than S's assumed reasons for believing that p is false; and (iii) if S believes he objectively should withhold p, then S's belief that p is based on reasons assumed by S to be either just as good as or better than S's assumed reasons for believing he objectively should withhold p.

Given conditions (i)–(iii) of SJ, it is epistemically permissible, from a subjective point of view, for S to believe that p. But this, of course, is not to say that it would be irrational for S to refrain from believing that p if (i)–(iii) were to obtain. For S may believe that his reasons for believing that $-p$ are just as good as his reasons for believing that p, and that it is irrational to believe that p while believing that $-p$.

Note, however, that we can summarize SJ by using the notion of *prima facie* subjective justification. Thus: S is *prima facie* subjectively justified in believing that p if and only if condition (i) of SJ obtains. *Prima facie* subjective justification for S's belief that p is defeasible in the sense that it can be overridden, for instance, by S's belief that his reasons for withholding p are much better than his supposed reasons for believing that p. Similarly, we may claim that if condition (i) of SJ obtains, then it is *prima facie* irrational, from a subjective epistemic point of view, for S to refrain from believing that p. In claiming this, we would be conceding that condition (i) may fail to determine what is rational or irrational for S to believe once additional beliefs of S's enter the picture. The important point for present purposes, however, is that SJ avoids the problem cases sketched above, and thus serves as a superior alternative to NC*. A fundamental weakness of NC* is its failure to acknowledge the essential role beliefs about good reasons play in subjective epistemic justification. The above problem from groundless conjecture reveals this weakness most clearly. But since clause (i) of SJ requires that S believe he has a good reason to believe that p, SJ successfully avoids the problem from groundless conjecture facing NC*.

SJ, of course, is concerned solely with what a person is subjectively justified *in believing*, that is, with subjective *doxastic* justification. The doxastic justification of one's belief that p, roughly speaking, is justification that depends on the manner in which one's belief that p is related to one's supposed good reasons. SJ says nothing about subjective *propositional* justification, that is, about when a proposition is subjectively justified for a person even if one does not believe that proposition. But we can introduce a notion of subjective propositional justification as follows: A proposition, p, is subjectively justified for a person, S, if S would be subjectively justified in believing that p if (i) S correctly determined p's objective relations to the propositions S is subjectively justified in believing, and (ii) S believed that p on the basis of those relations. So, for example, if S is subjectively justified in believing that all Olympian gods are mythical, then the proposition that Apollo is mythical is subjectively justified for S, even if S does not believe the latter proposition. Furthermore, if S is subjectively justified in believing a proposition p, then p is subjectively justified for S. But, of course, p can be subjectively justified for S even if S is not subjectively justified in believing that p. Basic to both kinds of subjective justification, however, are one's possibly mistaken beliefs about good reasons.

But how does subjective justification relate to the kind of justification required by the justification condition for knowledge? Are the two kinds of justification identical? Although some philosophers would answer 'yes', I shall argue that subjective justification of the kind under consideration cannot satisfy the justification condition for knowledge.

Let us summarize the most straightforward version of epistemic subjectivism as follows:

(ES)   For a person's (S's) belief that p to be justified sufficiently to satisfy the justification condition for knowledge, it is both necessary and sufficient that S believes that his belief that p is justified.

For present purposes, the most controversial implication of such subjectivism is the following:

66   CHAPTER III

(1)   If S believes that his belief that *p* is justified, then S's belief
         that *p* is justified sufficiently for the satisfaction of the
         justification condition for knowledge.

One likely argument purporting to falsify (1) runs as follows:

(2) (i)   No lucky guess (*i.e.*, coincidentally true belief) is a case of
          knowledge.
    (ii) Some true beliefs are lucky guesses.
    (iii) Hence, some true beliefs are not cases of knowledge.
    (iv) Further, some true beliefs which are believed to be justified
          are lucky guesses.
    (v)   Hence, some true beliefs which are believed to be justified
          are not cases of knowledge.
    (vi) All justified true beliefs are cases of knowledge.
    (vii) Hence, some beliefs which are believed be justified are
          not justified.

The major problem with argument (2), of course, is that premise
(vi) is evidently false. In light of Gettier-style counterexamples, it
appears that knowledge is not simply justified true belief; it evidently
requires a fourth condition. Consequently, the proponent of (ES) can
propose that true belief which is lucky guesswork need not be ruled
out as knowledge by the justification condition of knowledge. For it is
sufficient that such belief be ruled out as knowledge by the fourth
condition for knowledge, which is typically construed as something
like the following defeasibility condition: S's justification for his belief
that *p* must be undefeated in the sense that there is no true proposition which, when conjoined with S's justification for the belief that *p*,
undermines (or fails to provide) that justification.[5] But I doubt that a
typical fourth condition for knowledge can remove the deficiencies of
subjective justification. Thus, in what follows I shall show that there are
cases of undefeated subjectively justified true belief which are not
cases of knowledge.

A noteworthy argument one might use to forestall any counterexample to epistemic subjectivism is the following:

(3) (i)   Necessarily, if S is subjectively justified in believing that *p*
          on evidence, *e*, then the subjectivist epistemic principle, R,
          which implies that *e* subjectively justifies *p* for S, is true.
    (ii) Necessarily, if there is a counterexample, *x*, to R, then *x*
          falsifies R.

(iii) Necessarily, if justification, *y*, entails the truth of a proposition, *z*, and *x* falsifies *z*, then *x* defeats *y*.

(iv) Hence, necessarily, if *x* is a counterexample to R, then *x* defeats the subjective justification of S's belief that *p* on *e*.

(Note that one natural candidate for principle R is the principle (4) below.) But is the present argument sound? Note that if it is, then we can easily construct a sound argument also for a *non*subjectivist analogue of (iv) just by replacing the argument's talk of subjective justification with talk of some sort of nonsubjective justification. Premises (i) and (ii), it appears, are basically unobjectionable, and the same seems true of (iii) on a sufficiently broad construal of 'defeats'. If a counterexample, *x*, "defeats" an instance of justification, *y*, so long as *x* entails that *y* does not obtain, then (iii) seems as unobjectionable as *modus tollens*. Given this broad construal of epistemic defeat, argument (3) is evidently sound.

I doubt, however, that argument (3) can lend credibility to the sort of subjectivism summarized by (ES). One problem facing (ES), in spite of the soundness of (3), concerns the role of defeasibility on a subjectivist approach to justification. Recall that a genuine defeater of S's subjective justification for his belief that *p* is (at least) a true proposition, *q*, which when conjoined with S's evidence *e* for *p* fails to provide S with subjective justification for *p*. Recall also that given (ES) and the supposition that S believes that his belief that *p* is justified, then S is subjectively justified in believing that *p*; nothing else is required. By contraposition, then, S will fail to be subjectively justified in believing that *p* only if S does not believe that his belief that *p* is justified. Consequently, any genuine defeater of S's subjective justification for his belief that *p* will be (at least) a true proposition entailing that S does not believe that his belief that *p* is justified. But of course there will be no such true proposition so long as S actually believes that his belief that *p* is justified. Consequently, given (ES), so long as S actually believes that his belief that *p* is justified, then S has undefeated subjective justification for his belief that *p*.

(Of course the proponent of (ES) might set forth an alternative notion of epistemic defeat, such as the following:

q defeats S's evidence, *e*, for his belief that *p* if and only if (i) S believes that *q* is true, and (ii) S does not believe that (*e* & *q*) justifies *p*.

This notion of defeat does not require that a defeater be true, and so escapes the foregoing objection. But two obvious problems will threaten the notion of undefeated subjective justification that rests on the present notion of defeat. First, it is very implausible to hold that for every proposition, *p*, which we know on the basis of *e*, and for every proposition, *q*, which we believe to be true, we actually believe that (*e* & *q*) justifies *p*. After all, we might not have found time to conjoin (*e* & *q*) as would thus be required. Secondly, even if we have conjoined every relevant *q* with *e* in the required beliefs about the justification of *p*, it is still an open question whether the undefeated subjectively justified true belief that *p* is lucky guesswork. But of course the burden of a defeasibility condition, as construed by the subjectivist, is to rule out lucky guesswork as knowledge. Consequently, at the very least the subjectivist owes us a full account of epistemic defeat.)

On the other hand, if S does not believe that his belief that *p* is justified, then, given (ES), S will not have a subjectively justified belief which *might* be defeated, and which might satisfy the (subjective) justification condition for knowledge that *p*. So, once again it is doubtful that there can be defeaters of the subjective justification for S's belief that *p*; for, on the present assumption, there will be no such subjective justification. Consequently, although it seems useful to countenance possible defeaters of justification where the justification of *p* on *e* entails the reliability, or likelihood, of *p* on *e, and* the possibility of *p*'s being unreliable and thus unjustified on expanded evidence *e* & *q*, it is doubtful that a typical defeasibility condition can remove the deficiencies of subjective justification.

An example will clarify my present qualms about (ES). Conjoining (ES) with a typical defeasibility condition, we have seen that S will have an undefeated subjectively justified true belief, and thus knowledge, that *p* so long as S's belief that *p* is true, and S believes that this belief is justified. But we can imagine a case where these conditions are satisfied while S's belief that *p* is at best coincidentally true, and thus unreliable, from S's own standpoint. Consider, for instance, a case where S's belief that *p* is just a coincidentally true but unreliable groundless conjecture, and where S believes, simply because of wishful thinking, that his belief that *p* is justified. Perhaps in such a case S's *objective* justification for his belief that *p*, which requires the reliability of *p*, would be defeated, but, as suggested above, we cannot say the same for S's subjective justification for the belief that *p*.

We have, then, a case where undefeated subjectively justified true belief does not qualify as knowledge. And such a case, of course, provides a counterexample to the subjectivist's claim that undefeated subjectively justified true belief is sufficient for knowledge. Indirectly, such a case also provides a counterexample to the key implication of (ES), stated in (1), that if S believes that his belief that p is justified, then S is justified in believing that p at least insofar as the justification condition for knowledge that p is satisfied. For given a typical defeasibility condition, the proposed counterexample indicates that the justification condition for knowledge requires more than subjective justification of the kind characterized by (ES).

But it is also clear that the proposed counterexample does not defeat S's subjective justification for his belief that p. Should we say then that the existence of such a counterexample falsifies the conclusion of argument (3): the claim that, necessarily, if x is a counterexample to the subjectivist epistemic principle, R, (which implies that e subjectively justifies p for S), then x defeats the subjective justification of S's belief that p on e? It seems not. For the proposed counterexample does not falsify the epistemic principle required by S's being subjectively justified in believing that p on e, viz.: the subjectivist principle R implying that e subjectively justifies p for S. One such plausible principle is:

(4)   If S believes that his belief that p is justified, then S's belief that p is subjectively justified (but not necessarily justified adequately for the satisfaction of the justification condition for knowledge).

We can readily grant that (4) is a true principle of *subjective* justification, so long as we acknowledge that subjective justification does not entail the satisfaction of the justification condition for knowledge. Such a concession will not affect the foregoing argument. For the counterexample proposed above does not in any way purport to falsify (4) as a statement of a sufficient condition for *subjective* justification. Rather, that counterexample falsifies the more controversial subjectivist epistemic principles stating that (i) undefeated subjectively justified true belief is sufficient for knowledge, and that (ii) subjective justification is sufficient for the satisfaction of the justification condition for knowledge. But since neither of the latter principles is required by S's being subjectively justified in believing that p on e, we have no reason, at least from argument (3), to suppose that a counterexample to those principles defeats subjective justification. For subjective justification of the kind characterized by (4), it seems clear, depends on neither of the latter controversial epistemic principles.

In sum, then, even if we find argument (3) sound, we still have good reason to hold that epistemic subjectivism, as summarized by (ES), provides an unacceptable account of the sort of justification required by the justification condition for knowledge. And, more generally, the same seems true of any sort of subjectivism that bases epistemic justification on mere belief.

Having argued, then, that subjective justification cannot satisfy the justification condition for knowledge, and cannot plausibly be understood in terms of negative coherentism, I want briefly to return to a couple of noteworthy variations on *objective* negative coherentism to determine whether they avoid the central problems facing NC. The first natural alternative to NC above is:

NC1.   S is justified in believing that *p* if and only if S believes that *p*, and S believes that he does not have any good reasons to believe either that *p* is false or that he should withhold *p*.

NC1, I believe, states an inaccurate sufficient condition of objective epistemic justification. Suppose all of S's evidence, including the majority of S's beliefs, supports the fact that a proposition, *p*, is false. S, however, believes that he does not have any good reason to believe that *p* is false or that he should withhold *p*. S believes the evidently false proposition, *p*, we may assume, simply because it is in his best financial interest to do so. But clearly S would not be *epistemically* justified in believing that *p* in this situation, even if he believes that he does not have any good reason to believe that *p* is false or that he should withhold *p*.

We can fault NC1 on its necessary condition of justified belief also. Suppose S is justified in believing a proposition, *p*, on the basis of a proposition, *q*, which S justifiably believes to be true and to entail *p*. But S, let us assume, refrains from believing that he does not have any good reason to believe either that *p* is false or that he should withhold *p*. In fact, S happens to believe he has a good reason to believe that *p* is false and that he should withhold *p*, because he believes that *h* is true and that *h* entails −*p*. But actually *h* does not entail −*p*, and thus S may be justified in believing that *p* even if he does not believe that he lacks good reason to believe either that p is false or that he should withhold p. NC1, then, fares no better than NC.

Another noteworthy alternative to NC is:

NC2.   S is justified in believing a proposition, p, if and only if S believes that p, and S does not have any good reason to believe either that p is false or that he should withhold p.

NC2, however, must face the problem from groundless conjecture I raised above against NC. Suppose S does not have, *i.e.*, is not aware of, any good reason to believe either that p is false or that he should withhold p mainly because S has not assessed the truth of p and p is quite unrelated to anything else S believes. Assume also that S believes that p is true solely by way of a groundless conjecture. Contrary to NC2, S would not be epistemically justified in believing that p in this situation. For, since ordinary guesswork is neither generally nor apparently truth-conducive, and since S's groundless conjectures presumably are not relevantly different from ordinary guesswork, S's belief that p does not conform to the forementioned cognitive goal of truth. NC2, furthermore, obscures the basic distinction between mere belief and justified belief, and thus divorces epistemically justified belief from the goal of truth. Consequently, NC2 is unacceptable.

Evidently we need to introduce a clause like the following to salvage NC2: S has evidence supporting the truth of p, which is as good as, if not better than, the evidence for the withholding and the falsity of p, and S believes that p on the basis of the relevant evidence. But such a clause constitutes a departure from negative coherentism by requiring that S have some positive support for his belief that p. Negative coherentism, by definition, does not demand any such positive support. But since we must require such positive support in order to avoid the problem from groundless conjecture, we have good reason to reject NC2.

More generally, the problem from groundless conjecture counts against any variant of negative coherentism. For, necessarily, no variant of negative coherentism requires one to have positive support for one's justified beliefs. Accordingly, any version of negative coherentism is objectionable on the ground that it obscures the fundamental distinction between mere belief and justified belief, and thus divorces epistemically justified belief from the cognitive goal of truth. Hence, given the relevance of this objection, as well as the relevance of the other problems I have raised above, we may conclude that negative coherentism provides us neither with an acceptable theory of objective epistemic justification nor with an acceptable theory of subjective epistemic justification. Evidently, then, negative coherentism is not a worthy competitor for epistemic foundationalism and positive coherentism. Let us turn, then, to a different kind of epistemic coherentism — positive coherentism.

2. POSITIVE COHERENTISM

The various versions of positive coherentism share the assumption that a person is justified in believing a proposition only if he actually has good reasons to believe it. The leading contemporary versions of positive coherentism are holistic insofar as they construe coherence as a relation between a candidate belief and the set of all of the propositions a person antecedently believes. Holistic positive coherentism opposes any linear or axiomatic conception of empirical justification depicting the fundamental relation between justified beliefs as one of linear dependence with derivative beliefs depending on foundational beliefs. Rather, it advances a network or a systematic conception of justification depicting the fundamental relation between justified propositions as one of mutual support. Keith Lehrer has proposed the following as a schema for a coherence theory:[6]

> CT.   A person, S, is justified in believing a proposition, p, if and only if p coheres with the other beliefs belonging to a system of beliefs of kind K.

CT may state an accurate necessary condition of justification, but I suspect that its sufficient condition is inaccurate. For CT apparently neglects the standard distinction between *propositional* and *doxastic* justification. CT may state an accurate sufficient condition of propositional justification, but we must introduce an additional clause for CT to capture a correct sufficient condition of doxastic justification. We might add, for instance, the condition that S believes that p on the basis of p's coherence with a belief-system of kind K. In any case, at this early stage we should revise CT to allow for the distinction between doxastic and propositional justification.

We have another reason to revise CT. The belief-system of kind K mentioned by CT might include foundational propositions justified apart from any relations to other propositions. But the proponent of CT opposes the view that such foundational propositions are required for the justification of any propositions. Thus we should reformulate CT as follows:

CT*.   A proposition, p, is justified for a person, S, if and only if p coheres with the beliefs belonging to a belief-system of kind K that does not require foundational propositions for the justification of any propositions.

The proponent of CT must fulfill two basic requirements. He must provide us with an account of the relation called 'coherence,' and he must specify the kind of system with which a justified proposition must cohere.

Coherence theorists generally agree that coherence is not merely logical consistency. Brand Blanshard and some of the other idealists who espouse the coherence theory of truth construe coherence as a relation of necessary connection. More precisely, on Blanshard's theory a proposition, p, coheres with other propositions of a system, K, if and only if p logically entails or is logically entailed by every other proposition in K.[7] But surely this kind of logical coherence is not necessary for epistemic justification. For two propositions about quite unrelated perceptual objects can be justified for a person even though neither entails the other and they do not entail the same propositions. We should also deny that logical coherence is sufficient for empirical epistemic justification. Consider any consistent system of contingent propositions characterized by coherence in Blanshard's sense. We can form another coherent system simply by negating each of the propositions in the first system. The new system will of course contradict everything the first system says about the world. Thus if logical coherence is sufficient for epistemic justification, any contingent proposition justified for a person is such that its contradictory also is justified for that person. This problem, as well as the preceding problem, advises us against construing coherence as mutual entailment.[8]

2.1. Explanatory Coherentism

Some prominent coherence theorists connect coherence with explanation to produce explanatory coherence theories. Harman, Quine, and Sellars, among others, espouse such theories.[9] Keith Lehrer, however,

has set forth the most straightforward version of explanatory coherentism.[10] Thus I shall treat Lehrer's theory as a paradigm of explanatory coherentism. According to Lehrer's theory, called 'explanationism,' a belief is justified by its explanatory function in a system of
beliefs. A belief can have such a function in two ways. Either it can
explain or be an essential part of what explains something, or it can be
explained or be an essential part of what is explained. The justifying
system of beliefs for a person, S, must have a maximum of explanatory
coherence among the systems of beliefs understood by S. Thus Lehrer
provides the following statement of explanatory coherentism:[11]

> EC.   S is justified in believing that p if and only if (i) the belief of
> S that p is consistent with that system, C, of beliefs having
> a maximum of explanatory coherence among the systems of
> beliefs understood by S, and (ii) either the belief that p
> explains something relative to C that is not explained better
> by anything contradicting p, or the belief that p is explained
> by something relative to C and nothing contradicting p is
> explained better relative to C.

The following analysis of maximal explanatory coherence is central to
EC:

> MEC. A system, C, has a maximum of explanatory coherence
> among the systems of beliefs understood by S if and only if
> (i) C is among the systems of beliefs understood by S; (ii) C
> is consistent; and (iii) for any other system, C′, understood
> by S, if C′ is consistent, then C explains more than C′, or
> C and C′ explain the same things but some things are
> explained better by C than C′.

EC and MEC provide us with the basis of an explanatory coherence
theory.

For present purposes we may take the concepts of explanation and
of better explanation as primitive. In doing so we can happily avoid a
number of complex problems in specifying when one system explains
better than another. Philosophers generally agree that systemic tests
such as simplicity, familiarity, scope and fecundity are relevant to how
well a system explains.[12] For now, however, we can safely overlook
any problems with such tests. But we cannot overlook the problem in
determining just which propositions a belief-system should explain.

The above analysis of maximal explanatory coherence, MEC, states that a belief-system, C, has greater explanatory coherence than another system, C', if C leaves less unexplained or explains better what it does explain than does C'. But this condition enables a person to make his favorite system of beliefs maximally coherent by decreasing what should be explained. One could simply deny the truth of all the propositions one's belief-system leaves unexplained. But surely we should not limit the propositions requiring explanation in such an arbitrary way. Thus the proponent of EC must find a nonarbitrary way to restrict the propositions needing explanation.[13]

The EC-theorist might restrict the propositions needing explanation to singular observation propositions, singular propositions which if true entail the existence of physical objects. But even with this restriction we have an overly large set of propositions needing explanation. On this restriction a maximally coherent, justified belief-system might contain only probably false observation propositions and propositions explaining them. In this case empirical justification would be inappropriately divorced from empirical truth. The EC-theorist might tighten his restriction by requiring that the propositions needing explanation be *true* observation propositions. But he must then meet the following objection of James Cornman's. Assume that either Newton's theory or Einstein's theory (but not both) explains only true observation propositions. Given EC, for all we can determine, the Newtonian theory and what it explains might be justified for us because that theory explains only what is true. Following the orthodox contemporary physicists most of us believe, albeit mistakenly and with no easy way of discovering our mistakes, that Einstein's theory is justified. But anyone who believes Newton's theory would be justified in doing so, even though he cannot provide any support for his belief — except for saying that what Newton's theory explains is true. But surely we should not limit the set of propositions needing explanation in terms of the mere (lucky) truth of observation propositions.

Cornman's objection is, I believe, well-taken insofar as it relies on the following principle:

(3.1)   If a theory of justification implies that a person can justifiably believe a proposition (or theory), p, even though there is no way to support p except to say that what p explains is true, then that theory of justification is unacceptable.

The gist of (3.1) is that a proposition cannot be justified for a person simply by explaining what happens to be true. Obviously a proposition, p, can explain a true proposition, q, even if there is no reason to believe that q is true. But if there is no reason to believe that q is true, then similarly there will be no reason to believe that p explains what is true. But in that case there will be no reason whatsoever to believe that p is true. And without such reason, it seems, p cannot be justified for a person. Thus if p is to be justified for a person on explanatory grounds, we must be able to say more about p than that it explains what happens to be true.

But what else can we say about a proposition justified on explanatory grounds? One might reply that it must explain only those propositions confirmed by observation. On this view the propositions needing explanation are *confirmed* observation propositions, *i.e.*, observation propositions we may reasonably believe to be true. But given EC the observation propositions needing explanation cannot be confirmed independently of any explanatory belief-system. If the coherence theorist suggests otherwise, he departs from explanatory coherentism. Given EC, the observation propositions needing explanation must be confirmed by their explanatory function in some maximally coherent explanatory system. But this requirement returns us at once to the initial quandary: Which propositions need explanation? Without an answer to this question we cannot provide an adequate standard of maximal explanatory coherence.

Cornman has set forth and examined a noteworthy response for the EC-theorist.[14] On this response the EC-theorist, appealing to agreement rather than truth, advances the following principle:

AC.   An empirical proposition, p, of language L should be explained on occasion O if and only if it is a singular observation proposition and almost all members of speech community M (e.g., scientists who speak L) would, if queried, assent to the truth of p on witnessing occasion O.

Cornman's objection is that the right-hand side of AC is no more accessible to the EC-theorist than mere truth. Consider a person, S, who, given EC and AC, justifiably believes an observation proposition, p, explained by Einstein's theory but denied by Newton's. In order to be justified in believing that p should be explained, S must have good reason to believe that the right-hand side of AC is true with respect to *p*. Thus S must be justified in believing an observational generalization such as the following:

OG1.   Almost all members of community M would, if queried, assent to the truth of *p* on witnessing occasion O.

OG1 is an empirical proposition, although not a singular observation proposition, and thus, given EC, S is justified in believing OG1 if and only if it has an explanatory function in a belief-system having a maximum of explanatory coherence. But given EC how can S be justified in believing this?

Cornman has provided the following response for the EC-theorist. One might first assume OG1 and some generalizations similar to it, then use the set of observation propositions they and AC pick out to determine which explanatory systems are maximally coherent, and finally determine whether or not OG1 has an explanatory function in a maximally coherent explanatory system. If OG1 does not have such an explanatory function, then given EC it is unjustified. But one can always provide an explanatory function, and thus justification, for OG1 by enabling OG1 on occasion O to help explain q = 'Scientist A assents to p'. And since S must have good reason to believe that q needs explanation on occasion O, the EC-theorist may assume OG2, which is similar to OG1 except for its containing q instead of p. Then OG2 can be justified for S by explaining r = 'Scientist B assents to q'. And so on *ad indefinitum*.

The problem with such a procedure, as Cornman notes, is that it is arbitrary in what it justifies. If we substitute '$-p$' for 'p' in OG1, then $-p$ instead of p is justified for S. But this suggests that the above procedure makes EC run afoul of the following restriction:

(3.2)   A theory of empirical justification is adequate only if it does not provide a way to justify any empirical proposition for any person at any time.

Since EC violates this restriction when conjoined with AC as currently construed, AC does not enable the EC-theorist to limit the set of propositions needing explanation.

The proponent of EC might reply, however, that the foregoing argument against AC contains an erroneous assumption. The argument assumes that S must be somehow justified in believing OG1 if S is to be justified in believing a proposition on explanatory grounds. But according to AC, OG1 need only be true; S need not be justified in believing OG1. The above objection to AC is misguided, one might counter, since it misconstrues the right-hand side of AC.

But I believe there are good reasons to require that the right-hand side of AC be accessible to S, and so I shall try to explain a major motivation for this requirement. First we should recall the context in which the controversial requirement arises. According to EC a person, S, is justified in believing a proposition, p, if S believes that p and p plays an explanatory role in a maximally coherent system, C, understood by S. The simple question underlying the present problem is: What propositions must C explain? A natural reply is: true singular observation propositions. We saw, however, that (3.1) raises problems for that reply. I suggested that if S is justified in believing that p on explanatory grounds, then S must have good reason to believe that what p explains is true. For if S is epistemically justified in believing that p, S must have good reason to believe that p is true. But if EC is correct, what p explains cannot be justified apart from its explanatory function. Nor can we say that what p explains is justified by its explanatory function in C. For the very point at issue concerns just what propositions C includes. Principle AC proposes that C should explain all and only those propositions most members of a certain community would assent to on a certain occasion. This proposal constitutes a shift from truth to social consensus. But Cornman's claim is that AC is inadequate unless a person can, in accordance with EC, confirm an observational generalization such as OG1.

I believe Cornman's claim is correct insofar as it concurs with the following principle:

(3.3)   A person, S, is justified in believing an explanatory proposition (or theory), p, on explanatory grounds only if S is justified in believing that p explains a proposition needing explanation.

Suppose S believes a proposition, p, because p explains a proposition, q, which, being obviously false, should not be explained. S, we may assume, has no reason to believe either that q is true or that q should be explained, but S nonetheless believes that p because p explains q. In that case S may have no reason whatsoever to believe that p is true. But without such a reason S would not be justified in believing that p, even though p explains q. In order to be justified in believing that p on explanatory grounds, S needs good reason to believe that p explains what is probably true, or what should be explained. Thus we can justifiably employ (3.3) in the above argument against any coherence theory based on EC and AC.

We should notice one other problem with AC. The proponent of AC might claim that a person, S, is justified in believing a proposition, p, whenever (i) p explains a proposition, q, regarded to be true by almost all the members of S's speech community, (ii) S knows that q is so regarded, and (iii) S believes that p. But the majority might believe q to be true even though there is no good reason to believe that q. In that case it may be false that q should be explained, despite the majority consensus it enjoys. If q epistemically should be explained, there must be good reason to believe that q is true. Since mere social consensus about q does not provide such reason, as we saw in Chapter II, we should reject AC as an extension of EC.

In summary, the foregoing extended argument against EC enables me to reiterate Cornman's challenge to the EC-theorist: Refute the following dilemma or reject EC. Clearly the proponent of EC must find a way to limit the set of propositions needing explanation. He has only two alternatives: Permit a person to limit the set arbitrarily, or provide nonarbitrary specific restrictions that are accessible. Obviously we cannot accept the first alternative, since it permits a person to select just those propositions his favorite system explains. And we have found good reason to doubt that the EC-theorist can currently fulfill the second alternative. Hence, we have good reason to reject all versions of explanatory coherentism.

I want to anticipate two likely responses to the dilemma facing EC. The first response proposes that we limit the set of propositions needing explanation by introducing the notion of a self-explanatory belief. Lehrer once held that some ordinary observation beliefs, such as my current belief that I see a blue fountain pen, are self-explanatory in the sense that their existence is best explained simply by their truth. But it is doubtful that the truth of my belief that I see a blue fountain pen, for instance, is an adequate explanation of this belief's existence. For it seems that my educational and perhaps linguistic training will play a role in any adequate explanation of this belief's existence, since without such training I probably would not be familiar with the notion of a fountain pen. Furthermore, the existence of my belief that I see a blue fountain pen is explained in part by my subjective belief that I seem to see a blue fountain pen. In light of these considerations, one might try to salvage the notion of a self-explanatory belief by proposing that a belief is self-explanatory only if it is a subjective belief solely about one's own perceptual or sensation states and it does not presuppose any educational or linguistic training.[15]

But even on the present proposal the view that there are self-explanatory beliefs must overcome some major problems. First, the proponent of self-explanatory beliefs must tell us in what sense of 'explain' we can say that the truth of a particular belief "explains" this belief's existence. We need to know, in other words, whether there really is any explanatory principle that relates the occurrence of a belief to its truth. Second, there are some problems arising from the apparent appeal to a private language to preserve the notion of self-explanatory beliefs. Presumably, the relevant private language will be understood only by its single user; that is what makes it private. But the beliefs that must be inferentially justified by their explanatory relations to the self-explanatory beliefs are ordinary observation beliefs acquired through public languages; they are not restricted to some private language. How, then, do self-explanatory beliefs restricted to some private language relate to our ordinary observation beliefs requiring justification? The proponent of self-explanatory beliefs surely owes us an account of this relation. Third, a problem arises from the fact that a belief explains itself only if the truth of that belief is the best explanation of that belief. Normally, we say that something is an adequate explanation only if it is supported by good evidence. That is, as Chisholm has noted, an adequate explanatory hypothesis must have some positive epistemic status.[16] Thus, the present notion of self-explanatory beliefs apparently presupposes some hidden sense of justification. And the proponent of self-explanatory beliefs owes us an account of this hidden notion of justification. In light of the foregoing three points, I conclude that the doctrine of self-explanatory beliefs is seriously incomplete and unpromising as a response to the above dilemma facing EC.

The second likely response to the dilemma facing EC is that the dilemma has no bearing on the best construal of EC. On the best construal, one might propose, a belief-system possesses a maximum of explanatory coherence not because it explains the true or the confirmed propositions of a certain kind, but rather because it explains *either* the truth *or* the falsity of certain propositions of a certain kind. Or, more accurately, one might propose the following principle:

MEC*. A belief-system, C, has a maximum of explanatory coherence among the systems of beliefs understood by a person, S, if and only if (i) C is among the systems of beliefs understood by S; (ii) C is consistent; and (iii) for any other belief-system, C', understood by S, if C' is consistent, then for all the relevant empirical propositions, p_1, p_2, . . . , p_n, C explains either why p_i is true or why p_i is false for at least as many propositions as C' explains.

It seems that given the analysis of maximum explanatory coherence provided by MEC*, the EC-theorist need not worry about limiting the set of empirical propositions needing explanation. For given MEC*, the EC-theorist can claim that every empirical proposition is a candidate for explanation, that is, for explanation either why it is true or why it is false. And whatever belief-system provides such an explanation for the greatest number of empirical propositions will enjoy maximal explanatory coherence. Presumably, on this account a particular proposition, p, coheres with a maximally coherent explanatory belief-system, C, if and only if C explains why p is true. But notice that on the present account a belief-system, C, will be maximally coherent for a person, S, just in case C explains at least as many propositions as does any other belief-system, C', understood by S. This raises a likely problem for the present account. For according to many plausible accounts of explanation, if a belief-system explains a proposition, p_1, then it also explains infinitely many other propositions, since it also explains ($p_1 \lor p_2$), and ($p_1 \lor p_2 \lor p_3$), and so on. Thus the present account of maximal explanatory coherence is apparently faced with the odd situation in which any belief-system that explains at least one proposition explains as many any other belief-system, and thus is maximally coherent.[17]

Another problem facing the present account of maximal coherence is that although a maximally coherent belief-system might explain the truth or the falsity of the greatest number of propositions, it might also explain the truth of many propositions whose truth should *not* be explained because they are probably false. That is, a proposition that is probably false is not epistemically justified just because some maximally coherent belief-system explains its truth, for it may be that this belief-system should not explain the truth of this proposition, but should explain its falsity. The EC-theorist might reply that a maximally coherent belief-system explains the truth of a proposition only if this proposition is true or is probably true. And perhaps this reply is true of some notions of explanation. But if so, then the relevant notions of explanation are hiding some crucial notion of justification. And without this hidden notion of justification, the EC-theorist will be stopped by the problem at hand. In sum, then, the foregoing two problems suggest that the EC-theorist must provide us with a way to determine which propositions should have their truth explained and which propositions should have their falsity explained by some maximally coherent belief-system. Otherwise, the EC-theorist will be caught in the above dilemma.

Even if the proponent of EC can refute the above dilemma, EC is still objectionable. The EC-theorist must meet at least two additional objections. The first objection is less forceful than the second. It claims that EC is unacceptable insofar as it eliminates the standard distinction between propositional and doxastic justification, *i.e.*, the distinction between a proposition's being justified for a person and a person's being justified in believing a proposition. Recall that according to EC a person, S, is justified in believing a proposition, p, if p has an explanatory function in a maximally coherent system, C, understood by S. But this clearly is not a sufficient condition of doxastic justification, since nothing is said about S's belief that p being appropriately related to the conditions justifying p. Something must be said about this relation because S might believe that p for bad reasons even though there is justification for p available to S. The sufficient condition of EC states at most a sufficient condition of propositional justification. An additional condition must obtain if S is to be justified in believing that p, such as S's believing that p on the basis of its explanatory function in C. For if S is to be justified in believing that p, he must appropriately relate his belief that p to the conditions justifying p for him. Thus EC does not serve us as an adequate analysis of doxastic justification.

John Pollock has pressed a related but much stronger objection against explanatory coherentism. He claims that holistic positive coherence theories make it impossible for us to distinguish between justified belief and unjustified belief in a justified proposition.[18] According to EC, for instance, a proposition, p, is justified for a person, S, if p "coheres" with the maximally coherent explanatory set, C, of propositions understood by S. But if S is to be justified in believing a justified proposition, p, S's belief that p must somehow "arise out of" the fact that p coheres with C. Pollock claims that this is partly a causal notion and thus that p's cohering with C must be appropriately causally efficacious in the formation of belief. We may construe this requirement in two ways. The causal chain leading from p's coherence with C to S's belief that p might proceed via S's coming to believe that p coheres with C. In that case whenever S justifiably believes that p on the basis of its coherence with C, S believes that p coheres with C and believes that p on that basis. But Pollock objects that no plausible coherence relations have this character, and that one does not ordinarily believe that p coheres with C when he justifiably believes that p. One might propose, therefore, that the causal chain leading to justified belief that p is "nondoxastic" in the sense that it does not contain the belief that p coheres with C. But if we explicate the coherence relation in accordance with Lehrer's or Harman's explanationism, then coherence presumably could cause one to believe that p only via one's coming to believe that p coheres with C. Pollock concludes, therefore, that explanatory coherentism, as well as any other version of holistic positive coherentism, precludes the distinction between justified belief and unjustified belief in justified propositions.

I believe, however, the proponent of EC can meet Pollock's objection without much difficulty. One natural reply is that a person is justified in believing that p only if his belief that p is causally related, via inference, to the propositions forming a maximally coherent belief-system. However, the EC-theorist's simplest reply is that a person is justified in believing a proposition, p, only if he believes that p coheres with C, and believes that p on that basis. And the EC-theorist can transform this necessary condition into a sufficient condition of doxastic justification by adding the condition that p does in fact cohere with C. Furthermore, the EC-theorist can propose that a proposition, p, is justified for a person, S, if and only if p coheres with a maximally coherent explanatory system C understood by S. This proposal provides the EC-theorist with a notion of propositional justification. Pollock takes exception to that notion of doxastic justification on the ground that one does not ordinarily believe that p coheres with C when he is justified in believing that p. But that claim simply begs the question against the proponent of EC. To undermine EC we need to do more than simply to claim that a person can have justified belief even when the conditions stated by EC do not obtain. Thus Pollock's major objection to explanatory coherentism is hardly persuasive.

A much more forceful objection to EC stems from the fact that there are many examples of justified belief whose justification does not depend on explanatory considerations. Suppose, for instance, that a person knows that his backdoor is ten yards from his garage and that his dog is sitting halfway between the backdoor and the garage. Assume also that he has deduced from these propositions that his dog is five yards from his backdoor. In that case this person would presumably be justified in believing that his dog is five yards from the backdoor, even if he does not have any explanation why the dog is five yards from the backdoor. He may not even have an explanatory belief-system that can justify his beliefs about his dog on explanatory grounds. In that case a person has a justified belief independent of any explanatory relations to other beliefs. Consequently, we should reject EC.[19]

2.2. Coherentism and the Isolation Objection

One might attempt to salvage EC at this juncture by expanding the coherence relation to include non-explanatory relations. One might propose, for instance, that a proposition, p, is justified for a person, S, if and only if p either plays an explanatory role in a maximally coherent system, C, or stands in some (other) inferential relation, such as entailment, to some proposition in C. But once again the coherence theorist must take measures to preclude the possibility that any proposition whatsoever can be empirically justified for a person at a time. We can formulate the same caveat by saying that one must not cut empirical justification off from the empirical world. There are of course many outlandish coherent belief-systems − even in the expanded sense of coherence − completely unrelated to the empirical world in the sense that they are not even about the empirical world. The proponent of the coherence theory of empirical justification must explain why such belief-systems fail to qualify as maximally coherent justifying systems. Otherwise, we should reject his coherence theory due to the isolation objection, the objection that coherentism cuts empirical justification off from the empirical world. Yet thus far it is somewhat unclear just what this isolation objection amounts to.

Clearly the relevant isolation objection is not simply that epistemic coherentism entails that any contingent proposition might be justified under certain circumstances. Such an objection, it seems, would be equally applicable to non-coherentist accounts of epistemic justification, such as epistemic foundationalism and epistemic contextualism. Nor is the relevant isolation objection simply that coherentism entails that all one's justified beliefs can be false. Apparently this sort of anti-fallibilist objection would also be applicable to many non-coherentist theories of justification. Further, it is unhelpful to construe the isolation objection as claiming simply that coherentism entails that all one's justified empirical beliefs can be unrelated to the empirical world. For the relevant sense of 'being unrelated to the empirical world' is far from clear. What we need to know, on this construal, is precisely how a justified empirical belief should be related to the empirical world. We have, then, at least three unsatisfactory construals of the isolation objection.

A better construal of the isolation objection can be summarized as follows:

IO. Epistemic coherentism entails that one can be epistemically justified in believing a contingent empirical proposition that is incompatible with or at least improbable given one's total empirical evidence.

However, the talk of one's total *empirical evidence* in IO needs some elaboration. Clearly the proponent of IO should not restrict one's empirical evidence to one's empirical beliefs. For on this restriction, IO will be ineffective against any coherence theory that places a consistency requirement on one's evidence, and requires that a justified belief be probable given one's other justified beliefs. But IO becomes widely applicable to coherence theories once we expand the scope of empirical evidence. Assuming that one's *non*-belief sensory and perceptual states of awareness (such as one's feeling a pain or one's visually perceiving an apparent yellow disc) qualify as part of one's empirical evidence, we can see that IO becomes immediately relevant to a wide variety of coherence theories. For typically a coherence theory of justification analyzes epistemic justification exclusively in terms of coherence relations of some sort holding among *beliefs*, thus neglecting the epistemic relevance of non-belief states of awareness.

By way of example, consider a situation in which Sally has been gazing at the bright sun for five minutes, and so feels a painful burning sensation while visually perceiving an apparent yellow disc. Given EC and either MEC or MEC*, Sally could in the present situation be justified in believing that she is *not* feeling a pain while visually perceiving an apparent yellow disc. For the latter belief, it seems clear, could be a member of a belief-system that is maximally coherent for Sally in the sense of either MEC or MEC*, or even in Blanshard's entailment sense of 'coherence'. And for the same reason Sally could in the present situation be justified in believing some proposition that is consistent with but improbable given her total empirical evidence. Moreover, we can envisage a situation in which most, if not all, of the members of Sally's maximally coherent belief-system are incompatible with or at least improbable given Sally's total empirical evidence. But in such situations epistemic coherentism divorces Sally's justified empirical beliefs from her empirical evidence insofar as it permits those beliefs to be incompatible with or at least improbable on her total empirical evidence. Basically this problem results from the failure of coherentism to acknowledge the justificatory relevance of non-belief sensory and perceptual states. And with respect to explanatory coherentism in particular, the problem is basically that we have no non-arbitrary way to require that one's sensory and perceptual states need explanation.

Following Lehrer, however, one might object that non-belief sensory and perceptual states are not part of one's evidence, and thus do not determine what is probable or reliable for one, so long as one does not have an awareness of those states.[20] For if one has no awareness of one's being in pain, for instance, then one may very well *not* be justified in believing that one is in pain — even if one is in fact in pain. On the other hand, if one does have an awareness of one's sensory and perceptual states, then one will have a representation of those states, *i.e.*, a belief that they exist. And in that case, the evidence due to one's sensory and perceptual states will be reflected in one's beliefs. Consequently, the coherence theorist might counter that he has not neglected the epistemic relevance of non-belief sensory and perceptual states.

In reply to the present objection, we should readily grant that one's being in a particular sensory or perceptual state is insufficient for one's being justified in believing that one is in that state. For, clearly, if one is to be justified in believing that one is in a certain state, then one's belief that one is in that state must be "appropriately related" to one's relevant evidence supporting that belief. However, it does not thereby follow that one's sensory and perceptual states will make a proposition probable or reliable for one only if one believes that one is in those states. On the contrary, it seems quite plausible to hold that a sensory or perceptual state can make a proposition probable or reliable even if one lacks the belief that the relevant state exists. For instance, if one is in a state of pain, and the proposition that one is in pain is not disconfirmed by any evidence one has, then that proposition could very well be probable or reliable, indeed justified, for one, even if one failed to believe, and so was not justified *in believing*, that one is in pain. Borrowing Roderick Firth's terminology, we should recognize that one can have *propositional justification* for a proposition, in virtue of a proposition's being probable for one, even if one lacks *doxastic justification* for that proposition, insofar as one is not justified in believing it. Roughly speaking, let us say that one has propositional justification for a proposition, p, if and only if one would be justified in believing that p if (i) one believed that p, and (ii) one's belief that p was appropriately related to the justifying conditions of one's belief. Given this notion of propositional justification, one's having justification for a proposition clearly does not entail one's believing that proposition, and so does not entail one's being justified in believing that proposition. But one's being justified in believing a proposition does entail that proposition's being justified for one.

The objection at hand evidently neglects the important distinction between propositional and doxastic justification. For it apparently assumes that since one's being in some sensory or perceptual state is insufficient for one's being justified in believing some proposition (*i.e.*, for doxastic justification), sensory and perceptual states are not part of one's evidence. But in light of the forementioned distinction, this assumption seems unfounded. It gives us no reason to believe that sensory and perceptual states are insufficient for propositional justi-fication. But given the considerations of the following paragraph, it seems implausible to deny the evidential role of such states in empirical justification. Further, in neglecting the epistemic role of sensory and perceptual states, the coherence theorist is apparently wide open to the sort of isolation objection summarized by IO.

One good reason for us to acknowledge the epistemic significance of non-belief sensory and perceptual states arises from the epistemic regress problem. As noted above, this problem requires the epistemol-ogist to explain inferential justification, *i.e.*, one belief's being justified

on the basis of another, without being committed to an endless regress
of justification-requiring beliefs.[21] But if one accepts the common
coherentist assumption that only beliefs can function as justification-
providing evidence, it is doubtful that the regress problem will admit
of a plausible solution. For given that assumption, we evidently will
have to hold either that every belief is justified on the basis of some
other belief or that some beliefs are self-justified. The former option
will most likely leave us with an endless regress of justification-
requiring beliefs. And typically the notion of a self-justified belief is
unappealing to a coherentist, and, in any case, is no better than the
implausible notion of one belief's being justified on the basis of an
*un*justified belief. Each of these latter notions will provide at best
an *ad hoc* solution to the epistemic regress problem; for each of
these notions will divorce epistemic justification from one's having
good reasons for the (likely) truth of a belief. It appears, then, that
we have good reason to include non-belief states of awareness in
one's total empirical evidence. But if this is so, the isolation objection,
as summarized in IO, becomes immediately relevant to epistemic
coherentism.

Let us turn now to some likely replies to this objection.

John Pollock grants that the isolation objection counts against a
coherence theory of truth. But he denies that it is relevant to a
coherence theory of justification on the ground that according to such
a theory justification is not a matter of coherence with *all* propositions, but only with the set of propositions one believes.[22] Pollock
claims that the empirical world causally influences what one believes,
and thus that the coherence theory of justification does not unjustly
divorce justification from the world.

Unfortunately Pollock's reply to the isolation objection is much
too sketchy to help the coherence theorist. Although the empirical
world may causally influence some of a person's beliefs, we should
doubt that it causally influences all of one's beliefs. More importantly,
we should doubt that the empirical world *must* causally influence
all or even most of one's beliefs. But if the empirical world need not
causally influence most of one's beliefs, then the belief-system
maximally coherent for a person may be completely unrelated to the
empirical world in the sense that it is not even about the empirical
world. Thus if the empirical world need not causally influence most of
one's beliefs, then given the coherence theory empirical justification

may be divorced from the world. Accordingly Pollock's reply to the isolation objection can succeed only if one can show that the empirical world must causally influence most of one's beliefs. Since Pollock fails to show this, we may conclude that his response to the isolation objection is incomplete at best. The basic problem with Pollock's response, of course, is that it does not *require* that the *justification* of empirical beliefs be determined, or provided, by their (perhaps causal) relation to sensory input from the empirical world.

Michael Williams has set forth a different response to the isolation objection.[23] He claims that a reasonable and coherent belief-system must contain not only first-order beliefs, but also "epistemic beliefs," that is, beliefs about beliefs. The requisite epistemic beliefs, according to Williams, include beliefs about techniques for acquiring and rejecting beliefs (such as beliefs about how our encounters with objects in the world lead us to form beliefs about these objects) and beliefs about the conditions under which beliefs of certain kinds are likely to be true. Furthermore, Williams claims that the coherence theory of justification requires that any justified belief-system contain explanations of how our encounters with perceptual objects lead us to form beliefs about them.

But the basic issue here is whether a coherence theory of justification actually makes the requirement proposed by Williams. To put the question straightforwardly: What is the argument showing that a belief-system is maximally coherent for a person only if it contains certain epistemic beliefs? Unfortunately Williams has not provided the needed argument. Nor has he explained how epistemic beliefs are themselves justified. Moreover, he has overlooked the problem arising from the fact that many people have no epistemic beliefs. Clearly the belief-systems that are maximally coherent for these people can raise the kind of isolation problem summarized by IO. But if this is so, then it seems that coherentism will cut empirical justification off from the empirical world at least for some people. Given Williams' silence on this issue, we may conclude that his response to the isolation objection, like Pollock's, is at best incomplete. But, once again, the main problem appears to be that the coherence theory does not require that the justification of empirical beliefs be provided by their relation to sensory input from the empirical world.

I believe that Nicholas Rescher's response to the isolation objection is also inadequate and unpromising.[24] Rescher tries to relate coherence to empirical truth by introducing the notion of "truth-candidates" or "data." A truth-candidate, roughly speaking, is a proposition one should take not as true, but as potentially true; it is a *prima facie* truth in the sense that one should classify it as true if in doing so one generates no inconsistencies or other problems. Naturally Rescher includes first-person reports about sensation and perceptual states as well as certain other empirical propositions in the class of truth-candidates. But how can Rescher justify the status of a particular empirical proposition as a truth-candidate? Rescher's reply is that the criteria of truth-candidates are justified pragmatically; that is, they deliver the product we desire, namely factual truth, when we rely on them in conjunction with a certain criterion of truth. But what is the appropriate criterion of truth? Rescher construes a criterion of truth as a principle providing us with a strategy to determine which members of a set of conflicting truth-candidates we can justifiably accept as truths. The initial step of Rescher's strategy is to arrange the total set of truth-candidates in maximally consistent subsets, and then to eliminate all but one of these subsets in such a way that the remaining one is the subset of truth-candidates we are justified in believing to be true. Rescher proposes that we eliminate the competing subsets by assigning plausibility indices to the various truth-candidates. This amounts to assigning a numerical ranking to each truth-candidate that represents the initial epistemic strength of the truth-candidate. Given such a numerical ranking of all the relevant truth-candidates, according to Rescher, we can choose among the maximally consistent subsets in light of the overall plausibility of their members.

But there are at least two serious problems with Rescher's general strategy to avoid the isolation objection. First, it is doubtful that Rescher can justify his basic plausibility rankings without departing from coherentism and relying on some version of foundationalism. For coherentism, by definition, does not countenance any epistemic strength of a belief that is independent of this belief's relations to other beliefs. What Rescher needs to show, then, is that he can make and can justify plausibility rankings of the required sort without departing from coherentism. The second problem is that there is a troublesome circle in Rescher's strategy. I noted above that Rescher holds that certain criteria of truth-candidates and a certain criterion of truth can be justified by their pragmatic success. But Rescher holds that claims of pragmatic success are also truth-candidates. And this should lead us to ask whether truth-candidates are ultimately justified only by other truth-candidates. In any case, Rescher's strategy gives rise to a troublesome kind of circle at this point.[25] And in light of this problem in conjunction with the foregoing problem, I find Rescher's strategy for avoiding the isolation objection to be unpromising for nonfoundationalist purposes.

Laurence Bonjour has provided the coherence theorist with a better response to the isolation objection.[26] The first step of Bonjour's response aims to show how the coherence theory of justification can accord a significant epistemic role to observation. More precisely, it aims to show how observation beliefs can be justified by their inferential relations to other beliefs. Consider, for instance, my belief, resulting from my looking at my desk, that there is a blue book on my desk. This belief, let us suppose, is "cognitively spontaneous" insofar as it is not due to any conscious reasoning process, but simply occurs to me in a non-inferential manner. Bonjour holds that the following considerations are relevant to the justification of such a belief. First, the relevant belief is a visual belief, and I can be introspectively aware of this. Second, the conditions of observation are of a certain sort: for instance, the lighting is good, and my eyes are functioning properly. And again I can be aware of such facts by other observations. Third, there is a true law about me stating that my spontaneous visual beliefs about the relevant sort of subject-matter, under the specified conditions, are highly reliable, i.e., very likely to be true. And I can know this law.

On the basis of the foregoing considerations I might provide the following justification for my observation belief:

(1)   I have a spontaneous visual belief that there is a blue book on my desk.

(2)   Spontaneous visual beliefs about the color and general classification of medium-sized physical objects are, under normal conditions, very likely to be true.

(3)   The conditions are as specified in (2).

(4)   Therefore, my belief that there is a blue book on my desk is very likely to be true.

(5)   Therefore, there probably is a blue book on my desk.

Generalizing on this kind of argument, Bonjour claims that the justification of spontaneous observation beliefs must involve three elements. First, there must be a process producing cognitively spontaneous beliefs about a certain subject-matter. Second, the beliefs thus produced must be highly reliable regarding the relevant subject-matter; that is, it must be very likely that such beliefs are true. Third, the person whose belief is justified must know that the foregoing conditions obtain. He must know that his justified belief results from a reliable process and thus is itself reliable. Further, he must know that any necessary conditions of reliable belief are satisfied. Thus, he must know that the following schema for the justification of a spontaneous observation belief is satisfied:

    (i)   I have a spontaneous belief that p of kind K about subject-matter M.

    (ii)   Spontaneous beliefs of kind K about M are very likely to be true, if conditions C are satisfied.

    (iii)   Conditions C are satisfied.

    (iv)   Therefore, my belief that p is very likely to be true.

    (v)   Therefore, probably p.

The important question now is whether the above schema is compatible with the coherence theory of justification. Bonjour has attempted to show that it is. He claims that (3) and (iii) will normally be based on observation, and thus must be justified in the same way as observation beliefs. I find this claim indisputable, but it raises some unanswered questions. Is the justified belief that the relevant conditions obtain a *spontaneous* observation belief? Suppose a person arrives at this belief via a reasoning process even though the belief is observational. In that case this belief presumably would not be justified in the same manner as a spontaneous observation belief. But what then is the new schema for justification we must introduce? Let us hold this question in abeyance now in order to raise some more serious issues.

We should notice some unanswered questions about premises (2) and (ii) of the above justifying arguments also. Premises (2) and (ii) are obviously empirical premises. We may regard them as empirical laws about certain kinds of beliefs. Bonjour denies that we can arrive at such laws inductively, on the ground that no inductive argument would be possible unless one was already in a position to make warranted observations. He claims that confirming evidence for such empirical laws is available within the coherent belief-system. But this should lead us to ask what constitutes such confirming evidence within the coherent belief-system. And how is this evidence itself justified? Presumably empirical laws are not justified in the same way as spontaneous observation beliefs. But in that case the coherence theorist must explain just how empirical laws, including premises (2) and (ii), are justified given coherentist strictures.

A still more serious problem concerns how premises (1) and (i) of the above justifying arguments are justified. Bonjour proposes that we regard these premises as products of introspection and thus as justified in the same way as introspective beliefs. He claims that only the following premise is essential for the justification of introspective beliefs:

IJ.   Introspective beliefs (of certain sorts) are very likely to be true.

Premise IJ, according to Bonjour, is an empirical premise receiving justification within the coherent belief-system. If this is so, when one appeals to IJ to justify an introspective belief, the appeal is still ultimately to coherence.

But we must ask how an appeal to coherence can justify IJ. Bonjour has suggested that IJ is justified by its yielding coherent results in the long run. But we can derive a more informative answer to the question at hand from Bonjour's claim that the justification of a particular belief relies on the following four steps of argument:

1.   The inferability of that particular belief from other particular beliefs.
2.   The coherence of the overall system of beliefs.
3.   The justification of the overall system of beliefs.
4.   The justification of the particular belief in question by virtue of its membership in the system.

In light of these four steps, Bonjour probably would claim that IJ is justified for a person, S, if and only if IJ is a member of a maximally coherent belief-system understood by S. But suppose that IJ is not a member of a coherent belief-system understood by S. In that case, the maximally coherent belief-system understood by S may divorce empirical justification from S's empirical evidence insofar as it may justify beliefs that are incompatible with or at least improbable given S's total empirical evidence. Perhaps Bonjour's forementioned strategy shows how the coherence theory of justification can *allow* for inputs from the empirical world, so long as we understand those inputs in causal terms. But the coherence theory, being an account of *empirical* epistemic justification, must require, and not merely allow, input from the empirical world into one's maximally coherent belief-system. Otherwise, empirical justification may be cut off from one's empirical evidence.

Bonjour aims to solve the present problem on the basis of an observation requirement. The observation requirement states that for a belief-system to be a candidate for the status of empirical justification, it must include laws attributing a high degree of reliability (or probability) to a variety of kinds of cognitively spontaneous beliefs about the empirical world, including those kinds of introspective beliefs required for the recognition of other sorts of reliable cognitively spontaneous beliefs. Bonjour claims that the need for such a requirement is *a priori*. He holds that it is an *a priori* truth, according to the coherence theory, that a belief-system must attribute a high degree of reliability to cognitively spontaneous beliefs if it is to obtain empirical justification. But whether any cognitively spontaneous beliefs are actually highly reliable is an empirical issue decided solely on the basis of coherence within one's belief-system.

By way of reply, let us note first that Bonjour's solution to the isolation objection would succeed only by departing from a pure coherence theory of empirical justification. A pure coherence theory explains the epistemic justification of an empirical belief exclusively in terms of that belief's coherence with a maximally coherent belief-system. This maximally coherent belief-system is a justified system just because its members are more coherently related to each other than are the members of any competing system. Thus on the pure coherence theory, causal relations holding between beliefs and the empirical world are epistemically *in*significant. Maximal coherence is, from an epistemic point of view, the all-important feature. As suggested above, Bonjour introduces the following causal condition on grounds independent of coherence:

CC.   If a coherent belief-system is to be empirically justified, then it must include laws attributing high reliability to certain kinds of cognitively spontaneous, non-inferential beliefs about the empirical world.

According to the causal condition CC, the empirical justification of a coherent belief-system is not determined solely by its maximal coherence, but requires that the belief-system include certain laws that may or may not be conducive to maximal coherence. Suppose, for the sake of example, that a person, S, understands just two belief-systems, C_1 and C_2. Belief-system, C_1, let us assume, is much more coherent than C_2 and thus is maximally coherent for S. C_2, however, includes laws attributing high reliability to certain kinds of cognitively spontaneous empirical beliefs, whereas C_1 does not. Given CC, C_2 may be empirically justified for S, but C_1 cannot, even though C_1 is maximally coherent for S. But, of course, a pure coherence theory would assign empirical justification to C_1 rather than C_2. Consequently, we should contrast Bonjour's coherence theory, as well as any other theory including CC, with a pure coherence theory.

Nonetheless, Bonjour's coherentism is open to the same objection raised above against the responses from Pollock and Williams. For Bonjour's theory does not require that the *justification* of observation beliefs be provided by their relation to sensory input from the empirical world. Rather, on Bonjour's account observation beliefs are justified in the same way as any other beliefs: via inferential coherence. Consequently, the coherentism espoused by Bonjour, like the coherence theories of Pollock and Williams, fails to provide for the distinctive epistemic basis of observation beliefs.

Now even if an impure coherence theory like Bonjour's can avoid the isolation objection without introducing immediately justified, foundational beliefs, it raises a serious problem by giving rise to an infinite regress of required justified beliefs. As noted above, Bonjour holds that for a person, S, to be justified in holding some spontaneous observation belief that p, S must be justified in believing certain premises, such as (1)–(5) above. More specifically, one must be justified in believing that one's spontaneous observation belief results from a reliable process, and thus is itself reliable. Otherwise, one's spontaneous belief may be at best accidentally true from one's own epistemic perspective.[27] But according to any coherence theory of justification, one of the necessary conditions of any reliable proposition, p, is that p cohere with some maximally coherent belief-system. Thus, Bonjour's coherence theory relies on the following principle:

CN.   S is justified in believing that p because of p's cohering with a maximally coherent belief-system, C, only if S is justified in believing that (i) the beliefs cohering with C are reliable, and (ii) p coheres with C.

But in conjunction with a coherence theory, CN will obviously give rise to an infinite regress of required justified beliefs. For given CN and the coherentist thesis that p is reliable only if p coheres with a maximally coherent system, C, S will be justified in believing (i) of CN only by means of a justified belief that the belief that (i) coheres with C. And this latter belief must be justified by means of a further justified belief that it itself coheres with C. And so on *ad infinitum*. But, of course, it is doubtful that such an endless regress of required justified beliefs will allow for our having any justified belief whatsoever. For, among other things, it is highly doubtful that a temporally finite person has, or can have, an infinity of actual justified beliefs (although, of course, it may be that one can be *disposed* to believe an infinity of propositions.) (For more on infinite justificatory regresses see Chapter IV below.)

An additional problem facing Bonjour's impure coherence theory arises from its sufficient condition of empirical justification. The forementioned observation requirement implies that an empirically justified belief-system must include some cognitively spontaneous beliefs about the empirical world. And the coherentist's maximal-coherence requirement implies that one's justified belief-system must be at least as coherent as any other belief-system one understands. If these requirements are sufficient as well as necessary for empirical justification, we have:

CS.   A belief-system, C, is empirically justified for a person, S, if and only if C is maximally coherent for S, and includes some cognitively spontaneous beliefs about the empirical world.

Suppose, however, that S understands only two belief-systems, C_1 and C_2. C_2 not only is inconsistent, but contains no cognitively spontaneous observation beliefs, and hence by CS cannot be empirically justified for S. C_1, in contrast, contains a false cognitively spontaneous empirical belief and several other false beliefs that cohere with the former belief insofar as they are inferentially related to it. Given CS, we may infer that the mini-system C_1 is empirically justified for S. But it is highly doubtful that the fact that C_1 contains a cognitively spontaneous empirical belief and is more coherent that C_2 can, by itself, give S a good reason to believe that the member-beliefs of C_1 are true. After all, S may have acquired his cognitively spontaneous belief in a dream, and S may also have good reason to believe this. The basic problem, of course, is that C_1 acquired the status of a maximally coherent, and thus justified, belief-system much too easily. What we need from the coherentist, then, is an account of how, and under what conditions, a maximally coherent belief-system provides reliable and thus justified beliefs. Lacking such an account, the coherence theory of justification will remain seriously incomplete.

In sum, then, we have seen that a pure coherence theory of justification is open to a version of the isolation objection. Also, we have seen that a coherence theorist, following Bonjour, might try to avoid the isolation objection by introducing a causal condition like CC. But, as noted above, this will leave us with an impure coherence theory that faces some serious problems of its own, such as the problem of the endless regress of required justified beliefs, and the problem of over-simplifying empirical justification so as to divorce it from reliable belief. But more importantly, such an impure coherence theory fails to provide for the special epistemic basis of observation beliefs, *viz.*, their relation to sensory input from the empirical world. Overall, then, coherence theorists owe us, at the least, a resolution of the isolation objection and an explanation of how maximal coherence provides for empirically reliable, justified belief.

But we may need to qualify this conclusion. Thus far we have examined only objectivist coherence theories. Objectivist theories focus on some objective property or properties of beliefs, such as explanatory excellence and/or mutual entailment, to supply the conditions of maximal coherence and thus of justified belief. I have argued that the isolation objection raises problems for such coherence theories. But I have not shown that the isolation objection applies to non-objectivist coherence theories.

2.3. Subjective Coherentism

Keith Lehrer has developed the most refined non-objectivist coherence theory of justification.[28] I shall use his theory as a paradigm of a subjective coherence theory. In Chapter 8 of *Knowledge* Lehrer abandons the search for some objective feature justifying our beliefs, and appeals to a subjective feature instead. He develops a coherence theory stating that justification is based on a person's subjective probability assignments when one's only goal is to believe as many truths as one can and to avoid falsehoods. Lehrer holds that the justification of a belief cannot be based on a direct appeal to one's experience of the external world or to the testimony of others, but must be based on one's system of antecedent beliefs. Furthermore, Lehrer holds that a person's system of antecedent beliefs is able, without any external support, to provide complete epistemic justification to deserving beliefs.

To be justified, on Lehrer's theory, one's beliefs must cohere with a set of propositions articulating what one believes. Lehrer calls this set the "doxastic system" of a person. A doxastic system must be corrected to provide a person with what Lehrer calls "personal justification." That is, we must restrict the system to the propositions the person believes as an impartial and disinterested truth-seeker. Lehrer's analysis of personal justification is:

L1.   A person, S, is personally justified in believing a proposition, p, if and only if p coheres with the corrected doxastic system of S.

Thus to decide whether a person, S, is personally justified in believing a proposition, p, we must ask whether p coheres with the corrected doxastic system of S. If S believes within his corrected doxastic system that p has a good chance to be true, then p coheres with the corrected doxastic system of S. More precisely, if p is subjectively more probable than its denial and other competitors, relative to the corrected doxastic system of S, then p does cohere with S's corrected doxastic system.[29] Lehrer's more complete analysis of coherence is:

L2.   A proposition, p, coheres with the corrected doxastic system of S if and only if p is subjectively more probable, relative to the corrected doxastic system of S, than the denial of p and any other competitors.

On Lehrer's view, therefore, a person, S, is personally justified in believing a proposition, p, if and only if, within the corrected doxastic system of S, S believes p to have a better chance to be true than the denial of p and any other proposition competing with p.

Lehrer supplements the notion of personal justification to obtain his complete analysis of justification. He worries that all but one of the propositions a person accepts in his corrected doxastic system may be false. For we might deny that a person is justified in believing the single true proposition when it coheres with a system full of errors. This problem, as well as the familiar Gettier examples, leads Lehrer to introduce the notion of a *verific alternative* to a person's corrected doxastic system. A person believes a proposition in his verific alternative only if it is true. We thus arrive at a person's verific alternative by replacing any acceptance of a false proposition in that person's corrected doxastic system with the acceptance of the denial of that false proposition. Given this notion Lehrer sets forth the following principles:

L3.   A proposition, *p*, coheres with the verific alternative of S if and only if *p* is subjectively more probable, relative to the verific alternative of S, than the denial of *p* and any other propositions competing with *p*.

L4.   A person, S, is verifically justified in believing a proposition, *p*, if and only if *p* coheres with the verific alternative of S.

Given the notions of personal and verific justification, Lehrer offers this analysis of complete epistemic justification:

L5.   A person, S, is completely justified in believing a proposition, *p*, if and only if S is personally and verifically justified in believing *p*.

Lehrer requires both personal and verific justification for complete justification to insure that one's justified belief is based on what one antecedently believes, and that one does not lose one's justified belief through the correction of error.

Lehrer's analysis of coherence in terms of a network of probability is the most distinctive feature of his coherence theory. He construes beliefs about the chance of a proposition to be true as subjective probability propositions. But even if such beliefs are subjective, the actual chance of a proposition to be true need not be. If there are more losing than winning tickets in a lottery, and the tickets are consecutively numbered in a random way, there is a better chance that the *n*th number ticket is a loser than a winner. We may regard this as an objective feature of the world. And, following Lehrer, we may view beliefs about chances as subjective estimates about such features of the world. Lehrer regards beliefs about chances within a corrected doxastic system as conditional on other propositions in the system.

Thus we should understand any talk of a person's believing within his corrected doxastic system that one proposition has a better chance to be true than another as elliptical for the claim that a person believes that one proposition has a better chance to be true than another on the condition that the other propositions in his corrected doxastic system are true. A similar point pertains to the verific alternative to a person's corrected doxastic system: A verific alternative contains the belief that a proposition, p, has a better chance to be true than a proposition, q, if and only if p does have a better chance to be true than q on the condition of the truth of the other propositions in the corrected doxastic system.

I want now to argue that Lehrer's version of the coherence theory is objectionable on three grounds.[30] First, Lehrer must meet the forementioned isolation objection. He claims that his requirement that false beliefs must be deleted in the verific alternative ties justification to the world in a most appropriate manner — through the truth of our beliefs.[31] Let us call this requirement 'the deletion requirement' and assume that Lehrer's coherence theory is a theory of empirical justification. Suppose also that a person, S, believes many non-empirical but no empirical propositions in his corrected doxastic system and its verific alternative, and thus that no empirical propositions cohere with those belief-systems even though many non-empirical propositions do. On that assumption all the propositions S is empirically justified in believing would be divorced from the empirical world insofar as they are not about the empirical world. Thus if we construe Lehrer's coherence theory as a theory of empirical justification, the isolation objection applies. Clearly the deletion requirement does not meet this objection. To meet the isolation objection Lehrer must introduce a requirement similar to Bonjour's observation requirement, or principle CC, with the needed changes. But in doing so, he would depart from a pure coherence theory of empirical justification.

A more serious problem is that we have good reason to doubt Lehrer's claim that a person, S, is completely justified in believing a proposition, p, only if, within the corrected doxastic system of S and its verific alternative, S believes p to have a better chance to be true than any proposition competing with p. Recall that on Lehrer's theory a proposition, q, competes with a proposition, p, if and only if p is more probable antecedently than conditionally on q. Let us assume that p = 'S sees a blue book on his desk' and q = 'S sometimes but very rarely hallucinates.' According to Lehrer's theory, q competes with and is "negatively relevant" to p, since p is less probable given q than otherwise. We may assume that S believes that q is more probable than, and negatively relevant to, p. On this assumption Lehrer's theory implies that S cannot be justified in believing that p. But suppose that p has such a high probability, on S's total evidence, that the slight decrease in p's probability due to q does not rob p of its justification. Clearly, if the decrease in p's probability due to q is insignificantly minimal, p may remain justified for S even if S believes truly that q is more probable than p. Hence, we should reject Lehrer's necessary condition for complete justification.

Lehrer's sufficient condition of complete justification raises problems also. Lehrer claims that a person, S, is completely justified in believing a proposition, p, if, within his corrected doxastic system and its verific alternative, S believes that p has a better chance to be true than any proposition competing with p. But suppose S is a truth-seeker who believes that Monday's (generally unreliable) horoscope is the source of all current truth. On the basis of Monday's horoscope S believes that his wife is unfaithful to him, and he believes that the belief has a better chance to be true than any of its competitors. Let us assume also that S's wife is in fact unfaithful to him and that S's total evidence overwhelmingly supports this fact. S, however, has not based his belief about his wife's unfaithfulness on the supporting total evidence, because he holds that Monday's horoscope is the only source of current truth. In this situation the proposition that S's wife is unfaithful is justified for S, and S believes, within his corrected doxastic system and its verific alternative, that proposition is more probable than any of its competitors. Nonetheless, it is false that S is completely justified in believing that his wife is unfaithful, since his belief is based on a generally unreliable source. Admittedly, S's belief is true, but it lacks justification so long as it is not appropriately related to the justification-providing evidence of S's.

Lehrer might reply to the foregoing objection by denying that his theory implies that S can be justified in believing his wife is unfaithful on the basis of the unreliable horoscope. He might claim that an impartial and disinterested truth-seeker would not arbitrarily restrict his beliefs to the contents of Monday's horoscope. Thus one might doubt that S's beliefs based on Monday's horoscope can be beliefs of the *corrected* doxastic system of S.[32]

I am unconvinced, however, that a person would necessarily be biased if he based all of his beliefs on Monday's horoscope. A person might sincerely believe that Monday's horoscope is the source of all current truth. Given such a belief, a person could be genuinely veracious even if he bases all of his beliefs on Monday's horoscope. Such a person would probably have many false beliefs and few true beliefs, but he could nonetheless be a disinterested and impartial truth-seeker. And if he is such a truth-seeker, his beliefs based on Monday's horoscope could be components of his corrected doxastic system. Thus we may conclude that the anticipated reply is unsuccessful.

The previous two objections indicate that Lehrer's subjective coherence theory is unacceptable and apparently beyond simple repair. I believe they demand at least a modification of Lehrer's notion of competition and a shift from talk of doxastic justification to talk of propositional justification in principles L1–L5. The needed alterations would produce a theory very different from Lehrer's. And I doubt that the new theory would be a coherence theory in any ordinary sense of the term. Thus, instead of pursuing the needed alterations, I shall be content to conclude that the most refined version of subjective positive coherentism is unacceptable.

3. THE INADEQUACY OF COHERENTISM

In summary, then, I have argued that negative coherentism, objective positive coherentism and subjective positive coherentism raise serious problems suggesting that they are unacceptable theories of empirical justification. I believe these problems also suggest that these three kinds of coherentism, at least as exemplified in their most refined contemporary versions, are unpromising as general solutions to the epistemic regress problem.

One of the major defects in negative coherentism is that it permits groundless conjectures to play an important role in the inferential justification of observation beliefs. But it is doubtful that a groundless conjecture, being itself *un*justified, can figure prominently in the inferential justification of any belief. Thus, I find that negative coherentism provides an unacceptable solution to the regress problem. A major defect in objective positive coherentism's solution to the regress problem is that it fails to provide an adequate account of how membership in some maximally coherent belief-system entails propositional empirical justification. Good reasons for the truth of an empirical belief, according to objective positive coherentism, derive from this belief's cohering with some maximally coherent belief-system. But I have argued in connection with the isolation objection that this claim is at best dubious on pure coherentist accounts of maximal coherence. To avoid the isolation objection, the coherentist must introduce a causal condition like Bonjour's observation requirement. But even given a causal condition, objective positive coherentism is unpromising as a solution to the regress problem. One major problem is that the notion of maximal coherence is intolerably vague. I have illustrated this problem in my comments on principle (3.4). What we need from the coherentist, I have suggested, is a clear account of how maximal coherence excludes those belief-systems obviously unqualified for justification, and provides good evidence of the truth of certain empirical beliefs. Lacking such an account, the leading versions of objective positive coherentism are clearly unacceptable solutions to the regress problem. Finally, I have argued that Lehrer's subjective positive coherentism faces problems similar to those I raised for objective positive coherentism. Once again, my central challenge was that Lehrer has failed to show how his kind of maximal coherence provides good evidence of the truth of certain empirical beliefs. Given Lehrer's failure to meet this challenge, I find subjective positive coherentism to fare no better than objective positive coherentism as a solution to the regress problem.

Accordingly, given these verdicts regarding the leading versions of coherentism, I conclude that epistemic coherentism is currently unable to provide us with an acceptable solution to the regress problem. Perhaps some new version of coherentism can ultimately meet the objections I have raised, but those objections now lead me to conclude that the most refined versions of epistemic coherentism are beyond simple repair. Thus, I shall turn to epistemic foundationalism for a solution to the epistemic regress problem.

NOTES

[1] See Pollock, 'A Plethora of Epistemological Theories', in G. S. Pappas (ed.), *Justification and Knowledge: New Studies in Epistemology* (D. Reidel, Dordrecht, 1979), pp. 93–113, especially pp. 105–111. All subsequent parenthetical page-numbers in this section refer to this essay.

[2] Let us say that a person withholds a proposition if and only if he does not accept, or believe, that proposition.

104   CHAPTER III

[3] Note that I have substituted talk of "withholding p" for Pollock's talk of "rejecting p", since the latter talk, contrary to Pollock's usage, may suggest 'believing -p'.

[4] Here, of course, I am assuming that a person can believe contradictory propositions. For a persuasive defense of this assumption see John N. Williams, 'Believing the Self-Contradictory', *American Philosophical Quarterly* **19** (1982), 279—285. Yet for those doubtful about the possibility of self-contradictory beliefs, we might imagine a case where S believes that p while being aware of good reasons for the falsity of p (but not actually believing -p).

[5] This is the sort of defeasibility condition espoused, for instance, by Jonathan Kvanvig in 'Subjective Justification', *Mind* **93** (1984), 71—84, where the sort of subjective justification under consideration is defended as sufficient to satisfy the justification condition for knowledge. The present approach to defeasibility was originally suggested by Roderick Chisholm, 'The Ethics of Requirement', *American Philosophical Quarterly* **1** (1964), 147—153; and a similar approach has been defended recently by Peter Klein, 'Knowledge, Causality, and Defeasibility', *Journal of Philosophy* **73** (1976), 792—812. If one prefers an alternative defeasibility condition, my subsequent argument will not be affected so long as it is maintained that genuine (as opposed to misleading) defeaters are at least true propositions. On the important distinction between genuine and misleading defeaters, see Peter Klein, *Certainty: A Refutation of Scepticism* (University of Minnesota Press, Minneapolis, 1981), pp. 137—166.

[6] See Lehrer, *Knowledge* (Clarendon Press, Oxford, 1974), p. 154.

[7] See Blanshard, *The Nature of Thought*, 2 vols. (Allen & Unwin, London, 1939), 2: 265—266. A useful discussion of Blanshard's theory of truth is Nicholas Rescher's 'Blanshard and the Coherence Theory of Truth', in Paul Schilpp (ed.), *The Philosophy of Brand Blanshard* (Open Court, La Salle, Illinois, 1980), pp. 574—588. Cf. Rescher, *The Coherence Theory of Truth* (Clarendon Press, Oxford, 1973), pp. 27—31.

[8] Lehrer raises such objections in *Knowledge*, pp. 157—158. I shall return below to a variation on the second problem, in connection with the so-called isolation objection.

[9] See Gilbert Harman, *Thought* (Princeton University Press, Princeton, 1973), Chapters 8 and 10; idem, "Induction", in M. Swain (ed.), *Induction, Acceptance, and Rational Belief* (D. Reidel, Dordrecht, 1970), pp. 83—99; W. V. Quine and J. S. Ullian, *The Web of Belief*, 2d ed. (Random House, New York, 1978); and Wilfrid Sellars, 'Some Reflections on Language Games', in *Science, Perception, and Reality* (Routledge and Kegan Paul, London, 1963), pp. 321—358.

[10] See Lehrer, 'Justification, Explanation, and Induction', in M. Swain (ed.), *Induction, Acceptance, and Rational Belief* (D. Reidel, Dordrecht, 1970), pp. 100—133. Lehrer has since rejected this view. See *Knowledge*, Chapter 7.

[11] Lehrer, *Knowledge*, p. 165.

[12] James Cornman has provided a very useful examination of these systemic tests in *Skepticism, Justification, and Explanation* (D. Reidel, Dordrecht, 1980), Chapters 8 and 9.

[13] Cornman and Lehrer have stressed this requirement. See Lehrer, *Knowledge*, pp. 170—171 and Cornman, *Skepticism, Justification, and Explanation*, pp. 147—150.

[14] See Cornman, *Skepticism, Justification, and Explanation*, pp. 148—149.

[15] This proposal is suggested by Alan H. Goldman in 'Appearing Statements and Epistemological Foundations', *Metaphilosophy* **10** (1979), 227—246. Cf. idem,

'Epistemology and the Psychology of Perception', *American Philosophical Quarterly* **18** (1981), 46−47.

[16] See R. M. Chisholm, 'A Version of Foundationalism', in *idem, The Foundations of Knowing* (University of Minnesota Press, Minneapolis, 1982), p. 31. Cf. *The Encyclopedia of Philosophy*, s.v. 'Explanation in Science', by Jaegwon Kim.

[17] See on this point Cornman, *Skepticism, Justification, and Explanation*, p. 146, and *idem*, 'Foundational versus Nonfoundational Theories of Empirical Justification', *American Philosophical Quarterly* **14** (1977), 293.

[18] See Pollock, 'A Plethora of Epistemological Theories', in G. S. Pappas (ed.), *Justification and Knowledge*, pp. 104−105.

[19] Lehrer has provided different examples of justified beliefs whose justification does not depend on explanatory considerations. See *Knowledge*, pp. 178−180.

[20] See Lehrer, 'Knowledge, Truth and Ontology', in Werner Leinfellner *et al.* (eds.), *Language and Ontology: Proceedings of the 6th International Wittgenstein Symposium* (D. Reidel, Dordrecht, 1982), pp. 208−209. Cf. Lehrer, 'The Evaluation of Method: A Hierarchy of Probabilities among Probabilities', *Grazer Philosophische Studien* **12/ 13** (1981), 131−142.

[21] On the reasons for avoiding commitment to endless justificatory regresses, see Chapter IV below. Further argument for the epistemic significance of non-belief perceptual states can also be found in Chapter V. See also, in this connection, my article 'A Defense of Epistemic Intuitionism', *Metaphilosophy* **15** (1984), 196−209, and Marshall Swain, *Reasons and Knowledge* (Cornell University Press, Ithaca, 1981), pp. 74−82, 135−140.

[22] See Pollock, 'A Plethora of Epistemological Theories', in *Justification and Knowledge*, p. 102. Harman's coherence theory is in agreement with this point. See Harman, *Thought*, p. 159.

[23] See Williams, 'Coherence, Justification, and Truth', *Review of Metaphysics* **34** (1980), 248−251, and *idem, Groundless Belief* (Basil Blackwell, Oxford, 1977), pp. 106−107.

[24] See Rescher, *The Coherence Theory of Truth* (Clarendon Press, Oxford, 1973), pp. 53−70 and Chapter 5. Cf. *idem, Cognitive Systematization* (Basil Blackwell, Oxford, 1979), Chapter 5, and *idem, Methodological Pragmatism* (Basil Blackwell, Oxford, 1977), Chapter 3.

[25] For a helpful discussion of the circle in Rescher's account see Laurence Bonjour, 'Rescher's Epistemological System', in E. Sosa (ed.), *The Philosophy of Nicholas Rescher* (D. Reidel, Dordrecht, 1979), pp. 157−172, and *idem*, 'Rescher's Idealistic Pragmatism', *Review of Metaphysics* **29** (1976), 702−726.

[26] See Bonjour, 'The Coherence Theory of Empirical Knowledge', *Philosophical Studies* **30** (1976), 290−302.

[27] Bonjour has given an extended argument for the present requirement in 'Externalist Theories of Empirical Knowledge', in P. French *et al.* (eds.), *Midwest Studies in Philosophy, Vol. V: Studies in Epistemology* (University of Minnesota Press, Minneapolis, 1980), pp. 53−74. Cf. Bonjour, 'Can Empirical Knowledge Have a Foundation?', *American Philosophical Quarterly* **15** (1978), 6−8.

[28] My following statement of Lehrer's theory focuses on *Knowledge*, Chapter 8 and on the less programmatic sections of Lehrer's 'Self-Profile', in R. J. Bogdan (ed.), *Keith Lehrer* (D. Reidel, Dordrecht, 1981), pp. 80−90.

[29] In *Knowledge*, pp. 192–197, Lehrer construes the claim that a proposition, p, competes with a proposition, q, probabilistically as the claim that q is more probable antecedently than conditionally on p; that is, Prob(q) is greater than Prob(q/p). Cf. Lehrer, 'Coherence and the Racehorse Paradox', in P. French *et al.* (eds.), *Midwest Studies in Philosophy, Vol. V: Studies in Epistemology*, (University of Minnesota Press, Minneapolis, 1980), pp. 188–189. Lehrer's notion of competition is not equivalent to the one I employed in Chapter I, since his notion does not restrict competition to contraries.

[30] Cornman raises the second of the following three problems in *Skepticism, Justification, and Explanation*, p. 142.

[31] See Lehrer's 'Reply to Pastin', in *Keith Lehrer*, ed. R. J. Bogdan, p. 238.

[32] This anticipated reply stems from Lehrer, *Knowledge*, p. 209.

CHAPTER IV

EPISTEMIC FOUNDATIONALISM (I): INFINITE REGRESSES, EXTERNALISM, AND RELIABILISM

Given the foregoing arguments against epistemic contextualism and epistemic coherentism, we are left with two nonskeptical accounts of inferential justification, namely, inferential justification via infinite justificatory regresses and inferential justification via immediately justified foundations. Although the former account of inferential justification is unpopular at present, the foundationalist must nonetheless eliminate it before he can claim that a regress argument supports his foundationalism. In Chapter I, I have questioned the likely argument that an evidence chain extending infinitely is inadequate for inferential justification since no matter how far back in such a chain we go we always find a proposition that is only inferentially justified. This argument apparently assumes that an evidence chain is adequate for inferential justification only if this chain includes some proposition that is immediately justified. But since this assumption is the very point at issue in the debate between the foundationalist and the proponent of infinite justificatory regresses, the foundationalist cannot rely on the argument in question. We must determine, then, whether the foundationalist can say anything more substantive in opposition to infinite justificatory regresses.

1. INFINITE REGRESSES OF JUSTIFICATION

James Cornman and John Post, among others, have argued that an infinite justificatory regress is conceptually impossible on the ground that if there could be even one infinite regress such as:

(1) $\ldots, e_n$ justifies $e_{n-1}, \ldots, e_1$ justifies e_0,

then we could justify any logically contingent proposition we like.[1] Assuming that an entailment relation which includes a relevance condition is an inferential justificatory relation, we can construct the following endless regress:

(2) $\ldots, e_n, \ldots, e_1, e_0$,

107

where (i) e_i ($i > 0$) entails e_{i-1}; (ii) e_i is not entailed by any set of $e_{j<i}$; and (iii) e_i is not justified on the basis of any set of $e_{j<i}$. We shall assume that at every step of the regress there is a proposition satisfying conditions (i)—(iii). This assumption will guarantee deductive and justificational noncircularity in the regress. As a helpful example of (2), consider the following endless regress:

(3) $\ldots, p \& \{p \supset [q \& (q \supset r)]\}, q \& (q \supset r), r,$

where r is logically contingent and does not entail either q or p, and where the propositions related by '$\supset$' satisfy an appropriate relevance condition. *Modus ponens* is not the only entailment-form we can use to construct instances of (2), but it is perhaps the most familiar. The problem is that whatever entailment-form we choose, we can construct for any contingent proposition an instance of (2), such as (3), that satisfies (i)—(iii). The satisfaction of conditions (i) and (ii) by any proposition presents no problem. And we can show that (iii) may be easily satisfied as follows. Proposition r in (3) will not justify a universal set of propositions for a person, since if r justifies every proposition whatsoever, then r will justify every proposition plus its negation. But that is intolerable. Hence we may infer that there is some proposition q not justified by r. And if we let q entail r and assume that r does not entail q, then q will satisfy conditions (i)—(iii). Furthermore, the set $\{r, [q \& (q \supset r)]\}$ will justify at most a non-universal set, P, of propositions. Thus we may infer that there are propositions not in P. One such proposition, we may assume, is p. Let us also assume that p entails q and that $[q \& (q \supset r)]$ does not entail p. In that case p will satisfy (i)—(iii). Moreover, there will be at every step of the regress in question a proposition satisfying (i)—(iii). The upshot, then, is that for any contingent proposition we can construct an instance of (2) that satisfies (i)—(iii), from which we can construct a noncircular justificatory regress like (1). But surely our being able to justify any contingent proposition we like is quite unacceptable. Hence we may infer that there can be no infinite justificatory regresses. The foregoing argument thus appears to provide the foundationalist with some hope of success in his argument from elimination for founda-tions of justification.

But Ernest Sosa has argued that the above *reductio* argument is objectionable on the ground that it assumes, in effect, that the defender of infinite justificatory regresses cannot distinguish between *actual* infinite justificatory regresses and *merely potential* infinite justificatory regresses.[2] Apparently the argument assumes that if any infinite justificatory regress ever justifies the proposition at its head, then every infinite justificatory regress must do so. And since it is clear that not every such regress does so, it follows that no infinite regress is adequate for justification. Sosa, however, has argued that there is a definite distinction between actual infinite justificatory regresses and merely potential infinite justificatory regresses. Put abstractly, the distinction is that an actual infinite justificatory regress contains only justified propositions as members, whereas a merely potential infinite justificatory regress does not. Yet both kinds of infinite regress contain no member without successors that *would* jointly justify it *if* they were themselves justified. Sosa draws this distinction by examples also. Consider the proposition that there are perfect numbers greater than 100, and assume that there is a person whose mind is sufficiently powerful to believe every member of the following endless regress:

(4)   There is at least one perfect number greater than 100.
        There are at least two perfect numbers greater than 100.
        There are at least three perfect numbers greater than 100.

                          .
                          .
                          .

If such a person has no other belief about perfect numbers except the belief that a perfect number is a whole number equal to the sum of its whole factors less than itself, then, as Sosa notes, he is not justified in believing that there are any perfect numbers greater than 100. For he is unjustified in believing any of the members of (4). (4) is a merely potential infinite justificatory regress since no member of it is actually justified, but if any member were actually justified, then its predecessors would be justified also. As for an actual infinite justificatory regress, Sosa points out that someone (if not a human, then some superhuman mind) could believe the following infinite series of actually justified propositions:

(5)   There is at least one even number.
        There are at least two even numbers.
        There are at least three even numbers.

                          .
                          .
                          .

As Sosa notes, one apparently needs a proof that there is a denumer-
able infinity of even numbers to be the subject of the endless series of
justified beliefs (5). But the need for such a proof does not undermine
the infinite regress of justifiers, each of which is actually justified.

However, we need to clarify Sosa's distinction before we can relate
it to the above *reductio* argument. Regarding the so-called merely
potential infinite justificatory regress (4), Sosa claims that while it is
true that if any member of such a regress were justified, then its
predecessors would be also, still none is in fact justified. And regarding the so-called actual infinite justificatory regress (5), Sosa claims
that every member of this regress is actually justified. These claims, of
course, agree with the above suggestion that an actual infinite justificatory regress is an infinite regress all of whose members are justified,
and a merely potential infinite justificatory regress is an infinite regress
including at least some unjustified members. But we can improve on
this distinction by determining just why the members of a regress like
(4) are unjustified whereas the members of a regress like (5) are
justified. Regarding regress (4) Sosa notes that none of its members
is justified in the absence of further information external to, or epistemically independent of, the regress. (Let us say that information is
epistemically independent of a regress just in case the justification of
that information does not depend on the regress.) But regress (5)
differs from (4) insofar as the independent proof of the denumerably
infinite cardinality of the set of evens can provide a sufficiently
powerful mind with a terminating regress for each member of this
infinite series of justified beliefs. Thus, one might propose that Sosa's
distinction relies on the existence, or the lack, of information external
to, or epistemically independent of, a given infinite regress. That is, one
might propose that an infinite justificatory regress that is justificationally noncircular and devoid of immediately justified propositions is
actual if and only if there is information external to the regress that
ultimately justifies every member of the regress. Lacking such external
information, an infinite justificatory regress is merely potential.
Although Sosa docs not draw this distinction quite so explicitly, I
believe this is a plausible way to draw it.

But in drawing the distinction as above, one must avoid begging any
major questions against the infinitist who holds that one can have,
without relying on any external information, an actual infinite justificatory regress that is justificationally noncircular and devoid of any
immediately justified propositions. That is, one must be able to defend

the above distinction against such an infinitist. Let us try to determine whether the required defense is forthcoming by examining regress (4). Regress (4) clearly satisfies the entailment and noncircularity conditions (i)−(iii) satisfied, for example, by (2). Let us assume that a person, S, believes each member, e_n, of (4) and knows that e_n entails e_{n-1} and is entailed by e_{n+1}. Let us also assume that S has no other belief about perfect numbers aside from the belief about the standard definition of a perfect number. Now given just these assumptions, should we grant that S is justified in believing any member of (4), particularly the proposition, call it 'e_0' at the head of (4)? Clearly, S is justified in believing any member e_n *if* S is justified in believing its successor e_{n+1}. But is S justified in believing any successor e_{n+1}? More concretely, is S justified in believing, for example, the proposition that there are at least 10,000 perfect numbers greater than 100? Admittedly, S might attempt to meet any challenge to this proposition by appealing to its successor, and he may even know that the successor entails this proposition. But it does not obviously follow that S is justified in believing this proposition. For nothing we have assumed thus far gives S any reason to believe that the proposition in question is true. The most we can validly infer is that *if* S is justified in believing the successor of this proposition, then S is justified in believing this proposition itself. I submit that given only the present assumptions S is not rationally permitted to affirm the antecedent of that conditional, for he has no good reason to believe it true. The most S may affirm is that *if* the successor e_{n+1} of the successor e_n in question is justified, then e_n is itself justified. But once again S is not permitted to affirm the antecedent of the relevant conditional. And this problem recurs with respect to every member of regress (4). Of course if S had an independent proof of the denumerably infinite cardinality of the set of perfect numbers, the problem at hand would disappear. But on the present assumptions S has no such external information. Accordingly, we may say that (4) is a merely potential infinite justificatory regress.

My main contention at this point is that the correct way to portray the infinitist's noncircular infinite justificatory regress in which every member, including its terminus e_0, is purportedly justified by the next member (and not by any external information) is as follows:

(6)   . . . , *if* justified e_n justifies e_{n-1}, . . . , *if* justified e_1 justifies e_0.

An incorrect, or at least question-begging way for the infinitist to portray such a regress is:

(1) $\ldots, e_n$ justifies $e_{n-1}, \ldots, e_1$ justifies e_0,

since (1) begs the question whether the terminal member of such an infinite regress is justified. Obviously, the infinitist cannot assume from the start that all the members of an infinite regress like (4) are actually justified. For such an assumption would clearly beg the question at hand against the foundationalist. Thus, (6), being non-question-begging, is preferable to (1) as a portrayal of an infinite justificatory regress like (4). But the terminal member e_0 of a regress represented by (6) is merely conditionally justified; that is, e_0 will be unjustified for a person S unless the antecedent of the relevant conditional is true. S, in other words, must also be justified in believing e_1. But e_1 is also merely conditionally justified for S, since its justification depends on the justification of e_2, which is, in turn, merely conditionally justified. And the same point, *mutatis mutandis*, is true of e_3 and of every other member e_n of a regress represented by (6). Thus, once we portray an infinite justificatory regress like (4) along the lines of (6), as a regress of merely conditional justifications, we can readily see that such an infinite justificatory regress is inadequate to justify its terminal member. For, clearly, from the fact that e_1 entails e_0, and S knows as much and knows also that e_2 entails e_1 and so on, it does not follow that e_0 is justified for S. All that follows, of course, is that e_0 is justified for S *if* e_1 is. But why should anyone think the infinist can plausibly argue, without introducing external information, that every member of an infinite justificatory regress represented by (6) *is* justified by the next member? This is a crucial question, and unless the infinitist can answer it, we have good reason to believe that an infinite regress represented by (6) is inadequate to justify its terminal member.

    I should mention, however, the natural way, and apparently the only way, for the infinitist to argue that e_1, along with every other member e_n of a regress represented by (6), is justified for a person S. The infinitist will propose that S would be entitled to claim that e_1 is actually justified, and thus that e_1 actually justifies e_0, by arguing that e_1 is justified if e_2 is and claiming that e_2 is justified. If challenged about e_2, S could claim that e_2 is justified if e_3 is and that e_3 is justified. More generally, then, for each member e_n of a regress represented by (6), S can cite its successor e_{n+1} as the justification of e_n. But it follows, then, that e_0 is justified, since everything in its justificational ancestry is justified.

I find the foregoing kind of argument to be inconclusive at best. The inference from S's *claiming* that e_2 is justified to e_2's actually being justified is clearly invalid. And one cannot improve matters any by suggesting that S can claim that e_3 is justified and entails e_2. For the issue at hand is not what S can *claim* or can *cite* as a putative justification; the issue, rather, is whether any member of the endless regress trailing e_0 *is* actually justified, since it is supported by some actually justified e_i, and not merely conditionally justified. The infinitist holds that S is entitled to claim that every member e_i is justified because S can meet the challenge to his claim that e_i is justified. But precisely how can S meet the challenge to his claim? Surely the forementioned strategy involving an invalid inference is inadequate. That is, it is of no use for S simply to claim that e_{i+1} is justified and that e_i is justified if e_{i+1} is. For such a claim provides one at most with a string of merely conditional justifications represented by (6). And it is doubtful that a regress represented by (6) is sufficient to justify its terminal member. Hence, I doubt that the infinitist can answer my crucial question. And even if he can, he still must face the *reductio* argument I reiterate below.

I have already noted the possibility of an actual infinite justificatory regress such as (5), which can justify its terminal member for a person, S, because all of its members are ultimately justified for S by some information external to the regress. This raises at least two important questions. What is the fate of the earlier *reductio* argument for the conceptual impossibility of a noncircular infinite justificatory regress whose every member is justified by the next member? And what is the fate of the foundationalist's eliminative regress argument for immediately justified foundations of justification? I shall take up the former question first. I find that we must place a significant restriction on the above *reductio* argument of Post's. In light of the obvious and relevant difference between infinite regresses such as (4) and (5), we must specify that the above *reductio* argument applies only to noncircular infinite justificatory regresses in which every member, including the terminal member, is purportedly justified solely by the next member, and not by any external information. (For brevity, let us call the latter kind of regresses 'infinitist regresses.') For we can specify a relevant difference between an infinite regress like (5) and an infinitist regress, or a regress constructed on the basis of the *reductio* recipe I outlined above on pages 107–108. The relevant difference, of course, stems from the fact that a regress like (5) involves external information providing one with a terminating regress for each member of the infinite series of justified propositions. But there is no relevant difference between an infinitist regress, such as (4), and the infinite regress we can construct on the basis of the above *reductio* recipe. And since, as we have seen, we can construct an infinite regress, which is not relevantly different from an infinitist regress, for any proposition we like, the infinitist is committed to the view that any and every contingent proposition can be justified for a person at any time. But since this view is absurd, we can justifiably conclude that infinitist regresses are conceptually impossible. That is, there cannot be any noncircular infinite justificatory regress in which every member is justified solely by the next member. But, of course, this is not to say that there cannot be an infinite justificatory regress whose every member is justified by information external to the regress. The above *reductio* argument, I grant, does not bear on infinite regresses like (5). (Note at this point that even if the foregoing *reductio* argument turns out to be unconvincing, the infinitist will still owe us an account of how to distinguish actual infinite justificatory chains from merely potential ones in accordance with epistemic infinitism. Yet it is now doubtful that such an account is forthcoming.)

But does the possibility of an actual infinite justificatory regress such as (5) undercut the foundationalist's eliminative regress argument for immediately justified foundations of justification? I believe not, and I can begin to support a negative answer by raising two related questions. Must the foundationalist argue that an infinite justificatory regress like (5) can play no part whatsoever in the justification of its terminal member? Or, alternatively, need he argue simply that an infinitist regress is insufficient to justify its terminal member? I find that he need argue only the latter point. To illustrate this point, let us consider once again the belief at the head of regress (4), *viz.*: There is at least one perfect number greater than 100. The foundationalist need not deny that this belief could be justified for the person who has independent proof of the denumerably infinite cardinality of the set of perfect numbers and who can thus use (4) as an actual endless regress of justification. Rather, the foundationalist need deny only that (4) is sufficient to justify its terminal member without external information justifying its members. (And given the above *reductio* argument he can justifiably deny this.) In effect, the required external information provides a person with a terminating regress, for it entails that the members of (4), for instance, not only are justified if their successors are, but also are actually justified. Thus, such external information terminates the infinite regress of merely conditional justification. What the foundationalist must argue concerning infinite justificatory regresses is just that every inferentially justified belief is at the head of a terminating regress. But this requirement in no way commits the foundationalist to the impossibility of an actual infinite justificatory regress.

An important question at this point is: What is the nature of the external justification required for the members of an actual infinite justificatory regress? At least three points seem clear. First, once certain external information provides a person with the requisite terminating regress, the relevant infinite justificatory regress, (5) for example, becomes unnecessary for the justification of its terminal member. Second, the external justification involves more than a merely potential infinite justificatory regress represented by (6). Third, it is useless to assume that the external justification consists of an actual infinite justificatory regress, for such an assumption will only raise the question at hand once again. Accordingly, let us assume that the required external justification consists of a finite regress of mediate, or inferential, justification. And let us call this finite regress 'R.' I find that the first member e_n of R is either (i) justified by some information external to R; (ii) unjustified; (iii) justified by some set of members between e_n and the terminus of R; or (iv) immediately justified. Clearly, (i) either evades the issue at hand or begins an unacceptable regress. As for (ii), I have argued against this option in Chapter II in connection with my examination of epistemic contextualism. One serious problem facing (ii) is that it apparently enables us to justify any proposition we like. As for (iii), I have argued against the leading accounts of "circular" justification in Chapter III in connection with my examination of the leading versions of epistemic coherentism. This leaves me with (iv) and enables me to conclude that the external finite justificatory regress, if there be such, will probably rest on immediately justified, foundational propositions. But I cannot conclude at present that there are immediately justified foundations of justification; for, first, I have not yet provided a clear account of immediate justification, and second, I have not yet met the relevant skeptical objections to immediately justified propositions. Thus, I turn now to the first task of providing a clearer picture of epistemic foundationalism.

2. EPISTEMIC FOUNDATIONALISM

Talk of *the* foundational theory of justification can be just as misleading as talk of the coherence theory of justification. For 'foundationalism', like 'coherentism', is an imprecise catchword referring to several very different theories of justification. But these different foundational theories have at least one key feature in common: the assertion that there are foundational (or basic) beliefs that can be justified independently of any justificatory relations to other beliefs and can somehow epistemically support justified nonfoundational beliefs. The best way to clarify this common feature of foundational theories is to characterize the minimal foundational thesis.

Some philosophers have characterized the minimal foundational thesis in a way equivalent to the following:[3]

> MF.   (i) There are foundational beliefs justified noninferentially, that is, independently of any inferential relations to other beliefs; and (ii) every inferentially justified belief has at least one evidence chain leading from it to some foundational belief(s).

But MF needs some modification to serve as an accurate statement of minimal foundationalism. The foundationalist does claim that there are foundational beliefs justified independently of inferential relations to other beliefs. But he also makes the stronger claim that there are foundational beliefs justified independently of *any* justificatory relations to other beliefs. Notice that a coherence theorist such as Lehrer can consistently accept the weaker claim that some beliefs are justified apart from inferential relations to other beliefs. Lehrer distinguishes between two kinds of beliefs justified by coherence: the kind whose coherence depends on inferential relations and the kind whose coherence does not.[4] The justification of the latter kind of beliefs depends on coherence but not on inferential relations. Yet it is confusing to characterize Lehrer and many other coherence theorists as proponents of foundational beliefs. I propose therefore that we modify the foregoing characterization of foundational beliefs as follows:

FB.   A person's (S's) belief that p is foundational for S if and only if S's belief that p is justified for S but is not justified by any justificatory relations, inferential, coherence, or otherwise, to other beliefs.

Let us say that if a theorist denies that there are foundational beliefs in the sense of FB — and Lehrer, for example, does deny this — then he is not a foundationalist.

In light of FB, I propose the following modification of the minimal foundational thesis MF:

MF*.   (i) There are foundational beliefs justified independently of any justificatory relations to other beliefs; and (ii) every inferentially justified belief has at least one evidence chain leading from it to some foundational belief(s).

Clause (ii) of MF* requires some explanation. Inferential (or mediate) justification obtains when a person's belief that p is justified by evidence consisting of other justified beliefs. This kind of justification involves the notion of an evidence chain. As I mentioned in Chapter I, an evidence chain for a person's belief that p is a series of beliefs (or sets of beliefs) e_1, e_2, e_3, ... such that e_1 justifies the belief that p, and for any e_i in the series, e_i justifies e_{i-1}. Thus, according to minimal foundationalism, S's belief that p is justified if and only if either the belief that p is immediately justified (or foundational), or there is an evidence chain that justifies S's belief that p and any of S's evidence chains that justifies S's belief that p contains some belief that is immediately justified for S.[5]

But many important questions about minimal foundationalism still remain unanswered. A natural question is: How are a person's foundational beliefs justified? And which beliefs are foundational for a person? These are relevant questions since my above characterization of foundational beliefs is negative and does not specify just which beliefs are foundational. But, unfortunately, we have no foundationalist consensus providing answers to such questions. There are, however, three common kinds of answers that enable us to distinguish between radical, modest, and weak foundationalism. The radical foundationalist typically holds that only those beliefs that are infallible and indubitable are foundational for a person. The modest foundationalist, in contrast, holds that foundational beliefs need have only sufficient immediate justification to satisfy the justification condition of knowledge and to serve as justifying premises for other beliefs. And the weak foundationalist holds that foundational beliefs need have only a very low degree of immediate justification, much lower than that required to enable them to serve as justifying premises for other beliefs.[6] But notice that if we accept MF* as the minimal foundational thesis, then we should hold that weak foundationalism is not really a species of foundationalism. For weak foundationalism does not claim that foundational beliefs are sufficiently justified to satisfy the justification condition of knowledge; it claims only that foundational beliefs have "a degree of justification." But of course a belief may have a degree of justification but still be *un*justified in the sense that it does not satisfy the justification condition of knowledge; this, in fact, is true of many unjustified beliefs. However, if foundational beliefs are to provide justification for some observation beliefs, then these foundational beliefs must themselves be justified. This is one of the central lessons of Chapter II. Thus, I believe it is inadequate to claim that foundational beliefs have only a degree of justification. For in claiming that the degree of immediate justification had by foundational beliefs is insufficient for those beliefs to serve as justifying premises for observation beliefs, weak foundationalism fails to solve the epistemic regress problem. Clearly, if foundations of justification are to solve the regress problem, they must be able to provide other beliefs with more than just a degree of justification. Weak foundationalism, therefore, is unpromising as a solution to the regress problem.

Radical foundationalism, in contrast, does enable the foundations of justification to provide other beliefs with sufficient justification to satisfy the justification condition of knowledge. But it apparently goes beyond what is necessary to solve the regress problem. For the immunities invoked by the radical foundationalist to characterize foundational beliefs, such as infallibility, indubitability, and irrefutability, seem to be unnecessary for the epistemic justification of most, if not all, empirical beliefs. Consequently, we should be wary of any effort to question the immediate justification of a belief by questioning its infallibility, indubitability, or irrefutability.[7] However, I shall examine these alleged immunities in Chapter V, in connection with my assessment of C. I. Lewis' version of radical foundationalism.

Modest foundationalism, it seems at this early stage, is the most suitable of the three foundationalist solutions to the regress problem. It is neither too weak, unlike weak foundationalism, nor too strong, unlike radical foundationalism. For it states simply that the foundations of justification not only have immediate justification appropriate for knowledge, but also can serve as justifying premises for the epistemic justification of other beliefs. But before seriously considering any version of modest foundationalism, we must face a problem threatening any version of foundationalism.

2.1. *Epistemic Ascent Arguments*

Perhaps the most forceful anti-foundationalist argument is the epistemic ascent argument claiming that when we consider any putative immediately justified belief, we see that it requires for its justification certain reasons that are beliefs about its epistemic status. This argument is prominent in the epistemological writings of Wilfrid Sellars, but its clearest, most plausible formulation is found in some of Laurence Bonjour's recent articles.[8] I shall therefore focus on Bonjour's epistemic ascent argument.

In "Can Empirical Knowledge Have a Foundation?" Bonjour uses an epistemic ascent argument to support his claim that the standard argument from elimination for foundational beliefs fails because foundationalism cannot provide an adequate account of inferential justification and thus cannot solve the regress problem. Bonjour's central claim, more specifically, is that the foundationalist cannot explain how a justificatory regress terminates without resorting to *ad hoc* stipulation. The initial assumption of his anti-foundationalist argument is that if foundational beliefs are to be the sole basis for the justification of other empirical beliefs, then that feature in virtue of which a belief qualifies as foundational must also constitute a good reason for one's thinking that the belief is true. Letting 'F' represent this feature, Bonjour claims that for a person's (S's) belief that p to qualify as foundational in any acceptable foundationalist account, S must be justified in believing the premises of the following justificatory argument:

(7) (i)   S's belief that p has feature F.
     (ii) Beliefs having feature F are highly likely to be true.
     (iii) Therefore, S's belief that p is highly likely to be true.

In addition, Bonjour claims that if we assume that for S to be justified in believing that p it is necessary that S be in cognitive possession of the justification of his belief, then we get the troublesome result that S's belief that p is not foundational after all, since its justification depends on the justification of at least one other empirical belief. Clearly, if Bonjour's argument is sound, foundationalism fails to provide an acceptable way to terminate a justificatory regress.

I suspect that most foundationalists would readily grant that the premises and conclusion of (7) must be true if S is to be immediately justified in believing that p. For that would simply be to grant that the justifying feature F must be conducive to truth. But many foundationalists would not be so agreeable about the additional claim that S's foundational belief that p is justified only if S is in cognitive possession of the justifying argument (7). These foundationalists concede that S's foundational belief that p is justified only if the premises of an argument like (7) are true or are in principle available to S, but they deny that S must be justified in believing such premises or be aware of them in any way. Other foundationalists, however, hold not only that there must be a justificatory argument like (7) available to S, but also that S must have cognitive possession of such an argument. These foundationalists claim that S's cognitive grasp of the premises of the requisite justificatory argument involves not further beliefs but rather cognitive states called "intuitions" or "apprehensions." These intuitions, according to these foundationalists, do not themselves require further justification, but they are nonetheless able to justify foundational beliefs. We thus have two standard kinds of response to the forementioned epistemic ascent argument. The first kind of response I shall call "epistemic externalism," the second, "epistemic intuitionism." I shall examine externalism in this chapter and intuitionism in Chapter V.

2.2. *Epistemic Externalism*

Among the proponents of epistemic externalism are D. M. Armstrong, Alvin Goldman, and William Alston.[9] I shall focus here on the foundationalist views of Armstrong and Alston, which are versions of epistemic reliabilism, yet my general criticisms will apply to any version of epistemic externalism. I turn first to Armstrong's theory.

If we may construe Armstrong's epistemology as a theory of *justification* as well as a theory of knowledge, its central thesis is that a person's (S's) foundational belief that p is immediately justified by some natural relation holding between S's belief that p and the state of affairs that makes p true. Armstrong characterizes this natural relation by saying that there must be a law-like connection between S's belief that p and the state of affairs that makes p true such that, given that S believes that p, it must be the case that p. This view is externalist insofar as it makes the justification of S's belief that p depend solely on an external relation and not on S's cognitive grasp of reasons for his belief that p. If S's foundational belief that p is connected in a law-like way to the state of affairs making it true, then S qualifies as a reliable cognitive instrument with respect to that belief. In virtue of this reliability, according to Armstrong, S's foundational belief that p is epistemically justified. Thus, although on Armstrong's theory the premises of the above argument (7) must be true if S is to be justified in believing that p, S need not be justified in believing, or have any other kind of cognitive possession of, the premises. Armstrong's epistemology, accordingly, is externalist.

William Alston's account of "self-warrant" (or immediate justification) is similarly externalist. We may state the fundamental epistemic principle of Alston's account of self-warrant as:

(4.1)   Every given-belief of a person, S, (*i.e.*, every belief of S's solely about one of his own present conscious states, such as his perceptual and sensation states) is self-warranted (or immediately justified) just by virtue of being a given-belief.

The belief that I seem to see a blue book and the belief that I feel pain are examples of given-beliefs of mine. They are restricted to the intrinsic character of specific perceptual and sensation states of mine. (4.1) leads us to ask the question whether such given-beliefs are actually self-warranted, but for present purposes we may construe this question as the question whether we are justified in accepting principle (4.1). The latter question leads naturally to the further question of what conditions an epistemic principle must satisfy to be justified. One might begin to answer this further question simply by invoking the following principle:

(4.2)   Any belief is epistemically justified if and only if it is reliable, *i.e.*, highly likely to be true.

According to (4.2), a belief is justified if and only if there are relevant

facts about the way it is acquired or held such that given those facts it
is highly likely that a belief of that kind will be true. Some theorists
have held that an epistemic principle like (4.2) is the sole principle
of justification. But Alston prefers an analogue of rule utilitarianism
rather than act utilitarianism in taking reliability as a criterion
for epistemic principles governing specific types of beliefs. On his
criterion an epistemic principle stating certain conditions, C, as
sufficient for the justification of beliefs of type G is itself justified
only if (i) G's that satisfy C are reliable. Two additional necessary
conditions of a justified epistemic principle, according to Alston, are:
(ii) its conditions C must be applicable, i.e., useful in determining
whether a particular G is justified, and (iii) there must be no other
applicable conditions C' such that the proportion of true beliefs is
much greater among G's that satisfy C' than among G's that satisfy
C.[10] Conditions (i) and (ii), I believe, are sufficiently clear, but
condition (iii) demands some explanation. Alston introduces condition
(iii) because observation beliefs about the physical environment may
be true in most cases, and if they are, then every observation belief
will enjoy a high probability of truth. Given only conditions (i) and
(ii), one might be inclined therefore to accept an epistemic principle
claiming that every observation belief is immediately justified. But
surely any such principle would be unacceptable, since we can easily
add certain conditions to such a principle, such as conditions about
the state of the perceiver and his physical environment, and in doing
so we can increase significantly the proportion of true beliefs in the
relevant class of justified beliefs. Thus we should retain condition (iii).

The natural question now is whether (4.1) satisfies conditions
(i)−(iii). As for requirement (i), if we have good reason to believe that
given-beliefs are almost always true, then we are justified in believing
that given-beliefs are reliable. But do we have good reason to believe
that given-beliefs are almost always true? It seems so, since it is
difficult to find *actual* cases in which we can show that a particular
given-belief is false. Perhaps we can adduce a few such cases, but they
are rare by any standard. One might reply that such cases are rare just
because we have no independent checks on the accuracy of given-
beliefs. But I believe we do occasionally have such checks. When a
person is in severe pain or greatly depressed, for instance, we can
expect him to betray his feelings in his behavior. When we rely on
such an independent behavioral check, we rarely find that it conflicts
with the subject's reported given-belief. Thus, we may assume that

given-beliefs are reliable beliefs that satisfy requirement (i). It is even easier to see that (4.1) satisfies condition (ii). To satisfy (ii) we need only to be able to determine whether a particular belief is a given-belief. And given the simple notion of a given-belief, we should have no problem on this score. But to satisfy condition (iii) we cannot be quite so brief; for we need to show that there are no further applicable conditions that can reduce the proportion of false given-beliefs. This is not an easy task to accomplish. For it seems that by adding the condition that the person having the given-belief is a truth-seeker who is sincere, undistracted, unconfused, cautious, and "of sound mind," we can reduce significantly the proportion of false given-beliefs. The standard examples of false given-beliefs, which I shall discuss in Chapter V in connection with C. I. Lewis' intuitionism, rely for the most part on cases where the subject of the given-belief is insincere, distracted, confused, careless, or mentally unstable. By adding a condition that excludes such cases, we can significantly reduce the proportion of false given-beliefs. Alston, however, opposes the addition of such a condition on the ground that if a person's violating that condition entailed the falsity of some given-belief, that person would be in no position to form a belief about any of his current perceptual or sensation states. But I find this reasoning quite unconvincing. Surely we can, and indeed do, form false given-beliefs at times because of certain distractions, insufficiently cautious introspections, self-deception, subnormal mental dispositions, and so on. In the following chapter on epistemic intuitionism I shall adduce realistic examples to illustrate some of these possibilities. Thus, I find it gratuitous to assume that such cases involve only those people who are incapable of forming beliefs about their current perceptual and sensation states. And, consequently, I doubt that (4.1) satisfies condition (iii).

But instead of rejecting (4.1) because of its failure to satisfy condition (iii), let us simply relativize it to the appropriate kind of context. The appropriate kind of context, of course, is one in which the subject of the given-belief is a truth-seeker who is sincere, undistracted, cautious, etc. Very few foundationalists have recognized the need to relativize their epistemic principles like (4.1) to the appropriate kind of context, but given condition (iii), they surely should do so. Let us, then, relativize (4.1) to the appropriate kind of context, and grant that in its relativized form (4.1) satisfies conditions (i)–(iii).

The externalist feature of Alston's position is obvious. Principle (4.1) says nothing about S's own perspective of his epistemic situation; it says nothing about S's own reasons to believe that a particular given-belief is true or false. What is centrally important to the immediate justification of a given-belief, on Alston's account, is the external fact that a given-belief is an instance of a reliable kind of belief. According to that account, S need not have any awareness whatsoever of this fact to be justified in holding a particular given-belief. So long as the class of given-beliefs satisfies the reliability condition (i), those beliefs are candidates for immediate justification, even if S, along with everyone else, is completely unaware of their reliability. And a similar thesis arises from the externalist construal of the relativized principle (4.1). That is, to be justified in holding some given-belief, S need not be aware that he satisfies the requirement, due to (iii), of being a truth-seeker who is sincere, undistracted, cautious, etc. S need only satisfy this requirement. Some theorists have constructed an epistemic ascent argument against immediate justification by arguing that to be justified in holding any given-belief a person, S, must be justified in believing that there are no factors present that will probably cause him to be mistaken in his given-belief. But the externalist reply is now clear: S can be justified in holding some given-belief even if S is not justified in believing, or is not in any way aware, that the requirement that no mistake-causing factors be present is fulfilled. That requirement need only *be* fulfilled in S's case. According to epistemic externalism, then, a person need not have any cognitive awareness of the justifying conditions of his immediately justified belief; the fulfillment of those conditions may be quite outside one's own perspective of one's epistemic situation.

I shall argue, however, that epistemic externalism is an unacceptable solution to the regress problem. I agree with Bonjour that externalism is essentially an *ad hoc* evasion of this problem.[11] For what gives rise to the regress problem in the first place is the plausible requirement that for a person's (S's) belief that p to be inferentially justified, S must at least be justified in believing a set of beliefs providing a justification of S's belief that p. This requirement, stated more simply, is that S must *possess* good (*i.e.*, justifying) reasons for his justified belief that p. The externalist simply waives this general requirement in the case of the justification of foundational beliefs. But why should we permit the externalist to waive that requirement in this case, when it is not permissible to do so generally? The force of this question becomes clear once we notice that if it were generally acceptable to waive that requirement, then a person could be justified in believing any number of empirical propositions which are completely without evidential support from that person's epistemic perspective (*i.e.*, given all the evidence that person is, or has been, aware of). Thus, given externalism one can be justified in holding a belief even if one is not, and has not been, aware of anything providing a potential defense of that belief against skeptical queries. But these are surely implausible consequences of epistemic externalism. Such consequences, I believe, show that externalism runs afoul of any ordinary distinction between justified and unjustified empirical belief.

Following Bonjour, we can buttress this opposition to externalism by appealing to the forementioned normative conception of epistemic justification. On that conception epistemic justification is essentially related to the cognitive goal of truth. Thus any particular belief is justified only if its acceptance is directed toward the goal of truth. More precisely, one is epistemically justified in believing all and only those propositions one has good reason to believe are true. Consequently, to accept a proposition in the absence of good reason is to neglect the pursuit of truth. Such acceptance, we might say, would be "epistemically irresponsible". Consider, for instance, the person, S, whose belief that *p* is justified on externalist principles like Armstrong's or Alston's, but who possesses no reason at all for believing that *p* is true. From S's epistemic perspective, it is no more than an accident that his belief that *p* is true. Thus S's believing that *p* is no more responsible than his holding some belief for which the externalist's external conditions fail to hold. Consequently, given the normative conception of epistemic justification, we should conclude that externalism is unacceptable.

The central assumption underlying the normative conception of justification is that a person, S, is justified in believing that *p* if and only if S has not violated any epistemic duty or obligation in believing that *p*. But William Alston has raised this question about the above kind of anti-externalist inference from the normative conception of justification: Why should we suppose that one who believes that *p* without having adequate reason for supposing *p* to be true is violating any intellectual obligation?[12] Alston doubts that one would be violating some epistemic obligation by forming perceptual beliefs, for instance, in circumstances favorable to their truth even when one lacks any good reason to suppose that the circumstances are thus favorable. In addition, Alston rejects the normative conception of justification on the ground that it precludes justified belief and knowledge on the part of infants and lower animals. Since infants and lower animals are incapable of governing their conduct in accordance with norms or principles, we ought not to apply normative conceptions like obligation, duty, and reproach to them. Alston, however, finds it untenable to hold that such beings are devoid of knowledge. Alston's final objection to the normative conception of justification is that it presupposes what some philosophers have called "doxastic voluntarism". This is the view that what one believes is under one's direct voluntary control. Since ought implies can, the normative conception of justification presupposes that with respect to each candidate proposition for acceptance one has a choice whether or not to accept it. But Alston finds it obvious that belief is not always, or even generally, a matter of choice. And if he is right, it follows that a voluntaristic normative conception of justification does not apply to belief in general. In sum, then, Alston rejects the above kind of anti-externalist argument because the conception of epistemic justification basic to it is subjectivistic (or internalistic), normative, and voluntaristic.

I believe that Alston's three-pronged response to the above kind of anti-externalist argument leaves much to be desired. I shall consider each point in turn to air my doubts. My first problem with Alston's reply is that I cannot see that the normative conception of justification requires the assumption that what one justifiably believes is under one's *direct* voluntary control. All it requires, I believe, is that we can perform activities that affect our belief-forming habits. Such voluntary activities enable us to say that our believings and refrainings from belief are at least under *in*direct voluntary control. An example will perhaps clarify this point. Suppose I see, under normal circumstances, a police officer walking toward me on the sidewalk. Alston would deny that it will depend on my voluntary choice whether or not I believe that a police officer is walking toward me. He would claim that since he does not know how to control his believing under such circumstances, he will believe that there is a police officer coming down the sidewalk, and will not be able to believe the opposite. Admittedly, most of us will probably not believe, or even be able to believe, the opposite under such circumstances. But this concession is not directly relevant to the issue at hand. The relevant question is whether, under the assumed circumstances, one could *refrain* from believing that there is a police officer coming down the sidewalk. Such refraining is different from believing the opposite, and it seems to be psychologically as well as logically possible for the normal person. For it seems that one can train oneself to withhold believing anything that one does not have at least one good reason to believe. And the proponent of the normative conception of justification may hold that one is epistemically irresponsible if one does not train oneself in this way. In addition, he may hold that any believing that is not in accordance with such training is similarly epistemically irresponsible. Hence, even if a person's cognitive habits require us to hold that some acts of believing are not under *direct* voluntary control, we may still hold that such acts can be epistemically irresponsible because they are incompatible with epistemically responsible cognitive training. The possibility of such training, I believe, permits us to hold that most acts of believing are at least under *indirect* voluntary control. But if we deny even indirect voluntary control over most acts of believing, I do not see how we can maintain a normative conception of epistemic justification.

My second problem with Alston's reply is that its assumption that infants and lower animals have knowledge and thus justified belief seems gratuitous, if not irrelevant. It may be true that such beings have knowledge and justified belief, but, contrary to Alston's suggestion, it is less than obvious to many of us that they do. If the kind of justified belief enjoyed by adult humans is the product of reflective, rational inquiry, we surely should restrict such justified belief to those subjects capable of reflection on the epistemic status of their beliefs. I have no reason to believe that infants and lower animals are capable of reflection on the epistemic status of their beliefs. Accordingly, I doubt that they are capable of epistemically responsible actions. But if epistemic responsibility is indeed centrally important to justified belief, then it is doubtful that infants and lower animals are capable of justified belief. Furthermore, since we do not ordinarily attribute moral responsibility to infants and lower animals, I see no reason to attribute epistemic responsibility or justified belief to them. I suggested that the second prong of Alston's reply seems irrelevant also. This is because the proponent of the normative conception of justification is concerned solely with the kind of justified belief enjoyed by reflective

humans; he does not intend to apply his normative conception of
justification to infants and lower animals. Of course Alston, along with
most other externalists, would deny that even the kind of justified
belief enjoyed by reflective adult humans requires critical reflection.
For the externalist holds that a particular belief is justified so long as it
satisfies certain external conditions. It seems, therefore, that we have
arrived at a fundamental disagreement over the notion of justified
belief.

But I believe we can advance the discussion by examining some of
the implications of the externalist conception of immediately justified
belief. In doing so, I shall express my third problem with Alston's
reply. On a typical reliabilist version of externalism, a person, S, is
immediately justified in believing that p if and only if S's belief that p
satisfies certain external conditions that make the belief reliable, *i.e.*,
likely to be true. But obviously on this version of externalism S can be
justified in believing that p even though S believes that p on the basis
of no apparent reason. Moreover, S's belief that p might be quite
irrational and irresponsible from S's own epistemic perspective, but so
long as that belief satisfies certain external reliability-making conditions it is justified on externalist standards. Suppose, for instance, that
S's belief that p is reliable, but that S has very good reasons to believe
that p is false. From his own epistemic perspective S surely is epistemically irresponsible and irrational to believe that p. Contrary to
externalism, therefore, it seems wrong to hold that S is justified in
believing that p so long as that belief is reliable in the forementioned
sense.

But the externalist can take steps to avoid that problem. His first
step might be to qualify his view as follows:

(4.3)   S is justified in believing that p if and only if (i) S's belief
        that p satisfies certain external conditions that make that
        belief reliable, and (ii) S has no good reason to suppose
        that his belief that p is false or that it does not satisfy
        certain reliability-making conditions.

(4.3) enables the externalist to deny that S is justified in believing that
p when S has good reason to believe that his belief that p is false or
unreliable. But of course (4.3) does not bear directly on the above
objection that externalism implies that S's belief that p can be justified
even when that belief is unsupported by any reasons, accidentally true

at best (from S's own epistemic perspective), and thus epistemically irresponsible. The externalist might begin to meet the latter objection by noting that its talk of a belief's being "accidentally" true is ambiguous and thus potentially misleading. As I mentioned, the externalist does not grant epistemic justification to "accidentally" true beliefs for which there can be no reasons whatsoever. The external reliability-making conditions satisfied by a justified belief *can* provide good reasons for that belief. For instance, those conditions might provide the following justifying argument:

(8) (i)   S's belief that p is an instance of kind R.
    (ii) Beliefs of kind R satisfy certain (external) reliability-making conditions that make them likely to be true.
    (iii) Therefore, S's belief that p is likely to be true.

But my worry about "accidentally" true justified belief does not stem from an assumption that externalism minimizes the significance of the existence of reasons like premises (i) and (ii) of (8). Rather, my worry stems from the fact that externalism neglects the significance of S's *awareness* of reasons like premises (i) and (ii). Externalism, by definition, allows that S can be justified in believing that p even when S possesses no reason whatsoever to believe that p is true. Thus, on externalist principles like (4.3), S can be justified in believing that p even when from S's own epistemic perspective it is no more than an accident that his belief that p is true. But if S has an epistemic responsibility to believe only probably true propositions, then he has an epistemic responsibility to believe only those propositions he has some reason to believe are true. (How else could S consciously make an effort to believe only true propositions?) Hence, if S believes a proposition that he has no reason to suppose is true, he is epistemically irresponsible. But, given the normative conception of justification, S is not justified in believing any proposition that he is epistemically irresponsible in believing. Hence, S is justified in believing a proposition only if he has some reason to suppose it is true.

I want to anticipate a natural objection to the foregoing anti-externalist demand that S possess reasons for his justified beliefs. Some externalists have suggested that this kind of demand involves a kind of epistemic level-confusion.[13] Such a demand, we are told, involves a confusion of the notion of a person's being justified in believing that p with the notion of a person's being justified in believing that he is justified in believing that p; for such a demand implies that a person is justified in believing that p only if he is justified in believing that he is justified in believing that p. But I doubt both that the above demand implies any such thing, and that it involves any such confusion. The demand is simply that if S is to be justified in believing that p, then he must possess, in the sense of his having an awareness of some sort (to be specified in Chapter V), of a good reason to believe that p is true. But of course it does not thereby follow that to be justified in believing that p, S must be justified in believing that the belief that p is justified. Nor does it follow that if S is to be justified in believing that p, then he must be justified in believing some other proposition that justifies his belief that p. The present demand does not presuppose that the required awareness of a good reason is justified belief; nor does it assume that all good reasons are propositions. Consequently, the present anti-externalist demand neither involves a level-confusion nor rules out immediate justification. In the following chapter on epistemic intuitionism, I shall elaborate on this claim that the demand for reasons does not eliminate immediate justification. However, before considering epistemic intuitionism, I want to examine a version of reliabilism that avoids the forementioned problems facing externalism. Marshall Swain has developed this non-externalist version of reliabilism, which to my knowledge is the most refined one to date.[14]

2.3. *Internalism and Reliabilism*

Swain calls his version of reliabilism the 'probabilistic-reliability (PR) model of epistemic justification.' According to the PR model, a belief is justified if and only if it is a reliable indicator of the way the world is. The basic intuitive assumption underlying the PR model is that people are in significant ways analogous to barometers. By means of causal interaction with the world, we acquire beliefs about various features of the world. These beliefs, according to Swain, are related to the way the world is in the same manner as the point readings on a barometer are related to the atmospheric pressure. If in a given situation a belief is based on the right kinds of reasons, and if the believer has appropriate reliability-making characteristics, then the fact that the believer has this belief may make it highly probable that the relevant belief is true. In that case, according to the PR model, the belief is epistemically justified.

We need now to paint a clearer picture of Swain's reliabilism. As preliminaries, we need explanations of the notions of reliability-making characteristics, reason-based belief and high probability. For present purposes we may think of the reliability-making characteristics of a person as those characteristics making the person a reliable informa-tion-gathering and -processing entity. Good eyesight, good reasoning habits, and the ability to discriminate among kinds of entities are some typical examples of reliability-making characteristics. As for the explanation of a reason-based belief, matters are much more complicated. Swain proposes the following causal analysis:

(4.4)   S's belief that p is based upon the set of reasons, R, at time, t, if and only if S believes that p at t, and for every member, r_i, of R there is some time, t_n, such that (a) S has (or had) r_i at t_n and (b) there is an appropriate causal connection between S's having r_i at t_n and S's believing that p at t.

We can explain the notion of a causal connection in (4.4) by the notions of a causal chain and of event causation. A sequence of occurrent events, c, d_1, . . . , d_n, e, is a causal chain if and only if d_1 depends causally on c, d_n depends causally on d_{n-1}, and e depends causally on d_n. Causal dependence amounts to this: An occurrent event, e, depends causally on an occurrent event, c, if and only if c and e are distinct events and if c had not occurred, then e would not have occurred. Swain thus states his counterfactual theory of event causa-tion simply as follows: An occurrent event, c, is a cause of an occurrent event, e, if and only if there is a causal chain of occurrent events from c to e. He elucidates this definition by a possible worlds approach to counterfactuals, but we can safely skirt the details here. In constructing a causal account of the basing relation, Swain claims that the members of the set of reasons upon which a belief is based are causally efficacious and thus must be events or states. This claim leads naturally to a distinction between evidential and causal reasons for a belief. Evidential reasons consist of believed propositions and thus are not causally efficacious. Causal reasons, in contrast, are events or states of a person that can figure in a causal explanation of his having some belief. Belief states, for instance, are often among the causal reasons upon which a particular belief that p is based. However, Swain holds that the set of causal reasons upon which a belief is based can consist partly of certain kinds of *non*belief states a person is in. Perceptual states, such as being appeared to F-ly, and sensation states, such as being in pain, provide examples of such nonbelief states. Nonbelief reason states, according to Swain, are possible objects of direct awareness; that is, one's awareness of such states need not depend upon one's being aware of anything else. Swain countenances nonbelief states as reason states for two major reasons. First, they are internal states providing us with at least some of our access to the external world. By taking such states to be reason states we can give them a definite role in the acquisition of justified belief. Second, Swain's theory of justification requires that every justified belief be justified only on the basis of reasons; this includes beliefs whose justification is not based on other beliefs. Thus his theory requires that some beliefs be based on nonbelief reason states.

Clearly a person, S, can believe that p on the basis of a set of reasons, R, without having a *justified* belief that p. S's believing that p on the basis of R is epistemically justified, on Swain's account, if and only if S's believing that p on the basis of R is a reliable indication that p. Thus the PR model defines the concept of justified belief by means of the concept of reliable belief. And it defines the concept of reliable belief by means of the notion of conditional probability. Irrelevant complications aside, the central idea of the PR model is that a person's (S's) belief that p (where p is some proposition about the empirical world) on the basis of reasons, R, is a reliable indication and thus a justified belief that p if and only if the probability that p, given that S has the appropriate reliability-making characteristics and believes that p on the basis of R, is greater than the probability that q, given those same facts about S, for every q that is a competitor of p relative to S and R. Following Keith Lehrer, Swain espouses the following (somewhat simplified) definition of competition: q is a competitor of p relative to S and R if and only if p and q are such that the probability of each is greater than 0 and less than 1, and q is negatively relevant to p, given that S believes that p on the basis of R. To say that q is negatively relevant to p is simply to say that q, when conjoined with p, reduces the conditional probability that p is true. We now have the essential features of Swain's theory before us.

I believe that two troublesome issues concerning the PR model arise immediately. The first is the natural question about the conception of probability employed by the PR model. Is it the subjective conception, the frequency conception, or the logical conception? Or is the PR model employing some other conception? Swain claims that conditional probability expressions can "represent" statements about evidential support. But he takes the concepts of evidential support, *i.e.*, the notion of p's being better evidence for q than for $-q$, as undefined. Perhaps he intends to do the same for the concept of probability. In any case, we need to know which ways of construing his probability statements are acceptable and which are not. Thus we have here a rather large gap in Swain's model. My second point is more serious. Let us assume that p = 'I see a blue book on my desk' and that q = 'I occasionally, but very rarely, daydream'. Now q is negatively relevant to, and thus competes with, p, since q, when conjoined with p, reduces the conditional probability that p is true. But the probability of q (at least on any of the standard conceptions of probability) is just as great as, if not greater than, the probability that p. Hence, given the PR model's necessary condition of epistemic justification, I am not justified in believing that p. But presumably on my total evidence p is so likely to be true that its slight decrease in probability due to q hardly robs it of justification. The lesson of this example, I believe, is that the PR model of justification is inadequate on its present notion of competition and negative relevance. But let us pass over these problems now in order to move to an examination of Swain's solution to the regress problem.

The PR model raises the regress problem with its thesis that beliefs that are essential members of some set of reasons, R, upon which some further belief is reliably based, must themselves be reliably based upon some set of reasons R′. Presumably beliefs that are essential members of R′ must also be reliably based on some other set of reasons. But is the same true of this new set of reasons? if so, we need to explain just how this regress comes to an end. Swain's solution to the regress is provided by his thesis that many of our beliefs are reliable, and thus justified, on the basis of sets of reasons that do not include any belief states at all. An example will illustrate this point. Suppose Alfred is sitting in his study and is watching it snow outside his window. It is daytime, and Alfred has a clear view of the outdoors from his window. Further, Alfred is attentive, sober, and has normal vision, health, and intelligence. Thus Alfred is quite capable of distinguishing snow from other forms of precipitation. Now it is natural to assume that Alfred comes to be in certain reason states, such as the perceptual state of seeming to see snow, and comes to believe justifiably that it is snowing outside. But which reason is Alfred's justified belief based on? Swain holds that some members of this set of reasons are perceptual states, such as the state of seeming to see snow and the state of seeming to see a window, and that some members are belief states, such as the belief that snow looks just like what he now seems to see. Thus the total set of reasons, R, upon which Alfred's belief is based includes a subset R' that contains no belief states, but only perceptual states. Swain claims, furthermore, that, given Alfred's forementioned reliability-making characteristics, C, Alfred's belief that it is snowing on the basis of R' is reliable and thus justified. This claim amounts to the claim that the probability that it is snowing, given that Alfred seems to see snow, seems to see a window, etc., and given that Alfred has the characteristics C, is greater than the probability of any competitors, given those same facts about Alfred. But if the latter claim is correct, then we have an example of a belief that is reliable, and thus justified, on the basis of a set of reasons, *viz.*, R', that does not include any beliefs. Swain thus holds that Alfred's belief that it is snowing is immediately justified in the sense that its reliability does not necessarily depend on reasons that are beliefs. More generally, he holds that every justified belief is either immediately justified or based on an evidence chain that ends in a set of reasons whose belief members are immediately justified. And this view purports to block the regress problem.

A natural way to reply to Swain's example involving Alfred is to take issue with the claim that Alfred's belief is more probable than any competitor. One could do so by adapting the earlier objection I raised. But let us overlook this possibility, and assume that Alfred's belief is in fact more probable than any competitor. Does this assumption enable us to say that Alfred's belief that it is snowing is immediately justified? Notice that Alfred's belief is not a given-belief, but an observation belief. Thus on Swain's reliabilism the foundations of justification need not consist only of beliefs solely about our perceptual and sensation states; they can include beliefs about the external world. This kind of foundationalism has a couple of obvious advantages. It avoids the problem, stressed by John Pollock, that very few people have any beliefs about their own perceptual and sensation states, and thereby it does not automatically make justified belief the exclusive possession of a few traditional foundationalists.[15] Also, this view avoids the traditional foundationalist's notorious problem of somehow deriving the justification of all our observation beliefs from a small set of given-beliefs. In avoiding these problems, Swain's reliabilism is immune to at least two standard objections to foundationalism.

But the above advantages by no means vindicate Swain's reliabilist account of immediate justification. Consider once again Alfred's belief that it is snowing. By hypothesis, Alfred has the requisite reliability-making characteristics, and his belief is reliably based on a set of nonbelief reason states. Is his belief therefore immediately justified? If we answer 'yes', we return immediately to some version of externalism. For we would be granting that Alfred need not have had awareness of the justifying conditions of his belief. But, as seen, such externalism is unacceptable, even if we add the proviso that Alfred does not have any good reason to doubt that it is snowing. For such externalism attributes justification to Alfred's belief even though from Alfred's own epistemic perspective the fact that his belief is true seems purely accidental. But if the core notion of epistemic justification is epistemic responsibility, then Alfred's belief is surely unjustified. For in holding that belief he is irresponsible insofar as from his perspective the truth of that belief is at best accidental. The fundamental problem with such externalism, I have argued, is that it ignores Alfred's own epistemic situation. It may suffice as a theory of when an external observer is justified in believing that Alfred's belief is true. But in neglecting Alfred's own epistemic perspective it fails as an account of when *Alfred* is justified in holding his belief.

Fortunately, Swain's account is opposed to such externalism. One might have expected Swain to construct a version of internalism on the basis of his notion of direct awareness of nonbelief reason states. But he does not do so. Swain's view, rather, is that "having access to a reliable source of information does not render one's beliefs justified nor even reliable unless one justifiably believes that the source is reliable".[16] But does not this claim undermine the immediate justification of Alfred's belief that it is snowing? Swain's forementioned position was that Alfred's belief is justified just because it is reliably based on certain nonbelief reason states and Alfred has the requisite reliability-making characteristics. Nothing was said about Alfred's believing justifiably that his belief is reliably based and that he has certain reliability-making characteristics. But if we add such a requirement for the justification of Alfred's belief that it is snowing, then that belief is obviously not immediately justified. For its justification will then depend on the justification of Alfred's belief that it is reliably based and that he has certain reliability-making characteristics. Swain says nothing about this problem, but the proponent of his kind of reliabilism must deal with it, since it threatens to revive the regress problem.

Let us examine more closely the implications of Swain's departure from externalism. I have already noted that it undermines the immediate justification of the beliefs he takes to be immediately justified. I believe that his way of departing from externalism also commits him to an unacceptable infinite justificatory regress. Swain's reliabilism states, in effect, not only that a person's (S's) belief that p is justified only if it is reliable, but also that S is justified in holding a reliable belief that p if and only if he is justified in believing that his belief that p is reliable. But if S's belief that p is justified by its reliableness only if S is justified in believing that (i) his belief that p is reliable, then we are faced with an endless regress of justification. For, given the above principle, S is justified in believing that (i) only if he is justified in believing that (ii) his belief that (i) is reliable. And S is justified in believing that (ii) only if he is justified in believing that (iii) his belief that (ii) is reliable. And so on *ad infinitum*. But, as noted above, such a regress gives us no reason to believe that S's belief that p is justified. Hence Swain's reliabilism fails to block the regress problem.

The above kind of endless regress confronts any epistemic principle of the following form:

(4.5)   S's belief that p is justified only if it is F, and S is justified in holding an F belief that p if and only if he is justified in believing that his belief that p is F.

For given (4.5) S will be justified in believing that (i) his belief that p is F only if he is justified in believing that his belief that (i) is F. And this same requirement applies not only to this latter belief but also to the ensuing requisite beliefs. Clearly such a regress requires that we either reject or modify internalist epistemic principles of the above form.

Notice that foundationalist versions of internalism are not the only theories troubled by the above kind of regress. Bonjour's version of coherentism, as I noted in Chapter III, gives rise to just such a regress.

For Bonjour holds that for a person, S, to be justified in believing any particular proposition, S must be justified in believing some set of premises that provides a justifying argument for that belief. Clearly this kind of internalism leads automatically away from foundationalism to some version of coherentism. For it precludes from the start the justification of any belief independently of all other beliefs. Furthermore, Bonjour's coherentism cannot state simply that a person's belief that p is justified if that belief coheres with some maximally coherent belief-system. Given his anti-externalist strictures, Bonjour must adapt his coherentism to the requirements of the forementioned epistemic ascent argument (7) by formulating it as follows:

(4.6)   S's belief that p is justified by its cohering with some maximally coherent belief-system, C, only if S is justified in believing (i) that the beliefs cohering with C are likely to be true, and (ii) that p coheres with C.

But (4.6) leads to an endless regress. For given (4.6), S is justified in believing (i) of (4.6) only by justified belief that the belief that (i) coheres with C. And this latter belief is justified only by justified belief that it coheres; and so on *ad infinitum.* Hence Bonjour's internalism, like Swain's, commits one to an infinite justificatory regress that does not obviously justify any belief whatsoever. I argued earlier that there is no good reason to believe that such a regress is adequate to justify the belief at its head; and, consequently, I find Bonjour's internalism, as well as Swain's, to be an unacceptable alternative to epistemic externalism.

Ernest Sosa has suggested that the foregoing kind of regress arises from the internalist's denial that epistemic justification is supervenient on such *non*epistemic properties as a belief's basis in perception, memory, or inference.[17] Let us say, generally, that a normative property, J, supervenes on a non-normative property, N, provided only that N is necessarily such that whatever has it has J. Applying this notion of supervenience to Sosa's suggestion, we may say that there is a set of nonepistemic properties surrounding any justified belief, and no beliefs could have been surrounded by those properties without being justified. The internalist principles (4.5) and (4.6) obviously run afoul of such supervenience, because they entail that any source of epistemic justification must include an *epistemic* component.

In light of the regresses arising from principles like (4.5) and (4.6), I

concur with Sosa's opposition to epistemic principles entailing that any
source of epistemic justification must include an epistemic component.
Furthermore, I agree that such nonepistemic properties as a belief's
basis in perception, memory, or inference are centrally important to
the epistemic justification of a belief. But, given the earlier objections
to externalism, I want to resist any externalist implications of Sosa's
doctrine of supervenience. If the doctrine of supervenience implies
that a person can be justified in believing a proposition even though
he has had no awareness whatsoever of the justifying conditions of
his belief, then that doctrine is just as unacceptable as externalism.
Actually I doubt that either the above notion of supervenience
or those notions of supervenience in recent literature on physicalism
and values entail epistemic externalism. But Sosa does introduce his
notion of supervenience in connection with his apparently externalist
approach to epistemic justification. And in light of the earlier arguments against externalism, I find Sosa's apparent externalism to be no
real improvement on the kind of internalism espoused by Swain and
Bonjour.

3. CONCLUDING REMARKS

What we need now, I believe, is an epistemology that steers a clear
course between the Scylla of epistemic externalism and the Charybdis
of internalist epistemic principles like (4.5) and (4.6). Lacking such an
epistemology, we will be committed either to the externalist's *ad hoc*
evasion of the epistemic regress problem or to the internalist's
unacceptable infinite regress of justification. Or, to consider a third
undesirable alternative, we will have to grant that the epistemic regress
problem ultimately provides a powerful argument not for foundationalism but for epistemological skepticism of some form. But I
believe the foundationalist can provide a theory that successfully
avoids the pitfalls of externalism and internalism, namely, epistemic
intuitionism. It is the burden of the next chapter to develop a new
version of epistemic intuitionism and to defend it against some
powerful skeptical objections. Let us turn, then, to an intuitionist
solution to the epistemic regress problem.

NOTES

[1] See Cornman, 'Foundational versus Nonfoundational Theories of Empirical Justification', *American Philosophical Quarterly* 14 (1977), 290–291; idem, *Skepticism, Justification, and Explanation* (D. Reidel, Dordrecht, 1980), pp. 135–138; Post, 'Infinite Regresses of Justification and of Explanation', *Philosophical Studies* 38 (1980), 32–37. Cf. I. T. Oakley, 'An Argument for Scepticism Concerning Justified Beliefs', *American Philosophical Quarterly* 13 (1976), 227; and John Pollock, *Knowledge and Justification* (Princeton University Press, Princeton, 1974), pp. 27–28. I shall outline Post's version of the argument, as it is the most detailed.

[2] See Sosa, 'The Raft and the Pyramid: Coherence versus Foundations in the Theory of Knowledge', in P. French et al. (eds.), *Midwest Studies in Philosophy, Vol. V: Studies in Epistemology* (University of Minnesota Press, Minneapolis, 1980), pp. 12–13. Cf. Sosa, 'The Foundations of Foundationalism', *Noûs* 14 (1980), 548–549, 554.

[3] See, for example, George S. Pappas and Marshall Swain, Introduction to *Essays on Knowledge and Justification*, Pappas and Swain (eds.) (Cornell University Press, Ithaca, 1978), p. 32, and Mark Pastin, 'Social and Anti-Social Justification: A Study of Lehrer's Epistemology', in R. J. Bogdan (ed.), *Keith Lehrer* (D. Reidel, Dordrecht, 1981), p. 207.

[4] See Keith Lehrer, 'Reply to Pastin', in R. J. Bogdan (ed.), *Keith Lehrer*, pp. 234–235. Cf. Lehrer, 'The Knowledge Cycle', *Noûs* 11 (1977), 18–19.

[5] My characterization of minimal foundationalism is roughly equivalent to that of James Cornman's in 'Foundational versus Nonfoundational Theories of Empirical Justification', *American Philosophical Quarterly* 14 (1977), 288, and in idem, *Skepticism, Justification, and Explanation*, pp. 130–131.

[6] Three philosophers who apparently espouse weak foundationalism are: Bertrand Russell, *Human Knowledge: Its Scope and Limits* (Simon & Schuster, New York, 1948), pp. 157, 384, 392–395; Roderick Firth, 'Coherence, Certainty, and Epistemic Priority', *Journal of Philosophy* 61 (1964), 545–557; and Nelson Goodman, 'Sense and Certainty', *Philosophical Review* 61 (1952), 160–167. In subsequent discussion I shall use C. I. Lewis as a representative of radical foundationalism and William Alston as a representative of modest foundationalism.

[7] Two such dubious efforts occur in some of the writings of Keith Lehrer and Nicholas Rescher. See, for example, Lehrer, *Knowledge* (Clarendon Press, Oxford, 1974), pp. 78–80, 175, and Rescher, *The Coherence Theory of Truth* (Clarendon Press, Oxford, 1973), Chapter 13. Cf. Rescher, *Cognitive Systematization* (Basil Blackwell, Oxford, 1979), pp. 51–55.

[8] Sellars employs an epistemic ascent argument in *Science, Perception, and Reality* (Routledge & Kegan Paul, London, 1963), pp. 167–169, and in 'Epistemic Principles', in H. N. Castañeda (ed.), *Action, Knowledge, and Reality: Critical Studies in Honor of Wilfrid Sellars* (Bobbs-Merrill, Indianapolis, 1975), p. 332–343. Bonjour uses an epistemic ascent argument in 'Can Empirical Knowledge Have a Foundation?', *American Philosophical Quarterly* 15 (1978), 5–6, and in 'Externalist Theories of Empirical Knowledge', in P. French et al. (eds.), *Midwest Studies in Philosophy, Vol. V: Studies in Epistemology*, pp. 54–55. Cf. I. T. Oakley, 'An Argument for Scepticism Concerning Justified Beliefs', *American Philosophical Quarterly* 13 (1976), 222–224.

⁹ See Armstrong, *Belief, Truth, and Knowledge* (Cambridge University Press, Cambridge, 1973), pp. 157, 166–167; Goldman, 'What is Justified Belief?', in G. S. Pappas (ed.), *Justification and Knowledge* (D. Reidel, Dordrecht, 1979), pp. 1–24; *idem*, 'The Internalist Conception of Justification', in *Midwest Studies in Philosophy, Vol. V: Studies in Epistemology*, pp. 27–51; Alston, 'Self-Warrant', *American Philosophical Quarterly* **13** (1976), 267–272; and *idem*, 'What's Wrong With Immediate Knowledge?', *Synthese* **55** (1983), 73–95. See also Robert Nozick, *Philosophical Explanations* (Harvard University Press, Cambridge, 1981), pp. 172–196, 264–268. I discuss Goldman's reliabilism in the Appendix.

¹⁰ Alston introduces these conditions in 'Self-Warrant: A Neglected Form of Privileged Access', *American Philosophical Quarterly* **13** (1976), 268–269.

¹¹ See Bonjour, 'Can Empirical Knowledge Have a Foundation?', *American Philosophical Quarterly* **15** (1978), 7. Cf. *idem*, 'Externalist Theories of Empirical Knowledge', in *Midwest Studies in Philosophy, Vol. V: Studies in Epistemology*, p. 63. In the Appendix I have argued that externalism conflicts with the primary sense of 'justified belief' according to which if S is justified in believing that *p*, then S is *capable* of calling to attention evidence which justifies *p*.

¹² See Alston, 'What's Wrong With Immediate Knowledge?', *Synthese* **55** (1983), 73–95. Incidentally, Alston endorses the normative conception of justification in 'Self-Warrant', *American Philosophical Quarterly* **13** (1976), 271, but rejects it in the forementioned paper.

¹³ See Alston, 'Concepts of Epistemic Justification', *The Monist* **68** (1985). Cf. Robert G. Meyers, 'Sellars' Rejection of Foundations', *Philosophical Studies* **39** (1981), 74–76, and David B. Annis, 'Epistemic Foundationalism', *Philosophical Studies* **31** (1977), 350–351. On level-confusions in general, see Alston, 'Level-Confusions in Epistemology', in *Midwest Studies in Philosophy, Vol. V: Studies in Epistemology*, pp. 135–150.

¹⁴ The following outline of Swain's reliabilism is based on Swain, *Reasons and Knowledge* (Cornell University Press, Ithaca, 1981), Chapter 4; *idem*, 'Justification and Reliable Belief', *Philosophical Studies* **40** (1981), 389–407; and *idem*, 'Justification and the Basis of Belief', in G. S. Pappas (ed.), *Justification and Knowledge*, pp. 25–49. See the Appendix for more discussion of reliabilism.

¹⁵ See Pollock, *Knowledge and Justification* (Princeton University Press, Princeton, 1974), pp. 57–58, and *idem*, 'A Plethora of Epistemological Theories', in G. S. Pappas (ed.), *Justification and Knowledge*, pp. 98–99. Cf. page 204 below.

¹⁶ See Swain, *Reasons and Knowledge*, p. 107; cf. pp. 40–41, 102. The present quote seems to be inconsistent with parts of *ibid.*, pp. 101–102, but Swain supports the position of the quote more than once in his book.

¹⁷ See Sosa, 'The Raft and the Pyramid', in *Midwest Studies in Philosophy, Vol. V: Studies in Epistemology*, p. 18. Cf. Sosa, 'The Foundations of Foundationalism', *Noûs* **14** (1980), 552, and Chisholm, 'A Version of Foundationalism', in *idem, The Foundations of Knowing* (University of Minnesota Press, Minneapolis, 1982), p. 13. The following notion of supervenience is Chisholm's and, I presume, Sosa's as well.

CHAPTER V

EPISTEMIC FOUNDATIONALISM (II):
EPISTEMIC INTUITIONISM

Epistemic intuitionism provides an account of immediate justification that is currently unpopular among foundationalists. It is notorious particularly for its reliance on the doctrine of the epistemological given. Since there are various notions of the given in circulation, there are also various versions of intuitionism. To circumscribe the relevant versions of epistemic intuitionism, I find it useful to distinguish four general kinds of given: the phenomenological given, the factual given, the linguistic given, and the epistemological given.[1]

Two noteworthy senses of the phenomenological given are:

PG1. P's are given = Df. In perceiving, some perceivers are ostensibly presented with P's.

PG2. P's are given = Df. In perceiving, some perceivers are presented with P's noninferentially and without interpretation.

An essential characteristic of a phenomenological given is that its being given phenomenologically entails neither that it exists nor that it does not exist. We may think of a phenomenological given as the content of a perceptual experience, so long as we grant that something can be a content but not exist. Examples of such a given are the contents of illusory and hallucinatory perceptual experiences. The terms 'noninferentially' and 'without interpretation' in PG2 require some explanation. Let us assume that the content of a perceptual experience is presented noninferentially if and only if no process of inferring precedes or is causally relevant to that content. And let us assume that such content is presented without interpretation if and only if that content is not dependent on, *i.e.*, unaffected by, the perceiver's interests, attitudes, and ways of conceptualizing.

There are also two noteworthy senses of the second kind of given, the factual given:

FG1. P's are given = Df. P's are directly perceived by perceivers.

FG2. P's are given = Df. P's are presented to perceivers noninferentially and without interpretation.

141

Unlike being given phenomenologically, if something is given factually, then it exists. The direct realist holds that physical objects are factually given in the sense of either FG1 or FG2, whereas the indirect realist holds that sense-data are factually given in one of those senses. Fortunately I need not decide the issue of what is directly perceived for present purposes.

We can distinguish at least four senses of the third kind of given, the linguistic given:

LG1.   P's are given = Df. P-terms are correctly used by perceivers to report their perceptual experiences.
LG2.   P's are given = Df. P-terms are terms from which the meaningfulness of all empirical terms derives.
LG3.   P's are given = Df. P-terms stand for the extraconceptual and extralinguistic entities from which the meaningfulness of all empirical terms derives.
LG4.   P's are given = Df. P's are the entities which are experienced before any learning and independently of language, and with which a language must be associated if it is to be learned.

Notice that LG1–LG3 define the given solely in terms of linguistic entities. Many philosophers hold that sensations are given in the sense of LG1, but clearly one need not hold that only sensations are given in this sense. LG2–LG3 involve more controversial notions of the given than does LG1; they are relevant to the celebrated "myth of the given" that Wilfrid Sellars and others have opposed.[2] Many philosophers have assumed that these linguistic givens are centrally important to any doctrine of the epistemological given. But this assumption is not necessarily true of my construal of the epistemological given.

Two important senses of the epistemological given are:

EG1.   P's are given = Df. P's are entities about which some perceivers have immediately justified beliefs.
EG2.   P's are given = Df. Beliefs about P's are immediately justified and are the foundations for the justification of inferentially justified beliefs.

These notions of the epistemological given are modest. If one countenances an epistemological given in the sense of EG1 and EG2, one need be committed at most to some version of modest foundationalism. For EG1 and EG2 make no claim about the infallibility or indubitability of beliefs about the given. Furthermore, I doubt that a recognition of an epistemological given in either of those senses requires a recognition of any linguistic givens in the sense of LG2, LG3, or LG4. A recognition of such linguistic givens commits one to certain semantic claims, whereas a recognition of the epistemological givens commits one only to certain epistemic claims. In addition, I doubt that a recognition of the epistemological givens requires a recognition of either factual or phenomenological givens. But, as we shall see, some versions of epistemic intuitionism do involve factual and phenomenological givens.

In light of the foregoing distinctions, I can now begin to characterize the essence of epistemic intuitionism. A theory is a version of epistemic intuitionism only if it involves at least one of the above notions of the epistemological given. And there is an additional necessary condition of epistemic intuitionism. A theory is a version of epistemic intuitionism, let us say, only if it finds the solution to the epistemic regress problem in foundational beliefs justified not by reference to other beliefs, but by reference to an "intuition", "direct awareness", or "immediate apprehension" of the given. For simplicity, I shall use the term 'apprehension' as equivalent to each of these three terms. Unfortunately, intuitionists do not agree on the nature of apprehensions of the given. Some intuitionists appear to identify apprehensions with belief-like states, whereas others sharply contrast apprehensions and beliefs. R. M. Chisholm belongs to the former group, while C. I. Lewis belongs to the latter. I shall examine their views in turn.

1. INTUITIONISM AND IMMEDIATE JUSTIFICATION

1.1. *Chisholm's Intuitionism*

Chisholm understands the doctrine of the epistemological given to involve the following two theses about justified belief:[3]

> EG3a. The justified beliefs that a person has at any time form a structure or edifice, many parts and stages of which help to support each other, but which as a whole is supported by its own foundation.

EG3b. The foundation of one's justified beliefs consists (at least in part) of the apprehension of appearances or, more accurately, "ways of being appeared to".

Chisholm's less metaphorical statement of these two theses is:

EG4a. Every justified belief that a person has is justified in part by some belief that is self-justified, *i.e.*, immediately justified.

EG4b. There are beliefs about appearances, or ways of being appeared to, that justify themselves, or are immediately justified.

Notice that EG4b eliminates the talk of "apprehension" of appearances in EG3b. The talk of apprehension of appearances has given way to talk of beliefs about appearances. One may thus wonder whether Chisholm identifies an apprehension of an appearance with a belief about an appearance. Chisholm does cite with apparent approval Leibniz's notion of "direct awareness" of our own thoughts, and he does speak of a state of affairs being "apprehended through itself," but I believe that Chisholm either identifies apprehensions with beliefs about ways of being appeared to or fails to give them a significant role in the justification of foundational beliefs.[4] A natural question, then, is how foundational beliefs can be justified once apprehensions are identified with them or are eliminated. Chisholm's answer to this question requires some stage-setting.

A noteworthy preliminary is that Chisholm has come to hold that there are no first-person propositions. He holds that the first-person sentence 'I am F' expresses not a proposition but my direct attribution of the property of F-ness to myself.[5] But since Chisholm's theory of property attribution is not directly relevant to the issue at hand, and since this theory is readily adaptable to the standard view that the basic form of believing is propositional, I shall continue to talk of first-person propositions in connection with Chisholm's theory. This will raise no special problems, since even on Chisholm's theory of property attribution, whenever I directly attribute a property, F, to myself, I also accept a certain proposition, *viz.*, the proposition that someone is F.

Taking the notion of one proposition's being "epistemically prefer-

senses of the expression 'epistemically justified': (i) having some presumption in its favor; (ii) being acceptable; (iii) being beyond reasonable doubt; (iv) being evident; and (v) being certain. For present purposes we need to understand the last three senses. A proposition, p, is beyond reasonable doubt for a person, S, provided only that believing that p is more reasonable for S than withholding that p (where withholding a proposition is the state of accepting neither it nor its negation). And a proposition is evident for a person just in case it is beyond reasonable doubt for that person, and is one of those propositions on which it is reasonable for him to base his decisions. We can now define the concept of objective certainty. A proposition is certain for a person if and only if it is beyond reasonable doubt for him and there is no other proposition that is more reasonable for him to believe.

The above definitions enable us to approach the key notion of a "self-presenting" proposition. According to Chisholm, some propositions are *directly* evident for a person, and whenever something is directly evident for a person, some state of affairs "presents itself", or is "self-presenting", to him. To say that a state of affairs (or a proposition) is self-presenting to a person is just to say that it occurs (or is true) and that necessarily if it occurs (or is true), then it is evident for that person. Thus, if the proposition that I seem to have a toothache is a self-presenting proposition for me at present, then it is true that I seem to have a toothache at present, and, what is more, it is evident for me that I seem to have a toothache. Self-presenting properties and propositions necessarily involve psychological properties. That is, a self-presenting property is such that necessarily if one conceives that property, then one conceives some psychological property, such as one's way of being appeared to or of sensing. And self-presenting propositions are about just such properties. Self-presenting propositions and properties, according to Chisholm, are indubitable. Thus, if such a proposition is true of me, and if I consider it, then I cannot withhold belief from it. And if I have such a property and I consider my having it, then I cannot doubt that I have it. Furthermore, self-presenting propositions, on Chisholm's theory, are certain in the forementioned sense for the person considering them. Thus, they are also evident for a person if they are true of him and he considers

dently of any other propositions. Thus, self-presenting propositions are foundational in the sense that they are immediately justified, or in Chisholm's terminology, "self-justified".

But why should we grant that self-presenting propositions are self-justified? Chisholm's answer is that such a proposition is self-justified because the only way to describe its justification is simply to repeat the proposition itself.[6] This is obviously not true of the justification of propositions that are not self-presenting. Consider, for instance, my belief that I see a blue book on my desk. One can naturally ask the question, "What is your justification for believing that there is a blue book on your desk?" Or, "What is your justification for believing that it is a blue book that you see?" The possibility of such questions, according to Chisholm, indicates that we cannot stop questions about justification simply by an appeal to observation. For of the belief that I observe an F, one can always ask, "What is your justification for believing that you observe an F?" Obviously it would be inappropriate for me to answer such a question simply by reiterating my belief that I observe an F. But Chisholm claims that for some beliefs such an answer would be appropriate. Consider, for instance, my belief that I seem to see a blue book. This belief can play a role in answering the question about the justification of my observation belief that I do see a blue book. Furthermore, this belief about my perceptual state, according to Chisholm, is justified by its own occurrence, or simply by my reiterating the proposition that I seem to see a blue book. More generally, on Chisholm's theory, a self-justifying proposition, such as that I am appeared to F-ly, is justified simply by the fact that it is true.

I find Chisholm's strategy for arriving at and explaining the self-justification of certain beliefs to be unconvincing and implausible. For convenience, let us reintroduce the notion of a *given-belief* to refer to the allegedly self-justified beliefs solely about one's own current perceptual and sensation states. And consider, once again, my given-belief that I seem to see a blue book. Chisholm's basic assumption is that the only way I can possibly answer a query about the justification of such a belief is to invoke its truth, to reiterate the proposition that I do seem to see a blue book. But this assumption is dubious. For Chisholm has not eliminated the possibility that given-beliefs constitute a reliable kind of beliefs and each given-belief is justified by its being an instance of a reliable kind of beliefs. In Chapter IV, I outlined such a theory of immediate justification in connection with my examination of Alston's reliabilism, but I opposed such a theory because of its externalist features. Unfortunately, however, Chisholm cannot consistently oppose such a theory on account of its externalist features, because, as we shall see in the following paragraph, Chisholm's own accout of immediate justification is externalist. I submit, therefore, that Chisholm's strategy for showing the self-justification of given-beliefs is implausible even on Chisholm's own principles.

But there is a more powerful objection to Chisholm's account of immediate justification. His account, unfortunately, commits one to a version of epistemic externalism. As I have pointed out, Chisholm claims that my belief that I seem to see a blue book, for instance, is self-presenting in the sense that necessarily if it is true, then it is immediately justified for me, since it is directly evident for me. But nothing in this claim implies that I must be aware of my perceptual state of seeming to see a blue book, for on Chisholm's account a psychological state can be self-presenting for me even if I an unaware of this state. And Chisholm's notion of evidentness, being epistemic and *non*psychological, does not alter this point. In connection with the claim in question, then, I need only believe that I seem to see a blue book; I need not have been aware of my seeming to see a blue book. Thus, on Chisholm's theory, a person can be immediately justified in holding some given-belief even if he has had no awareness of the justifying conditions of that belief. Hence, Chisholm's foundationalism is a version of externalism and, consequently, is open to the objections I raised against externalist theories in Chapter IV.

In sum, then, I oppose Chisholm's account of immediate justification on at least two grounds. It relies on the unjustified claim that given-beliefs can be justified only by their truth. And it commits one to a version of epistemic externalism. Fortunately, the foundationalist can turn to a more traditional version of epistemic intuitionism to avoid Chisholm's externalism. One such version is C. I. Lewis' radical foundationalism.

1.2. *Lewis' Intuitionism*

Lewis' intuitionism relies on a notion of the epistemological given like EG2 and a notion of the factual given like FG1.[7] But, as we shall see, Lewis' notion of the epistemological given is not as modest as EG2. Lewis holds that what are factually given to perceivers are sense-data such as "the immediacy of redness or loudness." Some other examples of the factually given are a visual pattern, a feeling of pressure, and an appearance of paper. External objects, according to Lewis, are not among what is factually given to perceivers. He claims that the actually given is restricted to those appearances and sense-data that one can immediately apprehend with certainty. But what is immediate apprehension with certainty? Although commentators have debated this question, Lewis states explicitly that apprehensions of the given are not judgments. Thus apprehensions are not belief-states involving propositions. Rather, they are direct non-judgmental experiences or awarenesses of appearances or sense-data.

But what is a direct awareness of something? Is direct awareness involved in every non-cognitive stimulation of one's sense organs? If so, can insects and amoebas have immediate apprehensions of sense-data? Or, does direct awareness require interpretive and conceptual abilities, such as the ability to form judgments about objects? Of course intuitionists do not uniformly agree on the answers to such questions. Lewis, however, denies that perceivers first passively apprehend the given and then interpret it. On his view perception is shot through with interpretation. Yet Lewis holds that for theoretical purposes we can analytically distinguish the given from interpretation. As for direct awareness itself, some of Lewis' remarks suggest that it requires a kind of mental pointing to, or a focusing of attention on, a specific phenomenal object. If this is Lewis' view, then presumably he would reject the suggestion that insects and amoebas have apprehensions. Following Russell and Moore, Lewis explains his notion of direct awareness mainly by examples. Direct awareness occurs whenever a person sees a color, hears a sound, or smells an odor. Notice, however, that on this view a person is directly aware not of any external obejcts or dispositional psychological states, but of the phenomenal objects of occurrent psychological states, such as appearances or sense-data. Lewis suggests that we can be aware of certain appearances without being aware of anything else. This leads him to hold that we can have *direct* awareness or apprehension of certain phenomenal objects.

Notice, however, that Lewis' talk about the *certainty* of direct apprehensions raises a problem. Lewis frequently claims that apprehensions of the given are certain in the sense of being unmistakable or infallible.[8] But it seems meaningless to say that mere non-judgmental awarenesses of sense-data are certain in this sense. For what is certain or uncertain is necessarily something judgmental or propositional, something that can be true or false. I propose, therefore, that we regard Lewis' talk of the certainty of apprehensions of the given as elliptical for talk of the certainty of beliefs or propositions about the immediately apprehended given.

But which beliefs about the given are made certain, and thereby justified, by apprehensions of the given? Obviously, not every belief a person has about a particular sensation or appearance is immediately justified by reference to an apprehension of the given. Suppose a person believes that his current appearance of red is just like the appearance his brother had yesterday. Clearly this person's apprehension of his current appearance is inadequate to justify such a belief. What this person needs are additional reasons for believing that his brother's appearance is similar to his own. Consider also a person's belief that he has an appearance of a book given to him by his wife. The justification of this belief depends not merely on the apprehension of an appearance, but also on reasons for believing what a certain book looks like. Such examples clearly suggest that apprehensions of the given are inadequate to justify beliefs about the given when those beliefs involve more than the internal character of the given. Thus the intuitionist should hold that one's apprehension of a particular appearance, for instance, justifies at most one's belief about the internal character of that appearance. Let us assume, accordingly, that a person's apprehension of an appearance of a book, for instance, justifies at most his belief that he has an appearance of a book, or that he *seems* to see a book. Lewis calls such a belief restricted to the given an "expressive belief". But let us continue to use the term 'given-belief' for such a belief.

As I mentioned, Lewis holds that beliefs solely about the apprehended given are infallible; they cannot fail to be true. Of course a person's given-beliefs are not immediately justified solely by their infallibility. Presumably, all of our true beliefs solely about the principles of logic and mathematics are infallible, but they are not immediately justified for us because they are infallible and we happen to hold them. Thus, let us assume that a person's given-beliefs are immediately justified not because they are infallible, but because he has an apprehension of the phenomenal objects that make those beliefs true. Adapting Lewis' notion of infallible apprehensions, we might say that apprehensions of phenomenal objects constitute infallible evidence for the truth, and perhaps even the certainty, of given-beliefs. This suggests the following notion of infallible justification:

(5.1)   A person's (S's) given-belief that *p* about his appearance, X, is infallibly justified for S if and only if necessarily if S believes that *p* and has an apprehension of X, then S is immediately justified in believing that *p*.

In light of (5.1) we might say that S's apprehension of X guarantees not only the truth but also the justification of S's given-belief that *p*. On this reading of Lewis' intuitionism, then, given-beliefs are infallibly true and infallibly justified. Let us briefly take up the issue of the infallibility and indubitability of given-beliefs.

1.3. *Infallibility and Indubitability*

Why should we grant the radical foundationalist's thesis that given-beliefs are infallibly true? Before granting this thesis we should determine at least just how the radical foundationalist construes given-beliefs of the form 'I have an appearance of F'. He has, it seems, at least three options.[9] First, he might hold that the term (or concept) replacing 'F' in such beliefs is purely demonstrative, that it picks out its referent ostensively, unlike any multiply applicable classificatory or descriptive concept or term. Second, he might hold that the term (or concept) replacing 'F' describes or classifies its referent in some private language or system of mental representations. Third, he might claim that the term replacing 'F' is a descriptive or classificatory term in a public language (perhaps a language of thought), and thus that any perceiver using the term should use it in accordance with the standard practices of a certain linguistic community. As I am unable to determine which option Lewis himself prefers, I shall comment on each in turn.

The first construal of given-beliefs amounts to the claim that when a person believes that he has an appearance of F, he is stipulating the meaning of 'F' by ostensively applying it to some object of his direct awareness. In effect, this view makes given-beliefs about appearances ostensive definitions of appearance terms. Perhaps such given-beliefs are exempt from error in a trivial sense, just as any stipulative definitions are exempt from error. But it is doubtful that given-beliefs, on this construal, involve genuine empirical assertions. For on this construal my given-belief that I have an appearance of red, for instance, is equivalent to the belief that my appearance is *that* appearance. This is hardly a significant empirical claim. But it seems that if given-beliefs are to provide foundations for the justification of all our empirical beliefs, they must make significant empirical assertions. That is, they at least must involve multiply applicable classificatory or descriptive terms. Hence I find the first construal of given-beliefs to be quite unpromising.

Furthermore, I believe it is clear that on the second and third construals given-beliefs cannot be infallible. On these construals the terms replacing 'F' are reapplicable classificatory or descriptive terms, presumably mental or physical. But surely it is always possible for a person to misapply such terms either because of misremembering their proper application or because of an insufficiently cautious examination of the referents in question. Such misapplication, it seems, will give rise to false beliefs of the form 'I have an appearance of F'. And this possibility precludes infallibility. An example will illustrate my doubts about the infallibility of given-beliefs. Suppose that while gazing at an octagon Alfred believes that he has an appearance of a hexagon. (For simplicity we shall assume that if Alfred is employing a private language, the terms 'octagon' and 'hexagon' by some strange coincidence have the same meaning in that language as they have in current English.) But upon closer inspection of the matter, Alfred comes to see that he was insufficiently cautious in counting the sides of his appearance, and that he miscounted its sides. Surely this is a possibility. Consider also the case in which Alfred comes to see that he misremembered the meaning of the term 'hexagon', and thus that his belief about what appears to him is false. Surely this is a possible case also. But since such cases are possible, we should reject Lewis' thesis about the infallibility of given-beliefs.

Lewis, as well as other radical foundationalists, holds that given-beliefs are also indubitable for the person who has them in the sense that he cannot be led to doubt them, *i.e.*, withhold belief from them, either by reasoning or by subsequent experience. But I believe that the indubitability of given-beliefs is just as dubious as their infallibility. Let us consider once again the example of Alfred, who while gazing at an octagon, believes that he has an appearance of a hexagon. Suppose we inform Alfred that he is gazing at an octagon, and that therefore he probably has an eight-sided rather than a six-sided appearance. We might even suggest, accordingly, that he has miscounted the sides of what he seems to see, perhaps because of hasty introspection. In any case, if it is reasonable to suppose that a person like Alfred has an appearance of an eight-sided rather than a six-sided figure while gazing at an octagon, then it is reasonable to suppose that a person can be mistaken in his belief about what he seems to see. Similarly, it is reasonable to suppose that in the case under consideration we could provide Alfred with good reason to doubt the veracity of his given-belief. For a person can always make a mistake, verbal or otherwise, in describing what he seems to see, and in certain circumstances we can be reliable witnesses to the likelihood of such a mistake on his part. The case of Alfred, I believe, illustrates this possibility. Consequently, I am dubious about Lewis' thesis that given-beliefs are indubitable.

But the proponent of infallible and indubitable given-beliefs might reply that my example of a purportedly infallible and indubitable given-belief is inappropriate. He might propose that an appearance corresponding to an infallible and indubitable given-belief is exhaustively characterized by the given-belief itself; that the appearance is not something having determinate features independently of the relevant given-belief. If this is so, my example of Alfred's false belief about the appearance that has eight sides independently of Alfred's given-belief is inappropriate. But the present proposal about the relation between given-beliefs and appearances simply begs the question at hand in favor of the radical foundationalist. For it simply claims that the relation between given-beliefs and appearances is such that given-beliefs determine the character of appearances. I can find no good reason to accept such a claim. In fact, in light of the real possibility of hasty and incautious formation of given-beliefs, such as in Alfred's case, I submit that there is good reason to reject such a claim. And my objection is not restricted to given-beliefs involving the counting of the sides of an appearance; for the possibility of hasty and incautious belief-formation is relevant to almost all, if not all, given-beliefs. Perhaps the possibility of hasty and incautious belief-formation does not undermine the infallibility and indubitability of such beliefs as that I exist and that I believe something, but we have good reason to believe that this possibility counts strongly against the infallibility and indubitability of those given-beliefs that play a role in the justification of observation beliefs. If my examples involving Alfred fail conclusively to refute the radical foundationalist's thesis that given-beliefs are infallible and indubitable, then they at least challenge the radical foundationalist to provide us with the infallible and indubitable given-beliefs that can justify observation beliefs. And until the radical foundationalist can meet this challenge, his theory is unacceptable.

A natural reply is that Lewis' thesis about the infallibility and indubitability of given-beliefs applies only to those given-beliefs that one forms carefully and cautiously. Perhaps this is true of Lewis' thesis, but I am unconvinced that cautious belief-formation can preclude all the corrigible mistakes of the kind I have mentioned. Perhaps cautious belief-formation can do so if it entails the infallibility of given-beliefs, but I doubt that cautious belief-formation entails such infallibility. For the caution and care we take in belief-formation often turn out to be insufficient to provide us with truth. What the radical foundationalist needs to show, then, is how cautious belief-formation can eliminate the fallibility and dubitability of given-beliefs.

However, a better reply to my objections concedes their force but denies that they undermine the indubitability of given-beliefs. One might grant that there can be *prima facie* reasons to doubt a given-belief, but insist that one's given-beliefs can always override or defeat any reasons to doubt them. We can clarify this point by thinking of each person as the final epistemological authority about his own appearances (and sensations) in the following sense:

EA.   A person, S, is the *final epistemological authority* about his appearance of F at time *t* if and only if: necessarily if at *t* S sincerely aims to have only true beliefs about his appearances, and if S believes at *t* that he has an appearance of F after cautiously considering the matter and reflecting carefully on any available *prima facie* reasons to doubt that he has an appearance of F, then S will have no good reason to doubt that he has an appearance of F.

Let us say that a person has exercised his final epistemological authority with respect to a particular given-belief when he holds that belief after cautiously considering its truth and reflecting carefully on any available *prima facie* reasons to doubt that belief. The issue, then, is whether a person can have good reason to doubt a particular given-belief once he has exercised his final epistemological authority with respect to it. Of course one may come to have undefeated *prima facie* reasons to doubt a particular given-belief, but on the present view once one has exercised one's final epistemological authority in connection with these new reasons, one cannot have good reason to doubt that given-belief.

An example may clarify this kind of appeal to EA. Suppose that Sally, who has a jaundiced eye, believes that she seems to see yellow paper while gazing at the white paper on my desk. Upon hearing Sally report her belief, we inform her that she probably seems to see white paper since the paper on my desk is white rather than yellow. Our information provides Sally with a *prima facie* reason to doubt her given-belief, and presumably such a reason will prompt Sally to reconsider the nature of the appearance in question. Given her jaundiced eye, Sally will of course maintain her belief that she seems to see yellow paper, even though we have provided her with *prima facie* reason to doubt that belief. For her given-belief will override our *prima facie* reason to doubt it. We may thus say that Sally has exercised her final epistemological authority with respect to her given-belief. And it seems that having done so, Sally can hardly have good reason to doubt her given-belief. But notice that the kind of indubitability involved in the exercise of Sally's final epistemological authority does not entail that no one can have grounds for doubting the accuracy of Sally's given-belief. We who see the white paper on my desk may have good reason to doubt the accuracy of Sally's given-belief. But it does not follow that the same is true of Sally also.

Let us compare the kind of indubitability involved in EA with what some theorists call the "irrefutability" of given-beliefs. The irrefutability thesis is simply that it is impossible for anyone else to show that a person is mistaken in his beliefs about his current appearances, sensations, and psychological states. For example, you may have *prima facie* grounds for doubting my current given-belief, but you cannot show that I am mistaken in that belief. Some philosophers, however, have questioned the irrefutability of given-beliefs in light of certain cases of psycho-analysis.[10] Consider the classic case of the overprotective mother who prevents her daughter from going out into society in order to prevent her from becoming a threatening rival. The mother sincerely denies both that she wants to prevent her daughter's social development and that she believes her policy will have such a result. She claims that she simply wants to protect her daughter from harm.

Now surely it is possible that there are such cases in which a person has certain desires and beliefs without knowing he has them and attributes to himself certain desires and beliefs he does not actually have. Furthermore, in the case at hand we might have good grounds for doubting what the mother says, and, what is more, we might even be able to show (in some realistic sense of 'show') that she is mistaken about her beliefs and desires. But given the latter possibility, we should reject the irrefutability thesis.

In reply, I believe we should readily grant that a person can hide some of his beliefs and desires from himself and attribute to himself beliefs and desires he does not actually have. Freud has made a sufficiently compelling case here. But one might argue that the proponent of the irrefutability thesis is not thereby threatened. For he can easily restrict his thesis to those beliefs solely about *occurrent* appearances, sensations, and psychological states, including occurrent conscious belief and desire states. In fact, Lewis and other radical foundationalists do restrict their infallibility, indubitability, and irrefutability theses to such occurrent phenomena, and this much is clear from the fact that those theses are about *given*-beliefs. But I doubt that such a restriction is useful in the present context. In our example the overprotective mother has a dispositional unconscious belief that her daughter is a potential threat to her. I believe we might be able to show that the mother actually has such a belief and thus that her belief that she does not have such a belief is false. But her belief that she does not have such a belief is not a given-belief, since it is not a belief about an occurrent or conscious belief. Let us assume, however, that the overprotective mother has a conscious given-belief that she consciously believes that her daughter is not a potential threat to her. Does the above example show that this belief is refutable? It seems not, if we assume that the mother does consciously believe that her daughter is not a potential threat to her. Of course in that case her conscious belief would conflict with her unconscious belief. But let us assume that her given-belief is false and thus that she does not consciously believe that her daughter is not a potential threat to her. (This is an acceptable assumption, since irrefutability does not entail infallibility.) The question, then, is whether we can *show* that her given-belief is false. I believe we could show her given-belief to be false by showing that she really, albeit unconsciously, believes that her daughter is a potential threat to her, and further that her beliefs about her daughter are consistent. Presumably a skilled psychoanalyst could bring this unconscious belief to the surface of her consciousness. But in doing so, he surely would provide good reason not only for us but also for the mother to doubt the accuracy of her given-belief, especially given good evidence for the consistency of the mother's relevant beliefs. And in providing such good reason, he would show that some given-belief is false. Hence the irrefutability thesis is unacceptable.

I believe we can strengthen the case against the irrefutability thesis by invoking a version of D. M. Armstrong's "super electroencephalograph" (SE) argument against certain immunities of given-beliefs.[11] The argument purports to show that with the help of an SE we might be able to show that a person can be mistaken when he believes that he has a certain appearance or sensation. Suppose that on a particular occasion I believe that I have an appearance of green, but the SE reports that I have an appearance of red. If the neurophysiological theory on which the SE relies is highly confirmed, then one could, it seems, justifiably infer that my given-belief is mistaken. Moreover, it seems that one could justifiably infer that the SE has shown that my given-belief is mistaken. Perhaps we will never have access to an SE, but surely such a device is possible. And if the SE is based on a highly confirmed neurophysiological theory, we could justifiably regard it as capable of providing us with good reason to doubt the accuracy of certain given-beliefs. Moreover, if we assume that the SE can function as an *auto*-cerebroscope, then we should grant that it could possibly provide one with good reason to doubt one's own given-beliefs. But if the SE could provide such grounds for doubt, then presumably it would be able to show (at least in some realistic sense) that some given-beliefs are false. Thus this example confirms my doubts about the indubitability and irrefutability of given-beliefs.

But must we reject final epistemological authority with indubitability and irrefutability? I believe not. For the proponent of final epistemological authority in the sense of EA need not hold that all given-beliefs are indubitable or irrefutable. Nor need he hold that they are infallible. The proponent of EA need hold only that after one has exercised one's final epistemological authority, *i.e.*, cautiously considered the truth of one's given-belief and reflected carefully on any available *prima facie* reasons to doubt it, then one will not have any good reason to doubt that given-belief. This view is significantly different from the unqualified indubitability thesis that one cannot have grounds to doubt a given-belief and the unqualified irrefutability thesis that no given-beliefs can be shown to be false.

But how can EA fit into an account of immediate justification? A natural proposal is that a given-belief is immediately justified once a person has exercised his final epistemological authority with respect to it. But why should we grant that the exercise of final epistemological authority provides immediate justification? Does the exercise of such authority provide any good evidence for the truth of a given-belief? One might answer 'yes' to the latter question on the ground that in exercising final epistemological authority one finds that one's given-belief defeats all the available *prima facie* reasons to doubt it. That is, one finds that none of the reasons to doubt one's given-belief is a good reason. But what does this aspect of the exercise of final epistemological authority amount to? Is it simply the requirement that one *believe* that none of the available reasons to doubt is a good reason? Obviously this is too weak. For lack of a better candidate, I suspect that the requirement is that one be justified in believing that none of the available reasons to doubt is a good reason. But such a requirement makes the justification of a given-belief depend on the justification of some other belief; and, therefore, it robs the given-belief of immediate justification. Hence, the present use of EA does not advance foundationalist purposes.

Another noteworthy problem with EA is that it relies on the vague notion of "considering" whether one has an appearance of F. This notion is reminiscent of Chisholm's account of immediate justification, and it suggests some kind of introspection or perhaps intuition. But, it is intolerably unclear. Let us return, then, to Lewis' version of intuitionism to see whether matters are any clearer.

1.4. *Justification via Intuitions*

The above arguments against the infallibility, indubitability, and irrefutability of given-beliefs do not bear directly on the more important claim that given-beliefs can be infallibly *justified* independently of all other beliefs. The latter claim, recall, is that for any given-belief that *p* about some occurrent appearance, sensation or psychological state, X, it is necessarily the case that if a person believes that *p* and has an apprehension of X, then he is immediately justified in believing that *p*.

I find, however, that this intuitionist account of immediate justification must confront a serious problem. In raising this problem, I shall modify and develop an objection that Wilfrid Sellars has raised to a different kind of epistemic intuitionism.[12] The term 'apprehend', at least in its ordinary sense, is an achievement word. And in ordinary usage there is a possibility of "ostensibly apprehending" that does not entail achievement. But given this possibility, we may infer that the distinction between "apprehending" and "seeming to apprehend" requires a criterion that Lewis has not provided. Clearly Lewis cannot avoid this demand for a criterion by claiming that apprehensions are objectless and thus that 'apprehension' is not an achievement word. For on his view appearances are phenomenal objects that each perceiver immediately apprehends, and one can also apprehend occurrent psychological states.

How, then, can Lewis reply? Let us assume, for the sake of argument, that Lewis has the requisite criterion. Presumably this criterion will have one of three possible functions in the immediate justification of given-beliefs. First, a person apprehending an appearance, X, may need to be justified in believing that his apprehension of X satisfies the requisite criterion, if his given-belief that p about X is to be justified. Second, a person apprehending X may need only apprehend that his apprehension of X satisfies the requisite criterion. Third, a person apprehending X need not have any awareness whatsoever of the fact that his apprehension satisfies the requisite criterion; his apprehension need only satisfy the criterion.

The intuitionist of Lewis' persuasion should find each of these three options unacceptable. On the first option, the justification of given-beliefs would no longer be immediate, for it would depend on the justification of some other belief, *viz.*, the belief that the requisite criterion is satisfied. On the second option, we are faced with an infinite regress of apprehensions. For presumably the apprehension that one's apprehension of X satisfies the requisite criterion must itself satisfy the requisite criterion. But on the second option this requires yet another apprehension, and so on *ad infinitum*. On the third option, Lewis' version of intuitionism becomes a version of externalism. For it allows that a person can be immediately justified in holding some given-belief even though he does not have any awareness of a key justifying condition for his belief. The key condition, of course, is his apprehension's satisfying the requisite criterion. But intuitionism derives its plausibility largely as an alternative to externalism; thus it loses much of its appeal when it merges with externalism. Consequently, I find each of the above three options unacceptable.

In sum, then, we may pose the following dilemma for the intuitionist who explains immediate justification in terms of the immediate apprehension of occurrent appearances, sensations, and psychological states. Either he provides a criterion to distinguish genuine apprehensions from merely ostensible apprehensions or he does not. If he does not, then his intuitionism is seriously incomplete and provides at best an *ad hoc* solution to the epistemic regress problem. On the other hand, if he provides the requisite criterion, then he must hold either that the immediate justification of one's given-beliefs requires one's awareness of the satisfaction of the requisite criterion or it does not. On the former alternative, the intuitionist either gives up immediate justification or is faced with an infinite regress of apprehensions. And on the latter alternative, the intuitionist, contrary to his main objective, moves toward externalism. Until the intuitionist resolves this dilemma, we have good grounds to conclude that Lewis' intuitionism, as well as any other version of intuitionism involving apprehensions of occurrent appearances, sensations, and psychological states, is an unsuccessful solution to the regress problem.

Before anticipating some likely replies, I want to relate the dilemma I have developed to an objection due to Sellars and Bonjour that apparently applies to any kind of epistemic intuitionism.[13] As I see it, my dilemma plugs some large gaps in their objection. To state the objection I shall refer to what is allegedly intuited or immediately apprehended as "the given", and assume that the foundational belief justified by reference to the given state of affairs is just the belief that this given state of affairs obtains. Consider then the foundational belief that p justified by reference to the given state of affairs that p. The intuitionist cannot hold that this state of affairs alone justifies the belief that p, for such a view would constitute a return to externalism. Thus the intuitionist must hold that what justifies the belief that p is the apprehension of the state of affairs that p. This apprehension presumably is a cognitive state somehow related to the proposition that p, and it must be able to justify a belief with the same propositional content. But this raises the obvious question why the apprehension involving the propositional content that p does not itself require justification. If the intuitionist replies that the apprehension is justified by reference to the state of affairs that p, then we may counter with the question why this would not require a second apprehension of the state of affairs to justify the original apprehension. For otherwise one cognitive state will constitute both an apprehension of the state of affairs that p and a justification of that apprehension itself. And this is paradoxical.

The intuitionist might undercut this paradox by denying that an apprehension is a cognitive state involving a cognitive grasp of the state of affairs that p. Given that denial, he could also deny that the apprehension in question needs justification. But the resulting problem is that it is difficult to see how that kind of apprehension can justify the belief that p. Thus Bonjour understandably asks: If a person has no cognitive grasp of the state of affairs that p by virtue of having such an apprehension, then how does the apprehension give him a reason for thinking that his belief that p is true? The view under consideration, it seems, returns the intuitionist inevitably to externalism, the very position he aims to avoid.

In sum, then, Sellars and Bonjour pose the following dilemma for the intuitionist: If on the one hand the intuitionist construes his apprehensions as cognitive states, then they will be able to give justification, but will also require justification themselves. If on the other hand apprehensions are noncognitive, then they do not need justification, but are also incapable of providing justification for any beliefs. In light of this dilemma, Sellars and Bonjour conclude that the epistemological given is a myth.

But I believe that this dilemma is a serious threat to the intuitionist only if we supplement it with the dilemma I raised against Lewis' version of intuitionism. Bonjour and Sellars raise the first horn of their dilemma by assuming that if an apprehension "involves" some state of affairs, then it must be a belief-like cognitive state requiring justification. Admittedly, belief-like cognitive states involving propositional content do require justification, and, contrary to Chisholm, their truth will not provide their justification. But the foregoing assumption of Sellars' and Bonjour's is not directly relevant to the best versions of intuitionism. On those versions an apprehension can "involve" a particular occurrent psychological state, such as my seeming to see a blue book, without becoming just another belief state requiring justification. Lewis' intuitionism, as we have seen, depends on that possibility. The critical issue, of course, is the manner in which an apprehension involves the occurrent psychological state. A *de dicto* belief about an occurrent psychological state, X, places the believer in a conceptual relation to X that includes a judgment *that* something is the case. But a *de re* belief about X places the believer in a relation to X that is not merely conceptual, even though it does involve a judgment about X or a property attribution to X. For instance, in a *de re* perceptual belief about a certain perceptual object, the believer does not merely represent this object via concepts; he also has perceptual contact with it inasmuch as it affects his sense organs.[14] Some intuitionists hold that an apprehension also involves a non-conceptual relation to its object, but that, unlike *de re* belief, it does not require any judgment about or property attribution to the object. As I suggested earlier, we might think of such an apprehension as mental pointing to, or focusing of attention on, some occurrent appearance, sensation, or psychological state. Something like the nonconceptual awareness involved in apprehension apparently occurs when, for example, one counts objects or images without describing them or subsuming them under concepts.[15] The important point, however, is that the intuitionist does not, and apparently need not, hold that apprehensions are belief-like cognitive states requiring justification just because they "involve" phenomenal objects and occurrent psychological states. But if this point is correct, the intuitionist can easily escape the first horn of the above dilemma.

Unfortunately, however, the intuitionist is stopped by the observation that 'apprehend' is an achievement word and thus demands a criterion to distinguish genuine apprehension from merely ostensible apprehension. I have already developed this observation in connection with Lewis' intuitionism. The upshot, to summarize, is that Lewis' version of intuitionism appears to be unacceptable.

Given the present predicament, the intuitionist might find it advisable to deny that an apprehension involves any kind of cognitive grasp of the relevant occurrent psychological state. But on this view, the intuitionist is caught by the second horn of the foregoing dilemma. For on this view it is difficult to see how an apprehension could justify the foundational belief in question. Thus, the intuitionist must hold that an apprehension involves some kind of cognitive grasp of the relevant psychological state. But either such an apprehension is identical with the foundational belief in question or it is not. If it is not, then it is either an apprehension *de dicto* or an apprehension *de re* of the relevant psychological state. If it is an apprehension *de dicto*, then, like a *de dicto* belief, it will itself require justification. Such a view is thus caught by the first horn of the foregoing dilemma. And if the apprehension in question is an apprehension *de re*, then the intuitionist is caught by the objection I raised against Lewis' intuitionism. (Note that the problem at hand counts against even those more recent intuitionists, such as Anthony Quinton, who claim not only that the given does not necessarily involve infallible intuitions, but also that ordinary physical states of affairs, such as there being a blue book on my desk, are given to a perceiver.)[16] This leaves the intuitionist with the alternative that the apprehension is identical with the foundational belief in question. But this alternative not only constitutes a move away from intuitionism, but also leaves open the crucial question of how the foundational belief is justified. In moving away from intuitionism, this alternative, which is represented by Chisholm's theory, leads the intuitionist to some unacceptable form of externalism. Here we have, then, a dilemma that threatens any version of epistemic intuitionism. Can the intuitionist escape it?

I believe the most vulnerable aspect of the foregoing anti-intuitionist objection is its assumption that since 'apprehend' is an achievement word, the intuitionist must provide a criterion to distinguish apprehension from ostensible apprehension. The intuitionist can contest this assumption by arguing that 'apprehend' is not an achievement word, at least not in any ordinary sense, in his account of immediate justification. But how can the intuitionist construe 'apprehend' not to be an achievement word?

1.5. *Objectless Intuitions*

The most plausible way to avoid the achievement sense of 'apprehend' is to follow C. J. Ducasse in taking immediate apprehension as an objectless event of sensing.[17] Sensing, as we shall see, is just a species of experiencing. The distinction between the cognate and the objective accusative is central to Ducasse's account of immediate apprehension, as it enables him to distinguish between two kinds of apprehending. The difference expressed by this grammatical distinction is the difference, for example, between the hearing of a tone, such as middle C, and the hearing of a bell, or between the smelling of a smell and the smelling of a rose. This distinction requires us to distinguish between the sound-experience, the sound-stimulus (*viz.*, air vibrations), and the sounding object (*e.g.*, a bell), and between the smell-experience, the smell-stimulus (*viz.*, certain molecules in the air), and the object of smell (*e.g.*, a rose). On the present account, a sound-experience is just hearing sound, whether or not a sound-stimulus is present, and it is not identical with listening. And the same is true of a visual experience. A visual experience is just seeing some appearance, whether or not a visual stimulus is present, and it is not identical with the orienting of one's visual apparatus. Given these distinctions, Ducasse proposes that hearing is identical with hearing some sound, and thus that the *esse* of a sound consists in its being heard, just as the *esse* of a waltz consists in its being waltzed, and the *esse* of a stroke in its being struck. And a similar point holds for the sensing events of smelling, seeing, and tasting. But of course this does not imply that a stimulus of a sound, smell, appearance, or taste, or the generator (*i.e.*, the object) of such a stimulus consists just in our experience of it. I shall elaborate on this point in connection with appearances and visual experience.

If we may use a linguistic term such as 'accusative' for a non-linguistic entity, then we may think of an appearance as a cognate accusative of the sort of process called 'visual experience.' An appearance is a cognate rather than an objective accusative of visual experience, because it is identical with visual experience. The appearance of blue, for example, is not an object of my current visual experience as the sense-data theorists hold; rather it is a species or kind of visual experience. Thus, to sense blue is to sense "bluely," just as to dance a waltz is to dance "waltzily". Sensing blue is a species or kind of sensing. Thus, the noun 'blue' refers to a certain kind of experience. We do not sense an instance of blue; rather, our sensing bluely in some specific manner constitutes an instance of blue. Accordingly, in any case of awareness of blue, what one is aware of is the determinate nature of one's awareness. But this does not mean that sensing events or states of consciousness can have the property blue. We must distinguish between a property and a quality. A property is a power that a thing has to produce certain effects; for example, the property blue is a power that certain objects have to produce in us a sensation of blue. The quality blue, in contrast, is just the sensation of blue. Blue, then, is a quality or a content, but not a property or an object, of my current sensing event, in the sense that blue stands to my sensing blue as a species or kind stands to an occurrence of a case of it.

Following Ducasse, the intuitionist might hold that the relation between an event of sensing and a cognate accusative, such as the relation between my current sensing event and the appearance of blue, is the same as the relation called 'immediate apprehension by the mind'. Furthermore, he might hold that it is possible to apprehend some determinate appearance of blue, for example, without engaging in the additional activity of classifying what one is apprehending, *i.e.*, of deciding whether the appearance being apprehended is an instance of blue. For it seems clear that it is one thing to be aware of a specific appearance, and it is quite another thing to judge how that appearance is classifiable. The apprehension of an appearance, on the present account, has no object but does have a content, whereas a classificatory judgment about an apprehension does have an object, *viz.*, the content of the apprehension. In sum, then, an immediate apprehension is the experiencing or sensing of an accusative, or a content, that is cognate with, and not an object of, the event of experiencing or sensing. And the content itself, which is apprehended on a given occasion, is the determinate nature that the event of apprehending has on that occasion. Thus an apprehension is an act of experiencing in which what is experienced by that act is its own specific nature.

For present purposes, the most important feature of the foregoing account is its notion of the content of an objectless event of sensing. Given this notion, we fortunately can avoid the sense-data theorist's notion of appearances as "objects to a subject" and its well-known problems with puzzling questions such as those about the relations between appearances, or "visual sense-data," and the surfaces of physical things. The notion of appearance as object is replaced, on the present adverbial account of appearances, by the notion of appearance as manner of appearing, or of sensing. Given this account, we may hold that in normal, non-hallucinatory perception, the object appearing in a certain manner to a perceiver is not a sense-datum mediating between the stimulus-object and the perceiver, but rather is the stimulus-object itself. The stimulus object's "manner of appearing" to a perceiver, we may hold, is just a relational property of that object, *i.e.*, a property the object has by virtue of being related to the perceiver. But we may also think of an object's manner of appearing as an effect of it, for it is caused by the object when it affects a perceiver's sense-receptors. However, in the case of hallucinatory and other experience in which no physical object is perceived, we need not countenance hallucinatory objects. For the term 'F-ly' in 'sensing F-ly' is not an adjective attributing a property to some object; rather it is an adverbial description of the manner in which a perceiver is sensing, or is being appeared to. We may thus hold that in the case of hallucinatory experience, being appeared to F-ly is a nonrelational sensing event of the perceiver. And such an event, we may hold, is an effect of certain processes in the perceiver's brain.

Thus far, however, we have no grounds for construing any of our appearings as relational properties of external objects. That is, we have no reason to hold that we are appeared to in certain ways *by certain external objects*. From our present epistemic point of view, our events of sensing are just objectless events of sensing in certain ways. But like the dancing of a waltz, they are events with a determinate nature; that is, they have a specific phenomenological content. My current perceptual event of seeming to see a blue book, for example, is a sensing event of a determinate sort; specifically, it is an event of blue-book sensing. In this event of sensing, I am ostensibly presented with a blue book, but this event of sensing does not entail the existence of a blue book or even a sense-datum. I could very well be hallucinating. The ostensibly presented blue book, let us say, is the phenomenological content of my current sensing event.

It seems plausible to hold that a perceiver can immediately apprehend the phenomenological content of his current sensing events. In order to develop the epistemological import of this suggestion, let us introduce this notion of immediate apprehension:

IA.　　A person, S, immediately apprehends certain phenomenological content, C, of a particular sensing event at a time, $t =$ Df. S directly experiences C at t in such a way that the relation of experiencing between S and C is unanalyzable in terms of, and does not require, any other relations (including propositional and conceptual relations to C) or any other experiences or any inferences.

Given the unanalyzability of immediate apprehension in the sense of IA, I must resort to elucidation by examples. Some typical examples of immediate apprehension are one's seeing an ostensibly presented bright yellow sphere, one's tasting some bitter taste, and one's hearing some loud sound. I cannot justifiably assume at present that what one experiences in such cases are certain external stimulus-objects, but only certain phenomenological contents, such as ostensibly presented objects and properties. I see no reason to deny that one can experience such contents without having other experiences. But it may not be quite so clear that no processes of inferring need precede or occur with the content of such an experience. However, I can find no reason to believe that a perceiver must engage in certain processes of inferring either before or while being presented with certain phenomenological content. On the contrary, it seems clear that at least some such content must be independent of inferential processes, for these processes, presumably, must begin with such content. And the content with which they begin will not depend on inferential processes. Thus I doubt that the immediate apprehension of phenomenological content requires inferential processes.

Clearly, if an act of immediate apprehension is unanalyzable, then we cannot analyze it in terms of certain propositional or conceptual relations holding between perceiver and content. Let us assume that a conceptual relation to certain content consists of an act of classifying, categorizing, or attributing a property to this content in accordance with some classificatory scheme. Clearly, on this assumption, if immediate apprehension is nonconceptual, then it is also nonpropositional, since a propositional relation requires a mental act of classifying, categorizing, or attributing a property to this content. Thus, I can support the thesis that immediate apprehension is nonpropositional by arguing that immediate apprehension is logically independent of conceptualization. Note that on the present construal of conceptualization, any conceptual relation to content, insofar as it is at least a matter of property attribution, evidently requires a single-term judgment. For the linguistic expression of one such act of conceptualization might be 'Red', which apparently is simply an abbreviated version of the judgment 'This is red.' Thus, it seems that if immediate apprehension is logically independent of judgment, then on the present notion of conceptualization, immediate apprehension is logically independent of conceptualization also.

However, if immediate apprehension is logically independent of all conceptualization, what does it amount to? Is it mere sensory stimulation? If so, we must face once again the troublesome question whether insects and amoebas can immediately apprehend phenomenological content. I believe the best way to handle this question is, first, to deny that immediate apprehension is mere sensory stimulation, and secondly, to affirm that one immediately apprehends an ostensibly presented object or property only if this ostensibly presented object or property attracts, or engages, one's attention. Attention-attraction is best construed, for present purposes, as a psychological orienting response, a "what-is-it" response, whereby one is psychologically situated to maximize some apparent sensory stimulation.[18] I assume that when one attentively looks at the sun, for instance, an ostensibly presented bright yellow disk attracts, or engages, one's attention. In any case, if immediate apprehension requires the attraction of one's attention by certain phenomenological content, then immediate apprehension is not mere sensory stimulation. For it seems clear that a perceptual object can stimulate one's sensory apparatus even if one's attention is not attracted by this object. Further, I believe that the present view excludes insects and amoebas from the class of subjects of immediate apprehension, since I have no reason to believe that the attention of insects and amoebas is attracted by ostensibly presented objects and properties. More importantly, I deny that the present notion of immediate apprehension is equivalent to the notion of the focusing of one's attention on something as an isolatable individual. Apparently the latter notion necessarily involves a voluntary act of a subject, whereas the former notion does not. Also, it seems that the latter notion necessarily involves a primitive form of conceptualization, since it necessarily involves a psychological act of individuating. But the present kind of immediate apprehension does not necessarily involve any conceptual act of classifying or individuating content on the part of the subject. This latter claim, however, requires some argument. Note that if immediate apprehension necessarily involves the subsumption of ostensibly presented objects under empirical concepts, then since such subsumption requires at least single-term judgments, immediate apprehension will necessarily involve at least a primitive form of propositional attitude requiring justification. And, in that case, immediate apprehension obviously will be unable to serve as the basis of immediate justification.

But we have good reason to believe that the immediate apprehension of phenomenal content does *not* require conceptualization. For there is good reason to hold that one can have one's attention attracted by some ostensibly presented object, but refrain from subsuming this object under some concept, or general term, either because of one's cognitive indifference toward one's present perceptual situation or because of one's conceptual limitations. The relevance of conceptual limitation here is clearly illustrated by cases where a perceiver is confronted with, in the sense that his attention is attracted by, a completely novel perceptual object, something he knows not what. Consider also in this connection the common phenomenon of one's attention being attracted by something, say a gunshot, at one instant, while at the next instant something else, say a loud ringing of a bell, attracts one's attention. Typically in such a case one does not have *time* to conceptualize what initially attracted one's attention. Such a case thus provides a familiar example of nonconceptual attention-attraction.

Moreover, there is some reason to believe that the view that immediate apprehension requires conceptualization threatens to generate an unacceptable endless regress of conceptual events. Note, first, that if one is to conceptualize an ostensibly presented object, X, one must engage in the (mental) activity of subsuming, or classifying, X under some concept. But if one is to subsume X under some concept, one must be aware of X in such a way that one's attention is attracted by X; otherwise one will have nothing to subsume under the concept in question. But what kind of event of awareness of X must one have to conceptualize X? Is this event of awareness − call it 'A$_1$' − itself conceptual, and thus another event of conceptualization? On the view that all perceptual experience is conceptual, A$_1$ is, of course, itself conceptual. And thus we can say of the event of conceptualization A$_1$ that it also requires that one must be aware of X in such a way that one's attention is attracted by X. Accordingly, we can also ask what kind of event of awareness of X is presupposed by A$_1$. Is this latter event of awareness − call it 'A$_2$' − itself conceptual, and thus yet another event of conceptualization? Obviously, on the view that all perceptual experience is conceptual, A$_2$ is itself conceptual. Thus, on that view, A$_2$ also requires that one must be aware of X in such a way that one's attention is attracted by X. And when we assume that the kind of event of awareness of X required by A$_2$ is similarly conceptual, we are faced with an undesirable endless regress of required conceptual events. For, on that assumption, A$_2$ will require a conceptual event A$_3$, and A$_3$, in turn, will require a conceptual event A$_4$, and so on *ad infinitum.* Consequently, we are thereby threatened with an endless regress of required conceptual events. But there seems to be no reason to suppose that ordinary perceptual experience involves such a regress of conceptualization. Hence, the proponent of the view that all perceptual experience is conceptual owes us an explanation of how the threat of the foregoing sort of regress is to be avoided.

More generally, however, one might object that an immediate apprehension of the kind specified by IA, being nonconceptual, relates a perceiver at most to a mere homogenous *this*, and not to determinate perceptual content having definite ostensible empirical properties. According to this objection, the content of perceptual awareness acquires its determinate nature only via conceptualization, and thus preconceptual perceptual content, including phenomenological content, is indeterminate insofar as it does not exemplify definite ostensible empirical properties. Clearly, if this objection is sound, then nonconceptual immediate apprehension will be unable to play a significant role in the immediate justification of foundational given-beliefs.

But the present objection is hardly convincing, since it relies on the implausible assumption that the content of perceptual awareness is indeterminate without conceptualization. There are two major problems facing this latter assumption. First, it implies that all empirical conceptualization is misrepresentation, insofar as such conceptualization attributes definite empirical properties to the content of perceptual awareness. That is, given the assumption in question, the empirical conceptualization of any perceptual content as being definite in some specific way, *i.e.*, as having definite empirical properties, is erroneous. For on that assumption the content of perceptual awareness is indeterminate apart from conceptualization. Thus, on that assumption, all of our empirical judgments entailing the determinateness of our perceptual content are, strictly speaking, false. It follows also, then, that our use of incompatible empirical predicates to characterize different ostensibly presented (preconceptual) objects is always erroneous. But these are surely implausible implications of the view under consideration. Notice, furthermore, that it is not acceptable to reply, by way of defense of the assumption in question, that one always conceptualizes perceptual content that has a determinate nature because of some prior conceptualization. For such a reply will commit one to the forementioned kind of endless regress of required conceptual events.

The second problem is that the assumption in question evidently precludes our experiencing perceptual anomalies. That is, it precludes our being aware of any perceptual content having a determinate nature different from that attributed by our own conceptual activity. Thus, on the assumption in question, it will never be true of a perceiver that he is perceptually aware of perceptual content exemplifying ostensible empirical properties which are different from the ostensible empirical properties he has attributed to that content via conceptualization. But this means that, contrary to common opinion, one will never experience perceptual anomalies. Since only a subjective idealist might be content with such an implication, I find that the assumption in question is hardly acceptable.

Another likely objection to my notion of nonconceptual immediate apprehension concerns the so-called "ineffability" of the given. Some philosophers have claimed that since one's immediate awareness of the given is, by hypothesis, nonconceptual and thus nonpropositional, it is also "ineffable". But since one's awareness of the given is ineffable, some have argued, it cannot have any epistemic import.

The present objection, however, rests on at least one false assumption, *viz.*: If one's immediate apprehension of the given is nonconceptual and nonpropositional, it cannot have any epistemic import. In the following section I shall explain how one's immediate apprehension of the given can provide one with a good reason to hold that a belief about the given is true. Insofar as such an apprehension can provide a good reason for a belief about the given, I shall argue, it can have definite epistemic import. Further, as we shall see, one's immediate apprehension of the given can play a central role in terminating a regress of conceptual events requiring justification. Thus, such an apprehension can save us from commitment to an endless regress of justification-requiring cognitive events, and thereby can play a central role in the solution to the epistemic regress problem.

Another flaw in the objection under consideration is its false assumption that immediate apprehension of the given, being nonconceptual, is "ineffable". Insofar as one's immediate apprehension is characterizable, or expressible, by means of the forementioned notion of attention-attraction by ostensible physical objects or properties, such awareness is, at least in one sense, *not* ineffable. Perhaps, then, the real worry underlying the objection in question is that the given itself is ineffable insofar as it is uncharacterizable. But although some theorists, such as C. I. Lewis, have spoken, somewhat paradoxically, of the given as being ineffable, I see no reason to go along with this view. In fact, on the basis of some of the considerations just set forth, I believe we have good reason to hold that the given has a determinate nature independently of our conceptualization, and thus that it exemplifies characterizable ostensible empirical properties. If the above treatment of immediate apprehension of the given is sound, then by means of direct inspection of the phenomenological content of such apprehension, one can provide a description of the given. And since, as suggested above, ostensible objects and their properties, rather than sense-data, are given, one's description of the given need not be restricted to a characterization of those residual sensory qualities, the so-called 'qualia', typically discussed by sense-data theorists. Rather, in characterizing the given, one can speak justifiably of ostensible objects of various sorts and of ostensible properties of such objects.

I believe that the apprehension of ostensibly presented objects and properties is basic not only to empirical conceptualization but also to the understanding of the referential use of linguistic terms. For in order to understand any referential language, whether a language of thought involving only mental representations or a physical language involving uttered and inscribed sentence-tokens, one must be able to recognize correlations between the relevant linguistic terms and the ostensibly presented objects they refer to. One must be able to recognize, for instance, a correlation such as that between the term 'blue book' and the ostensibly presented blue book that this term refers to. For to understand the referential use of linguistic terms, one must be able to apply certain singular referring terms or predicates to certain ostensibly presented objects or properties. But one can recognize such a correlation between linguistic term and ostensibly presented object or property only if one has a *de re* apprehension of what is ostensibly presented. For if one's awareness of the relevant ostensibly presented object or property is just *de dicto*, or propositional, then one will not recognize a correlation between this object or property and some referring term. One will then recognize, at most, a correlation between some proposition and some referring term. But such a correlation is only a correlation between linguistic entities (in my broad sense of 'linguistic'). What we are at present concerned with, however, is a recognition of a correlation between certain linguistic terms and certain ostensibly presented objects or properties. And such recognition, I submit, requires *de re* awarenes, or immediate apprehension, of certain ostensibly presented objects or properties.[19]

In sum, then, I have been trying to elucidate the notion of immediate apprehension provided by IA. In addition to adducing examples of the immediate apprehension of phenomenological content, I have contrasted such apprehension with propositional and conceptual relations to certain content. Also, in order to emphasize the psychological nature of immediate apprehension, I have compared immediate apprehension favorably with the attraction of one's attention by an ostensibly presented object or property. And I have proposed that the immediate apprehension of phenomenological content is basic both to empirical conceptualization and to the understanding of the referential use of linguistic terms.

Perhaps, however, we can further advance understanding of immediate apprehension by modifying IA as follows:

> IA*.   A person, S, immediately apprehends certain phenomenological content, C, of a particular sensing event at a time t = Df. (i) S directly experiences C at t in a way specified by IA; and (ii) for any ostensibly presented empirical property, F, if, at t, S directly experiences C exemplifying F, then, at t, S directly experiences F, which is a property of C at t.

This modified notion of immediate apprehension is just the notion specified by IA plus the condition stated by clause (ii) of IA*. And one may plausibly regard IA* as providing a notion of direct acquaintance at least vaguely reminiscent of Russell's celebrated notion of direct acquaintance. In any case, one might be inclined to modify clause (ii) of IA* by adding the qualification 'under normal conditions of perception.' Such a qualification would definitely apply to (ii) if IA* were concerned with the immediate apprehension of *external* perceptual objects. But as IA* is concerned only with *phenomenological* content and thus with ostensibly presented perceptual objects, I doubt that any such qualification applies. Immediate apprehension, as specified by IA*, is a relation not only to the phenomenological content of normal perceptual experience, but also to the content of hallucinatory and illusory experience. Thus, the restriction of clause (ii) to normal conditions of perception seems inappropriate.

According to clause (ii) of IA*, a direct experience of a certain ostensibly presented empirical property is sufficient for a certain content C's having that property. If C were an external perceptual object, clause (ii) would obviously be false. But C is, by hypothesis, an ostensibly presented perceptual object, and therefore from our present epistemic perspective its properties are at most similarly ostensibly presented. Clause (ii), I believe, makes only a modest claim. It claims, in effect, that the ostensibly presented properties we directly experience an ostensibly presented perceptual object exemplifying *are* the ostensibly presented properties of that ostensibly presented object. Thus if, for instance, I am ostensibly presented with a blue book, and I directly experience this book's being blue, then, according to clause (ii), this ostensibly presented book has the ostensibly presented property of being blue. But immediate apprehension of an ostensibly presented perceptual object entails nothing about external perceptual objects. It concerns only the nature of what one *seems* to experience perceptually.

I find it useful to view IA* as providing a notion of the phenomenological given. Earlier I suggested that certain objects or properties are phenomenologically given if and only if in perceiving some perceivers are ostensibly presented with those objects or properties. I believe that certain objects and properties are phenomenologically given to normal perceivers in perceptual experiences, regardless of whether these experiences are veridical. IA* is useful for present purposes insofar as it enables us to characterize the objects and properties that are phenomenologically given. In light of IA*, we may hold that a perceiver immediately apprehends what is phenomenologically given to him in the sense that if he directly experiences the given (*e.g.*, an ostensibly presented sphere) exemplifying a certain empirical property (*e.g.*, bright yellow) at present, then the given has this property at present. But, once again, immediate apprehension in this sense does not entail anything about the properties of external perceptual objects. Its implications extend only to the determinate nature of some event of sensing.

1.6. *Apprehensions and Immediate Justification*

I propose that the notion of immediate apprehension can play a prominent role in a plausible intuitionist account of the immediate justification of given-beliefs. My proposal, more specifically, is that a justifying condition of my given-belief that I seem to see a blue book, for instance, is my immediate apprehension of an ostensibly presented blue book. I am not proposing, however, that if I immediately apprehend an ostensibly presented blue book and if I believe that I seem to see a blue book, then I am justified in believing that I seem to see a blue book. For such a proposal would be a version of epistemic externalism. If we grant that one can immediately apprehend an ostensibly presented object without being aware of one's immediate apprehension — and I see no reason why we should not grant as much — then given the latter proposal I could be justified in believing that I seem to see a blue book even though I am quite unaware of the justifying condition of this given-belief. Chisholm's account of immediate justification, I have suggested, tends toward externalism in this manner.[20] In any case, to avoid externalism and the problems it raises, we should require that one have some kind of awareness of the justifying conditions of one's given-beliefs. But what kind of awareness must one have?

On the face of it, the following principle appears to fill the order for a non-externalist principle of immediate justification:

(5.2)   If I immediately apprehend an ostensibly presented blue book, and I immediately apprehend my immediate apprehension, then I am immediately justified in believing that I seem to see a blue book.

William Alston, however, has raised a noteworthy objection to this kind of intuitionist principle.[21] He grants for the sake of argument that one might be directly aware of one's own sensing events. But since one's awareness that one is sensing F-ly is itself a mode of consciousness, Alston wonders what justifies one in the belief that one has that mode of consciousness. He claims that if that justification is again a direct awareness of the mode of consciousness, then the intuitionist is committed to an infinite hierarchy of direct awareness. The only way to avoid such a hierarchy, according to Alston, is to recognize some given-belief about one's sensing F-ly that is not justified by a direct awareness of one's sensing F-ly. And this of course is undesirable to the intuitionist.

I doubt, however, that Alston's threat of an infinite hierarchy of direct awareness is a genuine threat to the proponent of (5.2). Aside from Alston's misconstrual of the intuitionist's direct awarenesses as awarenesses *de dicto*, notice that Alston's central point amounts simply to the following claim: According to the intuitionist,

(B$_1$)   S's belief that he is sensing F-ly

is justified by:

(A₁)   S's direct awareness of his sensing F-ly;

and

(B₂)   S's belief that he has (A₁)

is justified by:

(A₂)   S's direct awareness of (A₁);

and so on *ad infinitum*. But there is no reason for the intuitionist to worry about such a regress. For, first, there is no reason to believe that anyone has an infinite number of justified beliefs following (B₁) and (B₂). Hence, there is no reason to believe that anyone has an infinite hierarchy of direct awarenesses based on (A₁) and (A₂). And, secondly, even if some superhuman being had such a hierarchy of direct awarenesses, we could not thereby reject versions of intuitionism committed to (5.2) on the ground that they entail an infinite justificatory regress. For the above kind of regress is not an endless justificatory regress in the sense that each belief (Bₙ) depends for its justification on the justification of some other belief (or set of beliefs) (Bₙ₊₁). Notice, for instance, that (B₁) obviously does not depend for its justification on (B₂). (B₁) depends *only* on (A₁). And (A₁) is not a belief-like cognitive state requiring justification. Hence, Alston's objection does not pose a genuine threat to the proponent of (5.2).

A more serious objection to (5.2) is that it uses 'apprehend', in its second clause, as an achievement term, and thus demands a criterion to distinguish genuine from ostensible apprehension. (5.2), it might be argued, is roughly equivalent to a central thesis of the intuitionism I earlier attributed to C. I. Lewis, and consequently it must face the dilemma I posed above for Lewis' intuitionism. A natural proposal, then, is that we modify (5.2) by replacing its second clause with 'and I believe that I have such an immediate apprehension.' But this proposal will surely elicit the objection that, first, I must have some evidential support for the latter belief concerning my immediate apprehension if it is to play a role in the immediate justification of my given-belief, and, secondly, if this belief must itself be justified, then this will evidently preclude the *immediate* justification of my given-belief.

Now, although I find the foregoing objections to (5.2) to be inconclusive, I believe they are important insofar as they force us to draw some overlooked important distinctions. The most serious flaw in (5.2), I find, is that it fails to relate the relevant immediately justified given-belief to the justifying immediate apprehension. Thus, I aim now to formulate a principle providing for this relation, and, in doing so, to answer the above objections to (5.2).

Let us reconsider, then, my proposal about a justifying condition of my given-belief that I seem to see a blue book. I submit that this given-belief itself can provide the kind of awareness one must have of the justifying condition in question, so long as one holds that belief *in light of* the relevant direct experience. We can begin to assess this claim by examining the justifying condition I proposed. Let us reformulate this condition simply as follows:

>   (5.3)   If I immediately apprehend an ostensibly presented blue book at a time, *t,* then, at *t,* I am immediately justified in believing that I seem to see a blue book.

We can alter the externalist image of (5.3) by supplementing it in accordance with my latest proposal. Hence:

>   (5.4)   If I immediately apprehend an ostensibly presented blue book at a time, *t,* and if, at *t,* I believe in light of this event of apprehending that I seem to see a blue book, then, at *t,* I am immediately justified in believing that I seem to see a blue book.

(5.4), as I understand it, is equivalent to the following jargon-free principle:

>   (5.5)   If I seem to see a blue book at a time, *t,* and if, and *t,* I believe in light of this perceptual state that I seem to see a blue book, then, at *t,* I am immediately justified in believing that I seem to see a blue book.

A key justifying condition of my given-belief, according to (5.4) and (5.5), is simply my perceptual state of seeing to see a blue book. And the requisite awareness of that justifying condition is provided by the given-belief held in light of the relevant perceptual state. In saying that I hold a given-belief "in light of" a certain perceptual state, I do not mean that this perceptual state causes my belief, although I would not deny that such a state, when manifested, can cause belief. Rather, I intend to suggest that my given-belief involves a *de re* awareness of the relevant perceptual state. Thus, we might rephrase (5.5) as follows: If I seem to see a blue book, and I believe with an awareness of that perceptual state that I seem to see a blue book, then I am immediately justified in believing that I seem to see a blue book. This talk of "believing with an awareness of, or in light of, a perceptual state" is intended, then, to imply that the relevant given-belief is not held without any awareness of the relevant perceptual state. And we may emphasize this implication by construing 'believes in light of' as implying also that in ordinary circumstances one would appeal to the relevant perceptual state if one were to try to show justification for the given-belief in question.

Returning to the above objection to (5.2), however, we must ask whether the required awareness of the perceptual state of seeming to see a blue book needs a justification of its own, and thereby threatens to generate a regress of required justifiers. To see that such awareness does *not* require a justification of its own, we should recognize that this event of awareness is to be construed, along the lines suggested above, as an event of immediate apprehension which, being nonconceptual, is incapable of epistemic justification. Thus, (5.4) and (5.5) require that we distinguish between (i) an immediate apprehension of an ostensibly presented blue book and (ii) an immediate apprehension of (i). I have proposed, and will explain below, that (i) can provide a key justifying condition of the given-belief that I seem to see a blue book. I have also suggested that (ii) is a key component of the given-belief justified in virtue of (i); for by means of (ii) one can have an awareness of a key justifying condition of one's given-belief.

It is useful now to distinguish between the conditions of propositional justification for a belief and the conditions of awareness of the former conditions. The latter conditions of awareness must obtain if *doxastic* justification is to be realized, *i.e.*, if one is to be justified in believing a proposition. (Recall here the distinction between propositional and doxastic justification sketched in Chapter I.) In the example under consideration, what provides propositional justification for my belief that I seem to see a blue book is, as suggested, my perceptual state of seeming to see a blue book. And what provides the awareness of this justifying condition is the *de re* component of my given-belief, *i.e.*, an immediate apprehension of this justifying condition.

Now, clearly, to say that a perceptual state is immediately apprehended commits one to an achievement notion of apprehending. For such talk implies that an event of apprehending has a distinct object. Does this mean, then, that principles like (5.4) and (5.5) presuppose that a criterion distinguishing between genuine and ostensible apprehension has been satisfied; and, if so, is not the above objection to (5.2) applicable here? Or, to put the question more directly, if I need to be aware of my seeming to see a blue book, in order to be justified in believing that I seem to see a blue book, and if my awareness of my seeming to see a blue book may be only ostensible and not genuine, do not I need to be justified in believing that this awareness is genuine and not merely ostensible? If so, the possibility of immediate justification is evidently ruled out; for the justification of my belief will then depend on the justification of some other belief, viz., the belief that I am genuinely aware of a justifying condition.

But the present worry stems from a misunderstanding of the proposed requirement of awareness. The requirement providing an alternative to externalism is simply that one *be* aware of a justifying condition for the propositional justification of one's belief. The requirement is not that one must be justified in believing that one is aware of a justifying condition. To reconstrue the requirement as the latter demand will commit one automatically to an implausible endless regress of required justified beliefs. For, given that demand, a person will be justified in believing one proposition only if he is justified in believing some other proposition, viz., the proposition that one is genuinely aware of a justifying condition of the former proposition. But a similar requirement applies also to this latter proposition, and to each of the members of the ensuing regress of required beliefs. The threat of such a regress can be avoided, however, once we clearly distinguish between the conditions for the propositional justification of a belief and the nonexternalist conditions for the awareness of the former conditions. The latter conditions do not set a requirement for a separate justified belief. The neglect of this fact is due perhaps to a level-confusion: the conflation of the requirements for one's being justified in believing that *p* with the requirements for one's being justified in believing that one is justified in believing that *p*.

Although (5.4) and (5.5) are equivalent on my account, I prefer to use (5.4) for present purposes, because its notion of ostensible presentation makes it quite clear that I am concerned at present only with the phenomenological content of events of sensing. Let us then modify (5.4) to make it a perfectly general principle of immediate justification:

(5.6)   A person, S, is immediately justified in believing that he seems to see an F at a time, *t*, if and only if, at *t*, S immediately apprehends an ostensibly presented F, and believes in light of this event of apprehending that he seems to see an F.

Before anticipating objections, I must clarify the kind of immediate justification involved in (5.6). Notice first that we would not raise any special problems by replacing the talk of seeming to see in (5.6) with talk of seeming to taste, smell, hear, or feel. For each such sensing event can have its appropriate phenomenological content. Notice also that (5.6) involves a species of infallible justification, which, incidentally, is not the same as Lewis' version of infallible justification in (5.1). In effect, (5.6) claims that a particular given-belief is immediately justified only if it is true. But it does not imply that all given-beliefs are infallibly true, indubitable, or irrefutable. The key implication of (5.6) is simply that if a given-belief is not true, then it is not *immediately* justified. And this implication, of course, is not equivalent to the claim that a given-belief is justified only if it is true; for a given-belief might be mediately (or inferentially) justified but false. (Yet I do not know of any adequate account of the mediate justification of false given-beliefs.)

The most important question concerning (5.6) is whether we should grant that a particular given-belief is immediately justified when it satisfies the conditions of (5.6). We may reformulate this question by asking whether a person would be epistemically responsible in holding a particular given-belief provided only that in doing so he satisfies the conditions of (5.6). Recall that a person is epistemically responsible in holding a particular belief if and only if he has good reason to believe it is true. I submit that a person satisfying the condition of (5.6) would be epistemically responsible in this sense. For this person would have good reason to believe that his given-belief is true. The good reason for this belief, according to (5.6), is neither that belief itself nor some other belief, but is that event of immediate apprehension which makes that belief true. Thus, with respect to my immediately justified belief that I seem to see a blue book, my good reason for that belief is my immediate visual apprehension of an ostensible blue book. This immediate apprehension can provide a justifying reason, since basically my having such an event of awareness is what *makes true* my belief that I seem to see a blue book. Further, given (5.6) one would be aware of one's good reason, since one would hold one's belief in light of the relevant immediate apprehension in the forementioned sense. Thus, if one satisfies the conditions set by (5.6), one will have some good reason for, and so will be justified in holding, a belief. Moreover, in satisfying those conditions, one will be *immediately* justified in holding some belief, since the justification of one's belief will not depend on the justification of any other belief. Evidently, then, (5.6) fortunately avoids the problems of externalism and fits quite well with the normative conception of epistemic justification.

     Another pressing question concerns how my intuitionist account of immediate justification fares with respect to the general dilemma I developed against certain other versions of intuitionism. The thrust of that dilemma, briefly, is that the requisite immediate apprehensions can be neither apprehensions *de dicto*, lest they themselves require justification, nor apprehensions in some achievement sense of 'apprehend,' lest they demand a criterion to distinguish genuine from ostensible apprehensions, nor apprehensions *de re*, lest they lack propositional content and thus be unable to justify any beliefs. Clearly, the notion of immediate apprehension I rely on, which is defined by IA and IA*, is neither an achievement notion nor a *de dicto* notion. It is not an achievement notion, because it does not relate a perceiver to facts, truths, perceptual objects, sense-data, or psychological states. Rather, my notion of immediate apprehension relates a perceiver to certain phenomenological contents, such as certain ostensibly presented objects and properties, which, on my current assumptions, have no existence independently of certain events of apprehending. Such contents, on my current assumptions, amount to no more than the determinate nature of certain sensing events. In due course I shall argue that we are justified in holding that some such contents are relational properties of perceptual objects, but obviously no such assumption is justified at present.

     My notion of immediate apprehension, furthermore, is clearly not a *de dicto* notion. It does not involve any apprehension *that* such-and-such is the case. We may think of immediate apprehension as a *de re* relation so long as we construe this relation in terms of the cognate rather than the objective accusative; that is, so long as we maintain my current assumption that ostensibly presented objects and properties are not existentially independent of some event of apprehending. Obviously, *de re* apprehensions in this sense do not require propositional content. But they do have phenomenological content, with respect to which given-beliefs can be justified. My effort in the present section has been to explain just how such content can play a role in the immediate justification of given-beliefs. And in light of this effort, I conclude that neither the general dilemma threatening earlier versions of epistemic intuitionism nor the epistemic ascent argument espoused by Bonjour and others is a genuine threat to my intuitionist account of immediate justification.

One likely objection to (5.6) is that, due to the possibility of inconsistent immediately justified given-beliefs, it should be modified as follows:

(5.7)   A person, S, is immediately justified in believing that he seems to see an F at a time, *t*, if and only if at *t*: (i) S immediately apprehends an ostensibly presented F; (ii) S believes in light of this event of apprehending that he seems to see an F; and (iii) S has no good reason to believe that he does not seem to see an F.

Consider the case in which S believes not only that (a) he seems to see a spherical object which appears to be the only object in his hands at present, but also that (b) he seems to see a cube which appears to be the only object in his hands at present. A natural question is whether S can be immediately justified in believing that (a) while he believes that (b). And this question amounts to the question whether S's belief that (b) provides a good reason for S to believe that his belief that (a) is false. Clearly, if S's belief that (b) provides such a reason, then we should modify (5.6) along the lines of (5.7), for it seems quite possible for S to believe that (a) and that (b) simultaneously. But S's belief that (b) provides S with such a good reason only if it is itself justified, since a good reason is a justifying reason. Let us assume, accordingly, that S's belief that (b) is immediately justified.

The question now is whether S can be immediately justified in believing that (a) while he is immediately justified in believing that (b). Apparently S's belief that (b) is true only if his belief that (a) is false. That is, it seems contradictory to claim that S seems to see a spherical object which (apparently) is the only object in his hands at present, and that S, at the same time, seems to see a cube which (apparently) is the only object in his hands at present. For this claim, as I undertand it, implies that what S currently seems to see is and is not a spherical object. If I am right about this implication, then I doubt that S can be immediately justified in believing that (a) and that (b) simultaneously. For, given (5.6), S's belief that (a) and his belief that (b) will be immediately justified simultaneously only if they are true simultaneously. But I doubt that they can be true simultaneously since I have no reason to believe that a determinate sensing event is describable by a contradictory expression. But if S's belief that (a) and his belief that (b) cannot be immediately justified simultaneously, and if S's belief that (b) is immediately justified at time *t*, then S will not be immediately justified in believing that (a). Of course, S may nonetheless believe that (a), but his unjustified belief that (a) will not provide a good reason for him to believe that his belief that (b) is false. On the contrary, S's immediately justified belief that (b) will provide him with a good reason to reject the belief that (a). The upshot, then, is that the sort of example under consideration does not force me to modify (5.6) along the lines of (5.7). For my account of immediate justification rules out the possibility of inconsistent immediately justified given-beliefs.

There is, however, another sort of example that appears to support (5.7) over (5.6). Consider the kind of case in which S has two consistent immediately justified given-beliefs, one of which makes the truth of the other improbable. Let us assume, for instance, that S is immediately justified in believing that (c) he seems to *see* something large and spherical in (what appear to be) his hands, and that (d) he seems not to *feel* something large and spherical in (what appear to be) his hands. Cornman, following a suggestion of Hans Reichenbach's, has suggested that it is improbable that a proposition such as (c) is true of a person, S, at a time, *t*, if a proposition such as (d) is true of S at *t*.[22] But if we follow Cornman in relativizing probabilities to persons, and construe probabilities epistemically, *i.e.*, as degrees of confirmation, then we can avoid the present problem. For we can then deny that S's belief that (c) is improbable for him if S's belief that (d) is true. Admittedly, if we were required to construe probability statements as estimates of relative frequencies, the example in question might present a serious problem. But I see no reason to employ the frequency interpretation of probability statements in the present context. In fact, the frequency interpretation seems quite inappropriate at present, since a given-belief concerns a *single case* at a particular time. Furthermore, I grant that for a person other than S, the probability of (c) being true of S while (d) is true of S may be low. But this possibility clearly does not affect the probability of (c) for S. Thus, I am unconvinced that Reichenbach's suggestion raises a serious problem for my account of immediate justification. And I doubt that his suggestion demands the modification of (5.6) along the lines of (5.7). (I am similarly doubtful, incidentally, about the force of the related objection that because, by some strange turn of events, all of S's numerous past given-beliefs have turned out, with S's knowledge, to be false, S might have good reason to believe that all of his present given-beliefs are false, even though the conditions of (5.6) are satisfied; for once again a questionable frequency construal of probability is evidently presupposed.)

My main worry about (5.7) is that it apparently provides a circular account of justification. The talk of "good reason" in clause (iii) evidently presupposes the very notion of epistemic justification in need of explanation. Or, to put the worry differently, since the notion of good reason required by clause (iii) is unexplained, (5.7) is, if not circular, at least uninformative in its distinctive clause. To this extent, (5.7) is inferior to (5.6).

Some philosophers would object to (5.6) on the ground that one can be justified in believing that one seems to see a blue book, for example, only if one has the independent information needed to enable one to distinguish the perceptual state of seeming to see a blue book from, for example, the state of wondering whether one is seeing a blue book and the state of seeming to see a green shoebox.[23] Unless one has such information, these philosophers claim, one is not justified in holding any given-beliefs. Chisholm has attempted to avoid this objection by distinguishing between the comparative and the non-comparative use of certain terms.[24] The central claim of Chisholm's reply is that my belief that I seem to see a blue book, for example, does not entail my comparison of my present perceptual state with some other perceptual state or with the features of certain external perceptual objects. Perhaps Chisholm is right about this, but it still seems that my belief that I seem to see a blue book entails the belief that my present perceptual state is of a certain kind. And, as Lehrer and Sellars have suggested, to be justified in believing that my present perceptual state is of that kind, I must have the information required to enable me to distinguish the present kind of perceptual state from another.

I find that the best way to handle the present objection is to concede that one must have the kind of information in question, and to propose that the information in question is *semantic* information. That is, it is information necessary for an understanding of what it means to claim that one is in a certain perceptual state rather than another.[25] The necessity of such semantic information is quite compatible with my proposal that certain given-beliefs are immediately justified. It seems clear that certain semantic information is necessary for believed propositions to be intelligible; and, therefore, we may hold that an understanding of certain semantic information is a necessary condition of a person's genuinely having any given-beliefs. But to avoid any objection from the importance of certain semantic information, let us revise (5.6) slightly as follows:

(5.8) A person, S, is immediately justified in believing that he seems to see an F at a time, *t*, if and only if at *t*: (i) S immediately apprehends an ostensibly presented F, and (ii) S understandingly believes in light of this event of apprehending that he seems to see an F.

By asserting in clause (ii) of (5.8) that S "understandingly believes", I intend to suggest that S has the semantic information enabling him to distinguish his present kind of perceptual state from another. Thus, the objection under consideration no longer presents a problem.

But the present objection is useful insofar as it requires us to recognize a familiar yet important distinction. We must distinguish between the conditions of the justification of a particular belief and the conditions of the existence of that belief. Clearly, epistemological questions about the justification of a particular belief can arise only once that belief exists. Accordingly, the relevant epistemological questions about the immediate justification of a certain belief presuppose the existence of that belief and thus any prerequisites of that belief's existence. I submit, then, that the immediate justification of one's belief that *p* is quite compatible with the requirement that one must have cognitive possession of certain semantic information basic to the existence of the belief that *p*. Further, I shall not concern myself in this book with the complicated issues regarding the nature of the required semantic information and the nature of belief-formation and concept-formation. Fortunately, for present purposes I can leave these issues to the cognitive psychologist.

A more troublesome objection to my foundationalist account concerns the manner in which the epistemic principle (5.8) is itself justified. The crucial question is whether and, if so, how I am justified in believing that (5.8) is a true epistemic principle. One possible line of response introduces semantic considerations, once again, and claims that (5.8) is true by virtue of the meaning of its constituent terms. But I find this claim to be unacceptable. Many skeptics, for instance, would deny that (5.8) is true, as they disagree with me about what is immediately justified. But I doubt that I can refute these skeptics simply by appealing to the meaning of the terms of (5.8). Of course, it is possible that the skeptic means something quite different by his epistemic terms from what I mean by mine. But, as Lehrer has argued persuasively, in many cases there is no good reason to believe that the skeptic has departed from the common meanings of epistemic terms.[26] Many skeptics, it seems, deny that any given-beliefs are immediately justified and, in doing so, mean what philosophers commonly mean by their epistemic terms. Thus, I find it unacceptable to hold that in rejecting a principle such as (5.8), the skeptic is necessarily attributing new meanings to the relevant epistemic terms. And I see no way to make a compelling case for the claim that (5.8) is true in virtue of the meaning of its terms.

Another line of response to the present question suggests that an epistemic principle such as (5.8) is justified because, like certain given-beliefs, it is immediately justified.[27] But, according to some critics, this line of response simply begs the question in favor of foundationalism and makes the choice of epistemic principles arbitrary.[28] I am inclined to agree with these critics that the present response is question-begging and dialectically ineffective. At least, I doubt that I would satisfy a coherentist, for instance, by telling him that principle (5.8) is immediately justified. But I also doubt that the coherentist's response to the present question is any less question-begging and dialectically ineffective when it states that a coherentist epistemic principle is justified by being conducive to coherence. In any case, it seems clear that (5.8) cannot be immediately justified on my intuitionist account of immediate justification, for an epistemic principle is not identical with or solely about phenomenological content. Thus, I need to look elsewhere for an answer to the present question.

Since (5.8) is neither analytically true nor immediately justified, it must be mediately (or inferentially) justified if it is to be justified at all; that is, its justification must depend on the justification of certain other beliefs. A likely objection at this point is that (5.8) cannot be mediately justified, since a foundational belief, by definition, does not depend for its justification on the justification of other beliefs. But I believe such an objection neglects an important distinction that William Alston has frequently stressed: the distinction between (i) being justified in believing that p (where p is some foundational belief), and (ii) being justified in believing that I am immediately justified in believing that p.[29] The foundationalist, of course, must hold that (i) does not depend on the justification of some other belief, but he need not, and I believe should not, hold the same regarding (ii). The foundationalist would have to hold the same regarding (ii) only if one's being immediately justified in believing that p required that one be immediately justified in believing that one is immediately justified in believing that p. But there is no good reason to suppose that immediate justification requires this. Similarly, there is no good reason to suppose that one's being immediately justified in believing that p requires that one be inferentially justified in believing that one is so justified. The latter requirement implies not only that (5.8) is false, but also that one is immediately justified in believing something only if one has an understanding of what it is to be immediately justified in believing something, since one can believe something only if one understands it. But the latter implication is quite dubious. Most people have no understanding of immediate justification, yet it seems that they can nonetheless be immediately justified in believing many things. Thus, the foregoing objection to the mediate justification of a foundationalist epistemic principle is dubious at best.

But how can an epistemic principle such as (5.8) be justified on the basis of other beliefs? I propose that (5.8) is justified by an inference to the best explanation from certain foundational given-beliefs. That is, (5.8) provides a better explanatory account of the immediate justification of certain given-beliefs than does any available alternative epistemic principle. I find the strongest support for this claim in the fact that (5.8) not only raises fewer general problems, but also enables us to solve the epistemic regress problem in a more trouble-free manner than do the competitors of (5.8). The competing epistemic principles, of course, are those of the contextualists, the coherentists, the foundationalists of externalist and internalist persuasions, and the epistemological skeptics. In Chapters II and III, I have raised my objections to the leading contextualist and coherentist epistemic principles, and I shall not rehearse them here. In Chapter IV, I have argued against the leading internalist and externalist foundationalist principles. The internalist principles, I have argued, give rise to endless regresses of justification, whereas the externalist principles provide only an *ad hoc* evasion of the epistemic regress problem. As for the skeptic's epistemic principles, which state that no beliefs are immediately or inferentially justified, I am now able to challenge only the principle stating that no beliefs are immediately justified. (In the following section I intend to challenge certain skeptical qualms about inferentially justified observation beliefs.) The objections I have been entertaining in the preceding several pages are the most forceful skeptical objections to immediate justification I have found. And I have argued that my intuitionist account of immediate justification is impervious to them. I conclude, therefore, that until better skeptical objections arise the epistemic principle (5.8) is justified by its explanatory superiority.

But one might understandably find this conclusion to be premature. For my solution to the regress problem is thus far only half of a solution. I believe I have shown how there can be immediately justified given-beliefs, but I have not shown how such beliefs can provide justification for any observation beliefs about external perceptual objects and properties. Let us turn then to the second half of my solution to the epistemic regress problem.

2. JUSTIFYING NONFOUNDATIONAL OBSERVATION BELIEFS

On my intuitionist account of immediate justification, only given-beliefs are immediately justified. These are beliefs about certain phenomenological content such as ostensibly presented perceptual objects, properties, and psychological states, including belief, perceptual and sensation states. The truth of such a belief does not entail the existence of any external perceptual object or property. The truth of an observation belief, however, does entail the existence of some external perceptual object or property. And on my account such a belief is inferentially justified at best; that is, it must be justified on the basis of certain immediately justified given-beliefs. Obviously, if I am to solve the regress problem concerning particular observation beliefs, I must show how those beliefs can be epistemically justified on the basis of certain immediately justified given-beliefs. In short, I must find some way to justify inferences from foundational beliefs to certain nonfoundational observation beliefs. Otherwise, no observation beliefs will be epistemically justified, and some form of epistemological skepticism will be reasonable. In that case, the epistemic regress problem will provide a powerful argument not for foundationalism, but for epistemological skepticism of some form.

There are three prominent strategies for the justification of inferences from foundational beliefs to nonfoundational observation beliefs: (i) Phenomenalist Deductivism, (ii) Chisholm's Critical Cognitivism, and (iii) Inductive Inference to the Best Explanation. I shall examine each of these strategies in turn.

2.1. *Phenomenalist Deductivism*

Let us ask first whether the foundationalist can rely on a deductively valid argument in justifying observation beliefs on the basis of foundational beliefs solely about phenomenological content. Suppose the observation belief requiring justification is:

N1.   At present there is a cat on the roof.

And assume that the relevant foundationalist belief is:

F1.   At present I seem to see a cat on the roof.

Let us assume, furthermore, that the talk of *seeming to see* in F1 indicates that the object of visual experience is phenomenological content, and thus does not refer directly to any physical object. And let us grant, if only for the sake of argument, the foundationalist assumption that the justification of F1 for me does not derive from any other belief. (We might assume, as above, that the justification of F1 derives, in virtue of a "making-true" relation, from a *non*belief perceptual state of seeming to see a cat on the roof; but this assumption is optional.) The question, then, is whether N1 can be deductively derived on the basis of F1. But let us not require that F1 be the only premise of the relevant deductive argument. That argument, let us

grant, can employ any beliefs solely about so-called phenomenological content as well as any beliefs that are true solely in virtue of
meaning. For we want to determine whether any such true beliefs,
individually or collectively, logically entail anything about physical
objects and their properties.

It is plain enough that F1 by itself does not logically entail N1.
Clearly, it is quite possible that at present I am having an hallucinatory
perceptual experience. And, obviously, if at present I am having such
an experience, then at present I seem to see a cat on the roof even
though there is no cat on the roof at present. F1, then, does not
logically entail N1; and, more generally, given the ever present
possibility of an hallucinatory perceptual experience, we evidently
should deny that a foundational belief solely about phenomenological
content entails an observation belief.

Recent phenomenalists such as A. J. Ayer and Georges Dicker,
however, have contested the present sort of argument against the
entailment of observation beliefs by foundational beliefs.[30] As Dicker's
reply is easily the strongest available, I shall focus on it in the present
section. Of course Dicker does not hold that by itself a foundational
belief like F1 logically entails an observation belief like N1. But,
following Ayer, he does hold that a foundational belief like F1
logically entails an observation belief like N1 when the former belief is
conjoined with other foundational beliefs predicting how a perceiver
would be appeared to under certain conditions.

Clearly, however, the foundationalist cannot conjoin the following
belief with F1:

F2a.   If I were to carry the object on the roof into direct sunlight
        and look at it, then I would seem to see a cat.

The antecedent of F2a does not refer to phenomenological content,
but rather to a physical object, and therefore F2a is not a foundational
belief. Thus, F2a, which obviously is not true solely in virtue of
meaning, is useless for the purpose of showing that foundational
beliefs entail observation beliefs.

Let us, then, reformulate F2a as follows:

F2.   If I were to seem to carry the object on the roof into direct
        sunlight and to seem to look at it, then I would seem to see
        a cat.

The antecedent of F2 does not refer directly to a physical object or a bodily action, and thus it does not raise the problem raised by F2. It is debatable, of course, whether a subjunctive conditional like F2 qualifies as a foundational belief, but let us grant, if only for the sake of argument, that it does qualify. Clearly, the conjunction of F1 and F2 does not logically entail N1. For that conjunction is logically compatible with the proposition that I am having an hallucinatory perceptual experience at present. To eliminate the possibility of such an experience, the phenomenalist must add further foundational beliefs to F1 and F2. For example, he might add the following belief:

F3.   If I were to seem to squeeze the object on the roof, I would seem to feel resistance.

But even when F1 and F2 are conjoined with F3, they do not logically entail an observation belief like N1. For the conjunction of F1 and F2 and F3 is logically compatible with the proposition that I am having an hallucinatory experience involving my touch as well as my vision. Moreover, it seems that no matter how many foundational beliefs we conjoin with F1−F3, the resulting conjunction will always be logically compatible with the proposition that I am having a comprehensive hallucinatory experience. Hence it is doubtful that any such conjunction of foundational beliefs logically entails an observation belief like N1.

Dicker's reply to this sort of argument is that it is not self-evident that no matter what foundational beliefs we add to a conjunction like F1−F3, it is still logically possible that I am having an hallucinatory perceptual experience (p. 193). Dicker claims not only that this point needs argument, but also that he can refute the best arguments for it. Dicker finds two arguments to be especially relevant to the point in question. I shall examine them in turn.

One argument rests on the assumption that no matter how extensive the conjunction of foundational beliefs F1 & F2 & . . . & Fn is, it is logically possible that some proposition, Fn + 1, which provides disconfirming evidence for N1 will be confirmed. But to provide an example of an observation belief that cannot be disconfirmed by new evidence, Dicker cites his belief that there is at present a typewriter on his desk. He claims that his "ways of being appeared to" with respect to his typewriter constitute a "coherent experiential history" leading up to his being appeared to in ways characteristic of typing. For his current perceptual state of being appeared to as if typing was preceded by such perceptual states as being appeared to as if walking into his study, being appeared to as if uncovering the typewriter, and being appeared to as if cleaning the typewriter keys. Given this kind of coherent experiential history, Dicker denies that further empirical evidence could disconfirm his belief that there is at present a typewriter on his desk. He claims that regardless of the kind of experience he might undergo in the future, it would be absurd for him to hold that a typewriter had never existed in his study. More generally, he claims that once there is a "sufficient accumulation of sensory evidence" in favor of an observation belief, it is false that further experience could disconfirm that belief (p. 195).

But Dicker's reply is quite unconvincing. What is especially unconvincing is his example of an observation belief that cannot be disconfirmed by further experience. Why should we grant that the apparent coherent experiential history leading up to Dicker's perceptual state of seeming to see a typewriter on his desk rules out the possibility that he is having an extensive hallucinatory experience? Surely it is logically possible, albeit improbable perhaps, that Dicker is currently hallucinating a typewriter on his desk and that this hallucinatory experience is characterized by what seems to be a coherent experiential history. Moreover, a certain kind of experience could disconfirm Dicker's belief that there is a typewriter on his desk, even though this belief is characterized by an apparent coherent experiential history. Suppose, for instance, that Dicker awakes one morning to find himself in the care of several advanced pharmacologists experimenting with hallucinogenic drugs for therapeutic purposes. They inform him that he has suffered a serious head injury in a car accident, has lost his memory, and is currently undergoing extensive tests with certain hallucinogenic drugs. Some of these drugs, he is told, cause extensive hallucinatory experiences, but nonetheless can be useful in treating special cases of amnesia, since they provide the patient with an apparent coherent experiential history. Now if we assume that Dicker's subsequent experience confirms the testimony of the pharmacologists, which includes the claim that he never had a typewriter or a study, then it is clear that a certain kind of experience could disconfirm Dicker's belief about his typewriter. More generally, then, given the ever present possibility that a person can come to realize that he has undergone such an experience, we should reject the claim that an apparent coherent experiential history eliminates the possibility of future experience disconfirming an observation belief.

Following Ayer, Dicker grants that we cannot actually specify a set of foundational beliefs constituting a logically sufficient condition for the truth of some observation belief (p. 195). He claims that any such set would be so extended and complex that it is impossible *for us* actually to specify its members. But, of course, he holds that we can list some of the foundational beliefs included in such a set. And these beliefs, according to Dicker, will form a set that can *in principle* be expanded in such a way that it logically entails the truth of some observation belief. But Dicker needs to show just how we can begin to expand the set in question to rule out the possibility of an extensive hallucinatory experience. The case imagined above shows that an appeal to an apparent coherent experiential history is insufficient to the task. Thus, it seems doubtful that some foundational beliefs logically entail an observation belief.

However, it will prove useful to consider Dicker's opposition to a related anti-phenomenalist argument. A prominent anti-phenomenalist variant on the Cartesian deceiving demon hypothesis claims that any sensory experience apparently produced by physical objects stimulating a perceiver's sense-receptors could be produced by advanced neurophysiologists directly stimulating the perceiver's brain with a computer. Let us call this claim the 'deceiver hypothesis.' The deceiver hypothesis, if correct, shows that no foundational beliefs logically entail an observation belief. But Dicker claims that the deceiver hypothesis cannot possibly show that any apparently veridical perceptual experience could be produced without the perception of physical objects. For, he believes, if any such experience can be so produced, then this possibility must apply not only to the experimental subject's experience, but also to the experience of the deceiving neurophysiologists. But given that the deceiver hypothesis applies to the neurophysiologists' perceptual experiences also, Dicker infers that the neurophysiologists would have no way of telling whether they are really performing the appropriate experiment or simply hallucinating such an experiment. But his major point concerns not just the neuro- physiologists' inability to discern what they are doing, but the inability of *anyone* to discern whether the hypothesis in question describes (i) the neurophysiologists producing the subject's apparently veridical perceptual experiences by directly stimulating his brain, or (ii) the neurophysiologists hallucinating that they are producing the subject's apparently veridical perceptual experiences. The crucial problem, according to Dicker, is that we cannot tell what the deceiver hypothesis describes if any of one's apparently veridical perceptual experiences can be produced without one's perceiving any physical object. And this problem, as Dicker sees it, shows the impossibility of describing the kind of deceiver hypothesis in question (p. 198).[31]

By way of reply, one might propose initially that the advanced neurophysiologists in question are actually deceiving Cartesian demons who have knowledge of human perceivers and the physical world because they created human perceivers and the rest of the perceptual world. Dicker, as suggested above, would claim that we cannot describe circumstances in which such demons produce our apparently veridical perceptual experiences by directly stimulating our brains. For, he would claim, no one can tell whether in such circumstances the demons are actually producing our apparently veridical perceptual experiences, or are simply hallucinating that they are doing so. Suppose, however, we just assume that the imagined demons are not hallucinating, but are producing our apparently veridical perceptual experiences in a deceptive way, and that these demons, being the creators, know that they are not hallucinating. Dicker objects to such an assumption on the ground that it implies that there is someone, *viz.* the deceiving demons, to whose experience it does make a difference whether one ever actually perceives physical objects rather than hallucinates such objects. He finds this implication to be contrary to what the deceiver hypothesis purports to show (p. 198).

But Dicker's objection stems from an ambiguity in the talk of "making a difference" whether one is actually perceiving rather than hallucinating a physical object. According to the phenomenalist, it makes a difference whether one is having a veridical perceptual experience in the sense that one can deduce from a certain set of foundational beliefs about phenomenological content of a veridical, but not of an hallucinatory, perceptual experience that one is perceiving a physical object. The deceiver hypothesis, I believe, counts against this claim. But it does not count against the plausible suggestion that the distinction between a veridical and an hallucinatory perceptual experience can make a difference *in some other way.* For instance, the deceiver hypothesis allows one to hold that it is significant that the imagined deceiving demons are portrayed as actually producing our apparently veridical perceptual experiences, rather than simply hallucinating that they are doing so.

Another weakness of Dicker's argument against the deceiver hypothesis is the use it makes of a certain verificationist premise. Dicker assumes that necessarily if the *existence* of the deceivers is possible, then it is logically possible for us *to tell* whether the deceivers would be producing our apparently veridical perceptual experiences. Further, on Dicker's argument, it is necessary that if it is possible for us *to describe* the circumstances of the deceiver hypothesis, then it is logically possible for us to tell whether the deceivers would be actually deceiving us rather than simply hallucinating that they are (p. 199). Thus, Dicker's argument rests on a kind of verificationism about what possibly exists and about what is describable.

We can concede the truth of verificationism about what is possible and describable, if only for the sake of argument, but question the support such verificationism provides for Dicker's anti-deceiver argument. An analogue of the above deceiving-pharmacologists example suggests that the relevant verificationist requirement can be satisfied by the deceiver hypothesis. Consider the possibility that the victims of the extensive deception are informed, by means of a verbal communication from the deceivers, that their previous apparently veridical perceptual experiences have actually been produced not by the presumed physical objects, but by the machinations of the deceivers themselves. This communication, let us further suppose, is accompanied by the announcement that the deceivers have changed their morally question- able ways, and now renounce all forms of deception. Obviously such a communication would be met *initially* with skepticism, if not ridicule or shock, from the victims. But in due course the former deceivers could prove themselves to be impeccably reliable, at least from the time of their startling communication, and in doing so they could provide the formerly deceived with good grounds for believing that they genuinely were formerly deceived. Admittedly, this case is far-fetched, but since we have good reason to believe that it is at least logically possible, we can conclude that it provides a way for the deceiver hypothesis to satisfy Dicker's verificationist requirement. Moreover, we now can conclude that such a verificationist requirement cannot be used to show the absurdity of the deceiver hypothesis.

But since Dicker's anti-deceiver argument can now be seen to be unsuccessful, we have no good reason to hold that some foundational beliefs logically entail an observation belief. On the contrary, given the ever present possibility of an extensive hallucinatory perceptual experience, we have good reason to reject that phenomenalist thesis.

Further, the present sort of deductive phenomenalism cannot be supported by a probabilistic analysis of observation beliefs. Consider, in this connection, the view of C. I. Lewis that observation beliefs should be given a phenomenalistic analysis not by subjunctive conditionals, but by probability statements of a certain sort.[32] Lewis' view can be illustrated with the following statements: P = 'A sheet of paper lies before me'; S = 'I seem to see a sheet of paper before me'; A = 'I seem to feel paper with my fingers, and seem to be tearing it; and E = 'Following S and A, I now seem to see a torn sheet of paper'. According to Lewis, the statement that the probability of E, given A and S, is almost unity entails P. It is doubtful, of course, that a statement about the probability of E given A and S qualifies as a foundational belief. But this is not the major problem for Lewis' proposal. The key difficulty is that Lewis' proposed entailment relation does not hold: It is false that the probability statement concerning E, A, and S entails P. More generally, it is doubtful that such a probability statement entails any observation belief, since the forementioned deceiver hypothesis is quite compatible with such a probability statement. Clearly, then, Lewis' probabilistic analysis cannot salvage deductive phenomenalism.

Let us turn now to an alternative approach to the justification of observation beliefs.

2.2. *Critical Cognitivism*

R. M. Chisholm's alternative to deductive phenomenalism, so-called 'critical cognitivism', relies on epistemic principles other than the principles of deductive and inductive logic. Chisholm initially proposed nine nondeductive, noninductive epistemic principles, among which are several principles stating how beliefs about physical objects and their properties can be justified on the basis of foundational beliefs.[33] Chisholm's original formulation of one of these latter principles was:

(B)   If S believes he perceives something to have a certain property, F, then the proposition that he does perceive something to be F, as well as the proposition that there is something that is F, is one that is reasonable for S.

In accordance with his foundationalist program, Chisholm formulated (B) in such a way that its antecedent concerns only a "self-evident" state while its consequent concerns the epistemic status of some nonfoundational observation belief. (B) will thus serve as a good initial example of the sort of nondeductive, noninductive epistemic principle the critical cognitivist uses to justify inferences from foundational to observation beliefs.

Herbert Heidelberger has shown that Chisholm's principle (B) is unacceptable.[34] Principle (B), as applied to a particular case, tells us that if a person believes that he perceives an object to be yellow, then the proposition that he does perceive that object to be yellow and the proposition that that object is yellow are reasonable for him. But Heidelberger asks us to suppose that the following facts are known by that person: there is a yellow light shining on the object, he remembers having perceived a moment ago that the object is white, and at that time there was no colored light shining on the object. Clearly, if we suppose that in spite of this evidence the person in question believes he perceives that the object is yellow, then it would be incorrect to say that for this person the proposition that the object is yellow is reasonable. For this person has evidence that definitely makes that proposition unreasonable for him. Consequently, principle (B) is unacceptable.

To avoid the foregoing counterexample to (B), Chisholm now proposes that we revise (B) as follows:[35]

(B*)   If S believes that he is perceiving something to be F, and if no propositions that are acceptable for S are such that they together confirm that he is not perceiving something to be F, then S is justified in believing that he perceives something to be F.

Principle (B*) is equivalent to the claim that if S believes, without good ground for doubt, that he is perceiving something to be F, then S is justified in believing that he perceives something to be F. And, on Chisholm's account of perceiving, if S is justified in believing that he perceives something to be F, then S is justified in believing that something is F. The second clause of (B*), which is equivalent to the clause 'without good ground for doubt', appears to block Heidelberger's counterexample to (B). Heidelberger, however, has anticipated a revision of (B) along the lines of (B*), but has objected to such a revision on the ground that it is inconsistent with the foundationalist program of justifying observation beliefs entirely on the basis of foundational beliefs. Apparently, this objection assumes that for a person, S, to believe without good ground for doubt that he perceives something to be F, S must be justified in believing some observation belief. But Chisholm has tried to avoid the present objection by rejecting the view that before one can be justified in holding an observation belief, one must be justified in holding some other observation belief. His view, rather, is that before one can be justified in holding some observation belief, one must be *un*justified in believing some other observation propositions. For (B*) claims, in effect, that so long as certain other observation propositions are unjustified, S's observation belief in question is justified.

But even if Heidelberger's objection to (B*) fails, there is another objection that succeeds. We need first to clarify Chisholm's use of the phrase 'S believes that he is perceiving' in the antecedent of (B*). On Chisholm's account, the notion of "believing that one perceives" is synonymous with the notion of "perceptual taking". Thus, if one believes that one perceives a cat on the roof, then one perceptually takes a cat to be on the roof. But one can perceptually take a cat to be on the roof even if there is no cat there; in that case one's perceptual taking will be unveridical. Chisholm's basic definition of perceptual taking is as follows:[36]

S *takes* something, X, to be F = Df. S believes (i) that X's being F is a causal condition of the way he is being appeared to, and (ii) that there are possible ways of varying X which would cause concomitant variations in the way he is appeared to.

Given this definition, if S takes something to be a cat, then S believes that a cat is a cause of the way he is appeared to, and that by varying the cat in certain ways he could cause concomitant variations in the way he is appeared to. But Chisholm stresses that taking need not be a kind of inferring. The relevant belief may be altogether spontaneous, and so not a result of inference.

A natural objection to (B*) can now be stated: (B*) does not characterize S as actually having a perceptual experience of seeming to see something that is F; rather, it characterizes S simply as *believing*, or *taking*, that he is perceiving something to be F. But it is doubtful that such a belief provides a justifying reason for S to believe that something *is* F; for one can believe almost anything about what one perceives. A way to illustrate this objection is to suppose that S believes he perceives something to be F *solely because of wishful thinking,* but that no proposition justified for S confirms that he is not perceiving something to be F. Contrary to (B*), it is doubtful that S would be justified in believing that he perceives something to be F in these circumstances. For S has no positive support whatsoever for his belief.[37]

Two additional problems face Chisholm's critical cognitivism. First, given Chisholm's definition of 'perceptual taking', it is doubtful that the belief referred to in the antecedent of (B*) is a foundational belief that is solely about phenomenological content or is analytically true. For that belief, basically, is S's belief that X's being F is a causal condition of the way he is being appeared to. It is very doubtful that S's justification for such a belief would be non-inferential. The second problem is that Chisholm's development of critical cognitivism simply *assumes* that skepticism about observation beliefs is false; it thus fails to challenge such skepticism in any way.

In the following section I shall develop an alternative account of nonfoundational justification that aims to challenge the skeptic. This account also acknowledges the central role of the perceiver's *non-*belief perceptual experiences in the justification of observation beliefs. In doing so, it accommodates a basic tenet of what Firth has called 'the traditional empiricist theory of evidence'.[38]

2.3. Explanatory Justification

It is, of course, highly doubtful that the foundationalist can rely on induction by enumeration or analogy to justify observation beliefs. But the value of another kind of inductive inference — so-called 'inverse inductive inference' — is not so doubtful in this connection. Roughly, the premises of an inverse inductive argument state, first, some of the things that are true if the conclusion is true, and secondly, that some of these things are true. Consider, for example, this argument:

(1) (i) If there is a cat on the roof at present, and if I attentively look at the roof at present, then I will seem to see a cat on the roof at present.
    (ii) I am attentively looking at the roof at present.
    (iii) I seem to see a cat on the roof at present.
    (iv) Hence, it is probable that there is a cat on the roof at present.

One obvious problem with this argument is that premise (ii) is an observation belief, and not a foundational belief. Another problem is that premise (i) is a contingent generalization that also fails to qualify as a foundational belief.

To avoid these problems, let us try to modify premise (i) in such a way that it is analytically true and (ii) is eliminable. What results is the following argument:

(2) (i) If there is a cat on the roof at present, and I am attentively looking at the roof at present under normal conditions of illumination and perspective, then I will seem to see a cat on the roof at present.

    (ii) I seem to see a cat on the roof at present.

    (iii) Hence, it is probable that there is a cat on the roof at present and I am attentively looking at the roof at present under normal conditions of illumination and perspective.

If premise (i) of this argument were analytically true, the foundationalist could perhaps rely on this argument to justify the observation belief N1. But it is doubtful that (i) is analytically true. For it is quite possible that the antecedent of (i) is true while a deceiving Cartesian demon makes me seem to see a cow on the roof at present.[39] Premise (i) of (2), like the first premise of argument (1), is a contingent generalization that must be justified on the basis of observation beliefs. Hence, argument (2) is unavailable to the foundationalist.

A much more promising inverse inductive argument is the following:

(3) (i) If there is a cat on the roof at present, and if I am attentively looking at the roof at present under reliable conditions of illumination and perspective and without any detrimental outside influence on my perceptual situation (such as the influence of a deceiving Cartesian demon), and if my processes of sense reception are reliable, then I will seem to see a cat on the roof at present.

    (ii) I seem to see a cat on the roof at present.

    (iii) I seem to be attentively looking at the roof at present under reliable conditions of illumination and perspective, and I seem to have neither any detrimental outside influence on my present perceptual situation nor any deceptive influence from my processes of sense reception.

(iv) I seem to be trying hard to evaluate all the evidence available to me that is apparently relevant to the truth of the observation belief that there is a cat on the roof at present, and it seems to me that none of this evidence conflicts with the truth of that belief.

(v) I have no other relevant information at present.

(vi) Hence, it is probable for me now that there is a cat on the roof at present.

It is plausible to hold that premise (i) is analytically true in virtue of the meaning of its antecedent. Clearly, whenever the consequent of (i) is false, we can correctly take its antecedent to be false also. Further, there evidently is no statement compatible with the antecedent of (i) which in conjunction with that antecedent entails the denial of the consequent. Admittedly, I cannot provide a full account of analyticity here,[40] but it still seems plausible, on the basis of the present considerations, to hold that (i) is true in virtue of its antecedent's meaning. Many philosophers have raised doubts about the general thesis that semantic relations hold between some observation statements and some "seeming-to-see" statements.[41] But such doubts invariably stem from an examination of insufficiently complicated conditionals. For instance, the conditionals examined frequently do not include in their antecedents considerations about the condition of the perceiver and his perceptual situation. Premise (i) clearly remedies this defect, and thus provides the desired semantic connection between the foundational and the nonfoundational. Further, since (i) qualifies as true in virtue of the meaning of its antecedent, its justification need not derive from the justification of a belief entailing the existence of a physical object. It appears, then, that premise (i) is available to the foundationalist. (And the same is obviously true of premise (ii).)

Premises (iii)–(v) demand some explanation. Premise (iii) is intended to be a conjunction of foundational beliefs. The notion of reliable conditions of illumination and perspective in the first conjunct of (iii) is meant to be equivalent to the notion of conditions of illumination and perspective that are appropriate for veridical perception. But I do not understand (iii) to imply that my present conditions of illumination and perspective *are* reliable. Rather, (iii) implies that I am experiencing what *appear to be reliable* conditions of illumination and perspective. Thus, let us construe the first conjunct of (iii) as the foundational belief that

I seem to be looking attentively at the roof and that what appear to be my present conditions of illumination and perspective appear to be appropriate for veridical perception.

The second conjunct of (iii) simply expands on the claim of the first conjunct. For the second conjunct is equivalent to the claim that what appear to be my present perceptual conditions do not appear to be unreliable either because of some detrimental outside influence or because of deceptive processes of sense reception. But I do not take this conjunct of (iii) to imply that I have conclusive reasons to believe that (a) there is no detrimental outside influence on my present perceptual situation, or that (b) my processes of sense reception are reliable. That is, I am not claiming in premise (iii) that it is logically impossible that my present evidence obtains, or is true, while (a) and (b) are false. The claim of the second conjunct of (iii) is much weaker than this; the claim is simply that I seem to have neither a detrimental outside influence (such as the influence of a deceiving Cartesian demon) nor a deceptive, or unreliable, influence from my processes of sense reception on my (apparent) present perceptual conditions. And for present purposes we should construe the latter claim as implying that the phenomenological content available to me fails to provide good grounds for the belief that I seem to have a detrimental outside influence on my present perceptual situation as well as for the belief that I seem to have a deceptive influence on my present perceptual situation from my processes of sense reception. Clearly, then, premise (iii) does not entail the existence of any external physical objects; it thus qualifies as a foundational belief.

To secure the conclusion (vi), it is useful to supplement (iii) with premises (iv) and (v). Clearly, we do not want the truth of the second conjunct of (iii), for instance, to be due to my unwillingness to evaluate rationally my present perceptual situation. I intend premise (iv) to make this a remote possibility from my perspective. Premise (iv) suggests that, from my perspective, I am doing my best to find good reasons to doubt the observation belief that there is a cat on the roof. It suggests that, from my perspective, the justification of that belief will not be due to my indifference, laziness, or special interest. As I understand it, premise (iv), like premise (iii), is a conjunction of foundational beliefs.

Premise (v), like premise (iv), provides added insurance that I lack evidence for the proposition that it is false that there is a cat on the roof. For instance, given (v), I cannot be a philosopher who has a general proof that all perception is unveridical. As it stands, premise (v) is

obviously not a foundational belief. Although we could easily replace it
with its corresponding foundational belief, I prefer to leave it in its
present form. For I doubt that the success of the argument requires that
I be justified in believing that (v) is true; I believe it sufficient that (v) is
merely true of me. (However, if there is any problem here, we can easily
replace (v) by 'I seem to have no other relevant information at present.')

The conclusion of (3) requires some explanation also. I intend
the kind of probability mentioned in (vi) to be epistemic. That is, I
understand the probability of the conclusion in question as its degree
of confirmation.[42] Given this notion of probability, we may regard
argument (3) as claiming that if premises (i)–(v) are true of me at a
certain time, then the proposition that there is a cat on the roof at
present (i.e., N1) is confirmed for me at that time. That is, according
to (3), the premises (i)–(v) are sufficient for N1 having a degree of
confirmation greater than 0.5 for me at a certain time. The conclusion
of (3) is really quite modest. It claims simply that the degree of
confirmation of N1 for me at a certain time is some small amount
greater than the confirmation of the denial of N1. And that claim, of
course, is quite compatible with the claim that N1 is not confirmed for
me at all other times. I submit that that key claim of argument (3) is not
only quite modest, but also quite plausible.

One might find it helpful to view (3) as involving a species of
inference to the best explanation. And this would be in accordance with
the tendency of Kyburg and others to think of an inverse inductive
argument as an inference to the best explanation. (Notice, however, that
the inductive inference involved in (3) is not itself a premise of (3).)
Further, if we may regard (3) as involving an inference to the best
explanation, then we can specify the way in which the skeptical critic
should proceed with his attack. Presumably, the skeptical critic will
charge that the premises of (3) may be true even though (vi) is false, that
is, even though it is *im*probable for me that there is a cat on the roof at
present. But given this charge, the skeptic must provide us with an
explanation of the premises of (3) that is better than the explanation
provided by the belief that there is a cat on the roof at present, or N1.
For on the present construal of (3), the skeptic's charge amounts to the
claim that he has a better explanation of the premises of (3) than that
provided by N1. But notice that the skeptic's alternative explanation
must account not only for premise (ii) of (3), but also for premises (iii)
and (iv). And given the latter premises, the skeptic will apparently be

unable to rely on his most familiar skeptical hypotheses. Suppose, for instance, the skeptic tries to refute (3) by claiming that I might be hallucinating a cat on the roof or that a deceiving demon might be directly causing me to have an appearance of a cat on the roof. I can readily grant these possibilities, but deny that they affect the conclusion of (3). For according to the premises of (3), I have no evidence whatsoever of my hallucinating or of a deceiving demon. What the skeptic needs to provide, then, is an alternative explanation that accommodates the premises of (3) better than, or at least as well as, N1 does. For without such an alternative his skeptical challenge will be quite ineffective.

Of course a skeptical challenge to the truth of observation beliefs might arise from skepticism about any kind of inference to the best explanation. But it is doubtful that any relevant kind of epistemological skepticism can itself be justified, or shown to be reasonable, if we reject inference to the best explanation. For the relevant skeptical objections derive their force from the alleged fact that they support a skeptical rather than a nonskeptical *explanatory account* of the relevant epistemological data. That is, in light of certain skeptical objections to nonskeptical accounts of inferential justification, the skeptic typically contends that his skepticism provides a better account of inferential justification than any nonskeptical account. But such a skeptical strategy itself relies on a kind of inference to the best explanation. Of course some skeptic might insist that the justifying evidence for an observation belief must logically entail the truth of that belief. But we should be unimpressed by any such skeptical ploy. For any worthwhile dispute between the skeptic and the nonskeptic depends on the fundamental assumption that the justifying evidence for an observation belief need not logically entail that belief. Once we abandon this assumption any worthwhile dispute disappears. Argument (3), then, apparently provides a challenge to the skeptical critic.

I suggested above that my account of nonfoundational justification would be in accordance with the traditional empiricist theory of evidence. The inverse inductive argument (3) will be in accordance with that theory so long as we hold that the foundational beliefs (ii)—(iv) are immediately justified for me only if I experience the appropriate phenomenological content (or, only if those beliefs are true). But it seems that the fact that premises (i)—(iv) of (3) are true of me is insufficient for my being justified *in believing* that N1 (= there is a cat on the roof at present). Perhaps this fact is sufficient for N1's being confirmed *for* me, so long as premise (v) is true. But for me to be justified in believing that N1, I must be justified in believing premises (i)−(iv), and I must believe that N1 *on the basis of* those premises.[43] Part of the analysis of this basing relation, it seems, will rely on a subjunctive conditional, which, in connection with the present argument, states that were I to try to provide a justificatory argument for N1, then I would invoke the premises of (3). In any case, my being justified in believing that N1 requires that my belief be appropriately related to my evidence.

Given argument (3), then, if I am immediately justified in believing premises (i)−(iv), and premise (v) is true of me, then I will be inferentially justified in believing N1, so long as I believe N1 on the basis of premises (i)−(iv). Moreover, we can construct an inverse argument like (3) for many of our justified observation beliefs. Hence, given a familiar form of explanatory inductive inference and analytically true conditionals, the foundationalist evidently can justify singular observation beliefs entirely on the basis of foundational given-beliefs.

Before commenting further on the significance of inductive arguments like (3), I want briefly to anticipate a natural objection to my account of justifying nonfoundational observation beliefs. Some philosophers have objected to certain foundationalist solutions to the regress problem on the ground that a person rarely, if ever, holds given-beliefs of the sort needed to justify observation beliefs.[44] But I believe such an objection betrays a misunderstanding of the traditional foundationalist program. I am not at all concerned, as a proponent of foundationalism, to describe the ways in which the ordinary person's beliefs about the external world actually arise. Rather, I am concerned to explain how one *could rationally* hold observation beliefs in spite of skeptical queries. That is, I am concerned to show just how certain observation beliefs can be epistemically justified. Consequently, I find it irrelevant for one to object that very few persons have foundational given-beliefs of the sort I have relied on.

In sum, then, the availability of inductive arguments like (3) has enabled me, in this section, to complete my solution to the epistemic regress problem that has vexed us from the beginning. More specifically, I have now provided an intuitionist foundationalist solution to the epistemic regress problem concerning singular observation propositions, that is, singular propositions whose nonlogical constants are, or are definable by, terms true of external perceptual objects and properties. But, of course, I have not tried to solve the regress problem either as it applies to theoretical propositions, that is, propositions entailing there is something that is unobservable, or as it applies to universal inductive generalizations. Nor have I attempted to justify any propositions about the unperceived present, the past, or the future. Such an attempt, I believe, would require an additional book at least the size of the present one. Yet I should note that I currently agree with James Cornman's arguments that the justification of those kinds of propositions requires the use of inductive inference to the best explanation.[45] Also, I believe that the inferential justification of such propositions must rely heavily on my foregoing foundationalist solution to the regress problem concerning singular observation beliefs about what we currently perceive.

3. GENERAL SUMMARY AND CONCLUSION

In conclusion I want to stress two points. First, I offer my intuitionist foundationalist account of inferential justification as the best available solution to the epistemic regress problem concerning observation beliefs about what we currently perceive. It qualifies as the best available solution, I have claimed, because it is the best available explanatory account of the inferential justification of such observation beliefs. That is, my foundationalist account, as I have argued, raises fewer problems and answers more questions regarding the inferential justification of such observation beliefs than does any competing explanatory account. The competing accounts, of course, are the leading versions of contextualism, coherentism, foundationalism, justification via infinite regresses, and epistemological skepticism. I have raised my objections to the first four of those competing accounts in Chapters II—IV and in the earlier sections of Chapter V, and I have defended my account against the relevant skeptical objections in the later, constructive parts of Chapter V. In light of these efforts, I submit that my version of intuitionist foundationalism is justified by its explanatory superiority.

The second point I want to stress is that my solution to the regress problem is not necessarily a final solution. It is, I believe, subject to revision. However, I also believe that any plausible solution to the regress problem will rely on some species of intuitionist foundationalism. But I cannot claim that any plausible solution to the regress

problem must include all of the details of my version of intuitionist
foundationalism. Such a claim would be at best gratuitous. But I can
justifiably claim, in light of the extended regress argument of this
book, that my version of intuitionist foundationalism is currently the
best available solution to the epistemic regress problem. At least, this
is the major claim I have tried to justify in the foregoing chapters.

NOTES

[1] Here I am following James Cornman's article 'Materialism and Some Myths about
Some Givens', *The Monist* **56** (1972), 216—226. For a helpful survey of various
theories of the given see J. J. Ross, *The Appeal to the Given* (Allen & Unwin,
London, 1970).
[2] See Sellars, *Science, Perception, and Reality* (Routledge & Kegan Paul, London,
1963), pp. 161—162, and idem, *Philosophical Perspectives* (Charles C. Thomas, New
York, 1967), pp. 351—353, 362. A direct reply to Sellars is William S. Robinson's
'The Legend of the Given', in H. N. Castañeda (ed.), *Action, Knowledge, and Reality:
Critical Studies in Honor of Wilfrid Sellars* (Bobbs-Merrill, Indianapolis, 1975), pp.
83—108. But for criticisms compare Charles G. Echelbarger, 'An Alleged Legend',
Philosophical Studies **39** (1981), 227—246.
[3] See Chisholm, 'Theory of Knowledge in America', in idem, *The Foundations of
Knowing* (University of Minnesota Press, Minneapolis, 1982), pp. 126—127. Where
Chisholm speaks of knowledge, I have substituted 'justified belief'. Chisholm's
subsequent remarks clearly indicate that he is concerned with justified belief.
[4] See Chisholm, *Theory of Knowledge* (Prentice-Hall, Englewood Cliffs, New Jersey,
1966), pp. 27—28, and idem, *Theory of Knowledge, 2d ed.* (Prentice-Hall, Englewood
Cliffs, 1977), pp. 21—22.
[5] On this point see Chisholm, 'A Version of Foundationalism', in *The Foundations
of Knowing*, pp. 5—6, and idem, 'The Directly Evident', in G. S. Pappas (ed.),
Justification and Knowledge (D. Reidel, Dordrecht, 1979), pp. 115—127. A more
detailed discussion of this point is Chisholm, *The First Person* (University of
Minnesota Press, Minneapolis, 1981), Chapter 3.
[6] See Chisholm, 'Theory of Knowledge in America', in *The Foundations of Knowing*,
pp. 136—137; idem, 'The Foundation of Empirical Statements', in *ibid.*, p. 82; and
idem, *Theory of Knowledge, 2d ed.*, pp. 21, 26.
[7] My sketch of Lewis' intuitionism is based on Lewis, *Mind and the World Order*
(Charles Scribner's Sons, New York, 1929), Chapter 2, idem, *An Analysis of
Knowledge and Valuation* (Open Court, La Salle, Illinois, 1946); Chapter 7 and idem,
'The Given Element in Empirical Knowledge', *Philosophical Review* **61** (1952),
168—175. See also in this connection Israel Scheffler, *Science and Subjectivity* (Bobbs-
Merrill, Indianapolis, 1967), Chapter 2, and Roderick Firth, 'Lewis on the Given', in
P. A. Schilpp (ed.), *The Philosophy of C. I. Lewis* (Open Court, La Salle, Illinois,
1969), pp. 329—350.
[8] See Lewis, *Mind and the World Order*, pp. 125, 131, and idem, *An Analysis of
Knowledge and Valuation*, p. 188.

[9] A. J. Ayer suggests the following options in 'Basic Propositions', in *idem, Philosophical Essays* (Macmillan, London, 1954), pp. 105−124. Cf. Alan H. Goldman, 'Appearing Statements and Epistemological Foundations', *Metaphilosophy* **10** (1979), 229−230. The first of the following options is defended by Pollock in *Knowledge and Justification* (Princeton University Press, Princeton, 1974), pp. 73−75.

[10] See William Alston, 'Varieties of Privileged Access', *American Philosophical Quarterly* **8** (1971), 231. Cf. Bruce Aune, *Knowledge, Mind, and Nature* (Random House, New York, 1967), Chapter 2, and *idem*, 'Chisholm on Empirical Knowledge', in E. Sosa (ed.), *Essays on the Philosophy of R. M. Chisholm* (Editions Rodopi, Amsterdam, 1979), pp. 240−241. A. J. Ayer espouses something like the irrefutability thesis in 'Privacy', in *idem, The Concept of a Person* (St. Martin's Press, New York, 1963), p. 73.

[11] See Armstrong, 'Is Introspective Knowledge Incorrigible?', *Philosophical Review* **72** (1963), 417−432. Cf. *idem, A Materialist Theory of the Mind* (Routledge & Kegan Paul, London, 1968), pp. 104−113, and Paul E. Meehl, 'The Compleat Autocerebroscopist', in P. Feyerabend and G. Maxwell (eds.), *Mind, Matter, and Method* (University of Minnesota Press, Minneapolis, 1966), pp. 103−181, especially Section 1.

[12] See Sellars, 'Epistemic Principles', in H.-N. Castañeda (ed.), *Action, Knowledge, and Reality*, p. 339. Cf. Lehrer, *Knowledge* (Clarendon Press, Oxford, 1974), pp. 107−110.

[13] See Bonjour, 'Can Empirical Knowledge Have a Foundation?', *American Philosophical Quarterly* **15** (1978), 10−11, and Sellars, 'Epistemic Principles', in *Action, Knowledge, and Reality*, pp. 336−338. Cf. Michael Williams, *Groundless Belief* (Basil Blackwell, Oxford, 1977), pp. 31, 102. In 'A Defense of Epistemic Intuitionism', *Metaphilosophy* **15** (1984), 196−209, I have tried to generalize the sort of dilemma under consideration to make it applicable to standard coherentist and contextualist theories of justification.

[14] Some philosophers have argued that we can replace all *de re* constructions by *de dicto* constructions. See, for example, David Kaplan, 'Quantifying In', in D. Davidson and J. Hintikka (eds.), *Words and Objections* (D. Reidel, Dordrecht, 1969), pp. 178−214, and R. M. Chisholm, *Person and Object* (Open Court, La Salle, Illinois, 1976), Appendix C. But for arguments against any such reduction see Tyler Burge, 'Belief *De Re*', *Journal of Philosophy* **74** (1977), 338−362.

[15] On such nonconceptual awareness, see William Robinson, 'The Legend of the Given', in H.-N. Castañeda (ed.), *Action, Knowledge, and Reality*, pp. 102−103, and Alan H. Goldman, 'Epistemic Foundationalism and the Replaceability of Ordinary Language', *Journal of Philosophy* **79** (1982), 145−149. I shall return to this issue below.

[16] See Quinton, *The Nature of Things* (Routledge & Kegan Paul, London, 1973), Chapter 5, and *idem*, 'The Foundations of Knowledge', in B. Williams and A. Montefiore (eds.), *British Analytical Philosophy* (Routledge & Kegan Paul, London, 1966), pp. 55−86.

[17] See Ducasse, *Nature, Mind, and Death* (Open Court, La Salle, Illinois, 1951), pp. 253−290, and *idem*, 'Objectivity, Objective Reference, and Perception', in *idem, Truth, Knowledge, and Causation* (Routledge & Kegan Paul, London, 1968), pp. 90−131. The following sketch of Ducasse's view is based on these two works.

[18] For a summary of and references to some of the important psychological literature relevant to this notion of attention-attraction, see David I. Mostofsky, 'The Semantics of Attention', in D. Mostofsky (ed.), *Attention: Contemporary Theory and Analysis* (Appleton-Century-Crofts, New York, 1970), pp. 9–24.

[19] For related arguments see Tyler Burge, 'Belief *De Re*', *Journal of Philosophy* **74** (1977), 345–348, and Bertrand Russell, 'On Verification', *Proceedings of the Aristotelian Society* **38** (1937–38), 8–13. And for more evidence in favor of nonconceptual awareness see Fred Dretske, 'Simple Seeing', in D. Gustafson and B. Tapscott (eds.), *Body, Mind, and Method* (D. Reidel, Dordrecht, 1979), pp. 1–15.

[20] The same is true of the accounts of immediate justification in Carl Ginet, *Knowledge, Perception, and Memory* (D. Reidel, Dordrecht, 1975), Chapter 3; John Pollock, *Knowledge and Justification*, Chapter 3; James Cornman, *Skepticism, Justification, and Explanation* (D. Reidel, Dordrecht, 1980), Chapter 2; and Alan Goldman, 'Appearing Statements and Epistemological Foundations', *Metaphilosophy* **10** (1979), 227–246.

[21] See Alston, 'Self-Warrant: A Neglected Form of Privileged Access', *American Philosophical Quarterly* **13** (1976), 267.

[22] See Cornman, *Skepticism, Justification, and Explanation*, pp. 33–34, and Reichenbach, 'Are Phenomenal Reports Absolutely Certain?', *Philosophical Review* **61** (1952), reprinted in R. M. Chisholm and R. Swartz (eds.), *Empirical Knowledge* (Prentice-Hall, Englewood Cliffs, 1973), pp. 354–356.

[23] See, for example, Wilfrid Sellars, *Science, Perception and Reality* (Routledge & Kegan Paul, London, 1963), pp. 146–147, and Keith Lehrer, *Knowledge* (Clarendon Press, Oxford, 1974), pp. 102–110.

[24] See Chisholm, *Perceiving: A Philosophical Study* (Cornell University Press, Ithaca, 1957), Chapter 4, and *idem, Theory of Knowledge*, 2d ed. (Prentice-Hall, Englewood Cliffs, 1977), pp. 30–33.

[25] Lehrer himself has suggested this proposal, and he apparently has no objection to it. See *Knowledge*, pp. 110–111. Cf. Alston, 'What's Wrong With Immediate Knowledge?', *Synthese* **55** (1983), 73–95.

[26] See Lehrer, *Knowledge*, pp. 114–119.

[27] See, for example, Chisholm, *Perceiving: A Philosophical Study*, Chapter 7, and James Van Cleve, 'Foundationalism, Epistemic Principles, and the Cartesian Circle', *The Philosophical Review* **88** (1979), 87–90.

[28] See, for example, Lehrer, *Knowledge*, pp. 121, 143–144, 152–153, and Alvin Plantinga, 'Is Belief in God Rational?', in C. F. Delaney (ed.), *Rationality and Religious Belief* (University of Notre Dame Press, Notre Dame, 1979), pp. 20–26.

[29] For elaboration on this distinction see Alston, 'Has Foundationalism Been Refuted?', *Philosophical Studies* **29** (1976), 296; *idem*, 'Two Types of Foundationalism', *Journal of Philosophy* **73** (1976), 165–185; and *idem*, 'Level-Confusions in Epistemology', in P. French *et al.* (eds.), *Midwest Studies in Philosophy, Vol. V: Studies in Epistemology* (University of Minnesota Press, Minneapolis, 1980), pp. 135–150.

[30] See Ayer, 'Phenomenalism', in *idem, Philosophical Essays* (Macmillan, London, 1954), pp. 134–139; *idem, The Problem of Knowledge* (Penguin Books, Ltd., London, 1956), pp. 125–126; and Dicker, *Perceptual Knowledge* (D. Reidel, Dordrecht, 1980), pp. 193–209.

³¹ Dicker's challenge to the deceiver hypothesis relies heavily on O. K. Bouwsma, 'Descartes' Evil Genius', *The Philosophical Review* **58** (1949), 141–151, reprinted in A. Sesonke and N. Fleming (eds.), *Meta-Meditations* (Wadsworth, Belmont, CA: 1966).

³² See Lewis, *An Analysis of Knowledge and Valuation* (Open Court, La Salle, Illinois, 1946), pp. 248–250. Cf. Lewis, 'The Philosopher Replies', in P. A. Schilpp (ed.), *The Philosophy of C. I. Lewis* (Open Court, La Salle, 1968), pp. 656–658.

³³ See Chisholm, *Theory of Knowledge, 1st ed.* (Prentice-Hall, Englewood Cliffs, New Jersey, 1966), Chapter 3. Cf. Chisholm, *Perceiving: A Philosophical Study* (Cornell University Press, Ithaca, 1957), Chapter 6.

³⁴ Heidelberger, 'Chisholm's Epistemic Principles', *Noûs* 3 (1969), 75–76.

³⁵ Chisholm, *Theory of Knowledge, 2d ed.* (Prentice-Hall, Englewood Cliffs, 1977), pp. 75–76; and *idem*, 'On the Nature of Empirical Evidence', in G. S. Pappas and M. Swain (eds.), *Essays on Knowledge and Justification* (Cornell University Press, Ithaca, 1978), pp. 269–276.

³⁶ See Chisholm, *Perceiving: A Philosophical Study*, pp. 75–77; cf. *idem, Theory of Knowledge, 2d ed.*, pp. 74–75. It should be noted that Chisholm restricts his definition of perceptual taking to "takings", or beliefs, about the so-called "common sensibles" and "proper objects of sense". Cf. *Perceiving*, pp. 83–90.

³⁷ To deny the need for some kind of positive support for observation beliefs will commit one to some form of contextualism or negative coherentism. For arguments against the prominent forms of such theories, see Chapters II and III above.

³⁸ See Firth, 'Ultimate Evidence', *Journal of Philosophy* **53** (1956), reprinted in R. J. Swartz (ed.), *Perceiving, Sensing, and Knowing* (Doubleday, Garden City, New York, 1965), pp. 486–496. For some further criticisms of Chisholm's critical cognitivism, see Cornman, *Skepticism, Justification, and Explanation*, pp. 91–98, 110, and *idem*, 'On Justifying Nonbasic Statements by Basic-Reports', in G. S. Pappas (ed.), *Justification and Knowledge* (D. Reidel, Dordrecht, 1979), pp. 138–141.

³⁹ A similar possibility undermines a related argument constructed by Henry Kyburg in 'On a Certain Form of Philosophical Argument', *American Philosophical Quarterly* 7 (1970), 233. Cf., in this connection, Cornman, *Skepticism, Justification, and Explanation*, p. 89.

⁴⁰ For some helpful suggestions in this connection, including a reply to Quine's notorious objections, see Hilary Putnam, '"Two Dogmas" Revisited', and 'Analyticity and Apriority: Beyond Wittgenstein and Quine', in *Realism and Reason, Philosophical Papers, Vol. 3* (Cambridge University Press, Cambridge, 1983), pp. 87–97, 115–138; and, especially, *idem*, 'The Analytic and the Synthetic', in *Mind, Language, and Reality, Philosophical Papers, Vol. 2* (Cambridge University Press, Cambridge, 1975), pp. 33–69.

⁴¹ See, for example, Chisholm, 'The Problem of Empiricism', in R. J. Swartz (ed.), *Perceiving, Sensing, and Knowing*, pp. 347–354; *idem, Perceiving*, pp. 189–197; and Cornman, *Perception, Common Sense, and Science* (Yale University Press, New Haven, 1975), pp. 119–125. Replies to Chisholm's argument can be found in C. I. Lewis, 'Professor Chisholm and Empiricism', in *Perceiving, Sensing, and Knowing*, pp. 355–363, and Roderick Firth, 'Radical Empiricism and Perceptual Relativity', *The Philosophical Review* 59 (1950), 164–183, 319–331.

⁴² On this kind of probability see Carnap, 'Inductive Logic and Rational Decisions', in

R. Carnap and R. Jeffrey (eds.), *Studies in Inductive Logic and Probability* (University of California Press, Berkeley, 1971), p. 25; and Henry Kyburg, 'Epistemological Probability', in *Epistemology and Inference* (University of Minnesota Press, Minneapolis, 1983), pp. 204—216.

[43] Here, of course, I am alluding to the forementioned distinction between propositional and doxastic justification. My present talk of "believing on the basis of" is intended to be basically equivalent to the above talk of "believing in light of". For some other ways to construe 'believes on the basis of' see George Pappas, 'Basing Relations', in *Justification and Knowledge*, pp. 51—63. Cf. Robert Audi, 'The Causal struture of Indirect Justification', *Journal of Philosophy* **80** (1983), 398—415.

[44] See, for instance, John Pollock, 'A Plethora of Epistemological Theories', in *Justification and Knowledge*, pp. 98, 100; and Carl Ginet, *Knowledge, Perception, and Memory* (D. Reidel, Dordrecht, 1975), p. 125. Cf. Gilbert Ryle, *The Concept of Mind* (Hutchinson, London, 1949), pp. 242—243.

[45] For Cornman's elaborate arguments see *Skepticism, Justification, and Explanation*, Chapters 7—10.

CHAPTER VI

EPILOGUE:

THE EPISTEMIC AND THE RATIONAL

Having argued that an intuitionist foundationalist approach to epistemic empirical justification provides the best solution to the notorious epistemic regress problem, I want now to ask how epistemic justification is related to rationality in general. Many philosophers have assumed that an account of epistemic justification provides, by itself, an account of rational belief. Such an assumption, as we shall see, is correct in one sense, but seriously incorrect in another sense. One major problem with such an assumption is that rational agents sometimes find themselves in a predicament where the fulfillment of a morally rational obligation, for instance, requires that they believe a proposition that is unlikely to be true, and thus epistemically *un*justified, on their total evidence. In such a predicament, typically, one rational obligation — a *morally* rational obligation — conflicts with another rational obligation — an *epistemically* rational obligation. We then have a case of rational dilemma. In this epilogue I aim to characterize three types of rational obligation that sometimes come into conflict, to specify the nature of conflict found in rational dilemmas, and to propose a straightforward resolution of such dilemmas — a resolution in terms of "all-things-considered" rationality. In doing so, I aim not only to lay to rest a central problem in the so-called ethics of belief, but also to clarify the relation of epistemic justification to rationality in general.

1. RATIONAL CONFLICTS

Consider the following not unlikely situation. Ed and Edna have been devoted partners in marriage and business for the past twenty years. Lately, however, Ed has acquired strong evidence indicating that Edna is disloyal to him in both the marriage and the business. For instance, Edna's own parents, who are trustworthy friends of Ed's, have recently informed Ed of Edna's privately confessed disloyalty toward her marriage and business relationships with Ed. In addition, Ed recently has found several very recent love letters addressed to Edna by an unknow author. Moreover, Ed has just uncovered Edna's hitherto undisclosed involvement in some very dubious business transactions which violate the ground-rules on which their business partnership was founded. Such evidence, we may plausibly suppose, makes likely to be true, and so epistemically justifies, for Ed the proposition that Edna is disloyal in both the marriage and the business. But given the past twenty years, Ed is heavily dependent upon his marriage and business relationships with Edna. Indeed, without these relationships Ed would be psychologically as well as financially devastated; and Ed painfully realizes this. What's more, Ed is well aware that his believing that Edna is disloyal would have at least two undesirable consequences: it would result in the breakup of his marriage and business partnership with Edna, which in turn would spell his psychological and financial doom, and it would bring him to despise and even to mistreat Edna. (And it is easily imaginable that Ed's merely refraining from believing that Edna is loyal would have similar undesirable consequences.) Consequently, it would not be surprising for Ed to refuse to believe that Edna is disloyal, and to persist in his belief that Edna is a model of loyalty.

But let us assess Ed from a rational point of view. Would he be rational to refuse to believe in accordance with his evidence? That is, should he, on pain of being irrational, believe that Edna is disloyal? Or, alternatively, is it rationally obligatory for Ed to believe, in accordance with his "practical" interests, that Edna is loyal? Such questions, in any case, force us to face a basic problem in the ethics of belief: the problem of the priority of conflicting rational obligations concerning what one should believe. But, more basically, such questions force us to characterize the sorts of rational obligation in conflict.

Let us begin by distinguishing the following two general questions:

(1)   Under what conditions is one rationally obligated to believe a proposition?

(2)   Under what conditions is it rationally permissible, or justified, for one to believe a proposition?

These questions, of course, need to be distinguished, since a person can be rationally permitted to believe a proposition even if he is not rationally obligated to believe it. (Compare the analogous situation in the ethics of conduct where an action is right or permissible, but not obligatory, for a person.) Further, the present distinction needs to be drawn even if we accept the familiar view that one is rationally obligated to believe only what is rationally permissible. For the thrust of the latter view is not, of course, that whatever is rationally permissible is also rationally obligatory, but rather that whatever proposition one believes, it should provide for a belief that is at least rationally permissible. Perhaps the easiest way to distinguish (1) and (2) is to note that the conditions providing an answer to (1) can be violated only at the expense of being irrational, but the same is not true of (2). For present purposes I shall be concerned primarily with question (1), and I shall accept the natural assumption that if one is rationally obligated to believe a proposition, then one is also rationally permitted to believe it. But the converse implication must be rejected.

Before dealing with (1) directly, let us note that our concern with this question does not commit us to extreme doxastic voluntarism, the implausible view that all of a person's beliefs are voluntarily chosen. We can take (1) seriously even if we grant that many beliefs are involuntary. For it seems plain enough that even if many beliefs are involuntary, some psychological events or so-called states that qualify as beliefs are voluntary. For instance, we often voluntarily assent psychologically to a proposition, and such assent, when sincere, frequently qualifies as belief. In any case, I shall use the term 'belief' to refer primarily to such psychological assent. It should be stressed, however, that voluntary belief can be either indirectly or directly voluntary. Many beliefs taken to be involuntary are really indirectly voluntary at least insofar as they have arisen from a noncompulsory, albeit perhaps habitual, belief-forming process. Like many habits, such belief-forming processes are noncompulsory to the extent that one can, perhaps only with considerable effort, dispense with them, and thereby eliminate or preclude the beliefs arising from them. Thus, even if one holds that every belief is directly *in*voluntary and at most *in*directly voluntary, one could, it seems, make sense of question (1). For the sort of obligation mentioned by (1) could be taken to require only indirect control over belief.[1]

But what constitutes one's having a *rational* obligation? I shall assume that one can have a particular moral obligation, for instance, even if this obligation does not qualify as a morally rational obligation for one. Such a distinction rests on the rough assumption (to be refined below) that obligations of a particular kind, *e.g.*, moral, qualify as rational for one if and only if one has certain preferences, or desires, whose satisfaction is evidently best provided for by the fulfillment of obligations of that kind. Yet it seems quite implausible to hold that such preferences provide a necessary condition of one's having a (nonrational) moral obligation, for instance. In any event, I find that rational obligations fall into at least three main categories: the epistemic, the moral, and the prudential. I shall briefly characterize each of these kinds of rational obligation in turn. To do so, I begin with a characterization of (nonrational) epistemic, moral, and prudential obligation.

A familiar characterization of epistemic obligation states that it is the (*prima facie*) obligation one has, *qua* truth-seeker, to maximize true belief and to minimize, if not to avoid, false belief. (Here and in what follows I insert '*prima facie*' parenthetically to leave open the possibility that an obligation is overridable or defeasible.) Note that on the present characterization both prongs of the obligation are essential. Without either prong the fulfillment of the obligation would be a cinch: Believe everything, and true belief will be maximized; believe nothing, and false belief will be minimized, even avoided. But we need to modify this characterization to account for the fact that some true beliefs are more important than others from an epistemic point of view. For instance, assuming that explanatory value is a determinant of epistemic importance, a person could be epistemically obligated to believe a single true proposition with considerable explanatory value instead of several true propositions with lesser explanatory value, in a situation where he cannot believe all these propositions. But whatever determines epistemic importance, it seems clear that one's general epistemic obligation cannot be satisfied simply by a purely quantitative maximization of true belief and minimization of false belief. Let us assume, then, that the general obligation to maximize true belief and to minimize, if not to avoid, false belief concerns true beliefs of equal epistemic importance, the holding of which does not preclude one's holding any beliefs of greater epistemic importance.

Let us consider how these general considerations bear on a particular case. In the above example, Ed has a (*prima facie*) epistemic obligation to believe that Edna is disloyal, if we assume that his believing this proposition does not preclude his holding a belief of greater epistemic importance. For it is likely to be true on Ed's total evidence that Edna is disloyal, and Ed, by hypothesis, recognizes as much. Further, if Ed has the forementioned general epistemic obligation in its appropriately qualified form, then this obligation of his will be fulfilled most consistently in particular cases if he believes only those propositions that are likely to be true on his total evidence. This, it seems, is the most responsible way for Ed to fulfill his general epistemic obligation. In fact, were Ed to believe that Edna is actually loyal, despite his evidence, we could plausibly claim that he is epistemically irresponsible; for in that case he would believe a proposition that is unlikely to be true on his total evidence. Further, in assuming a familiar normative notion of epistemic permissibility as epistemic responsibility,[2] we also could plausibly say that Ed is not epistemically permitted to believe that Edna is loyal. For whenever one would be epistemically irresponsible in believing a proposition, one is not epistemically permitted to believe it. But of course if one is not epistemically permitted to believe a proposition, then one is not epistemically obligated to believe it. In sum, then, let us say roughly that a person, S, is epistemically obligated to believe a proposition, p, on his evidence, e, if and only if p is likely to be true on e, and S's believing that p is not incompatible with S's believing a proposition, q, which is also likely to be true on e, and which is epistemically more important than p. And let us say that a proposition is likely to be true on one's total evidence if and only if it has a better chance of being true, given that evidence, than its denial does.[3]

In addition to epistemic obligation, there is also moral obligation. When restricted to acts or states of believing, this is the (*prima facie*) obligation one has, *qua* moral agent, to believe a proposition if and only if the moral advantages of believing it for oneself probably, on one's total evidence, outweigh the moral advantages of denying (*i.e.*, disbelieving) it and of withholding (*i.e.*, neither believing nor disbelieving) it. Let us say that the moral advantages of believing a proposition for a person outweigh the moral advantages of denying it and of withholding it if and only if believing it is more conducive to the moral goodness of the person than is denying it and withholding it.[4] What precisely moral goodness is, let us assume, is determined by the set of correct, or at least warranted, moral principles. But it seems plain enough that one's being morally good minimally requires one's refraining from despising and mistreating one's marriage and business partner. If this is so, then it should be clear that a person can have a moral obligation to believe, deny, or withhold a proposition. For it seems clear that in some cases one's believing, denying, or withholding a proposition is conducive to one's moral goodness.

To illustrate the present point, suppose, in accordance with the above example, that if Ed believed Edna to be disloyal, he would despise and mistreat her. Given this supposition, it follows that Ed's treating Edna morally properly, and thus his being morally good, requires that he not believe that she is disloyal. It appears, then, that Ed has a moral obligation to refrain from believing a proposition which he has an epistemic obligation to believe. Further, if we assume that Ed's treating Edna morally properly requires not only his not believing her to be disloyal, but also his believing her not to be disloyal, then a proposition which Ed has a moral obligation to believe contradicts a proposition which he has an epistemic obligation to believe. In sum, then, let us say that one's moral obligation, at least with respect to believing, is to believe only those propositions the believing of which probably, on one's evidence, makes a greater contribution to one's moral goodness than does their denial and withholding (or, equivalently, those propositions probably most conducive to one's moral goodness). Given this proposal, we should not assume that one's moral obligation is just the obligation to maximize belief in true moral principles and to minimize, if not to avoid, belief in false moral principles. This latter obligation is more appropriately regarded as a feature of one's general epistemic obligation.

In addition to epistemic and moral obligations, there are also prudential obligations. Let us say that prudential obligation is the (*prima facie*) obligation one has, *qua* prudential agent, to satisfy one's nonepistemic, nonmoral interests, and thereby to advance one's nonepistemic, nonmoral well-being. Among our most valued prudential interests are, of course, the interests to have psychological, physiological, social, and financial well-being. What counts as psychological and physiological well-being, we may plausibly assume, is determined by the best psychology and physiology of our day. Social and financial well-being, however, appear to be somewhat more variable. Yet we might plausibly hold that generally social and financial well-being consists of one's having adequate social relationships and financial resources to satisfy one's psychological and physiological interests. On this proposal, one's social and financial well-being could be regarded as essential ingredients of one's psychological and physiological well-being.

In any event, let us say that prudential obligation, when restricted to believing, is the (*prima facie*) obligation one has, *qua* prudential agent, to believe a proposition if and only if the prudential advantages of believing it for oneself probably, on one's total evidence, outweigh the prudential advantages for oneself of denying it and of withholding it.[5] The prudential advantages of believing a proposition for a person, let us assume, outweigh the prudential advantages of denying it and of withholding it if and only if believing it is more conducive to the prudential well-being of that person than is denying it and withholding it. In the above example, for instance, it is clear that Ed has a prudential obligation not to believe that Edna is disloyal, since, by hypothesis, his believing that she is disloyal will probably result in the breakup of the marriage and business partnership, and thereby gravely damage him psychologically and financially. And it is plausible to suppose that this obligation would stand even if we consider what is prudent for Ed in the long run. Further, if we make the natural assumption that Ed's believing that Edna is loyal is probably more conducive to Ed's prudential well-being than is his denying and his withholding that proposition, then we may say that Ed has a prudential obligation to believe that Edna is loyal.

But, once again, the example in question presents us with a conflict of obligations. For, on the forementioned assumptions, Ed has an epistemic obligation to believe that Edna is disloyal, but also has a prudential as well as moral obligation to believe that Edna is loyal. One might propose of course that Ed's epistemic obligation has actually been overridden, since it is outnumbered by his prudential and moral obligations. But this proposal is seriously inadequate. For it not only conflicts with the fact that a single obligation can be more important, from a normative point of view, than the conflicting obligations out-numbering it, but also fails to provide a hint of a strategy for cases where there are just two conflicting obligations, neither being supported by a third obligation. But of course we need just such a strategy if we are to provide a uniform account of conflicting obligations. Before developing such a strategy, I shall refine and extend some of the distinctions already suggested.

2. THREE KINDS OF RATIONALITY

My account of obligations has thus far been decidedly objective, characterizing obligations not in terms of what one believes, but rather in terms of what is actually likely to be epistemically, morally, and prudentially advantageous. But I find that the above notions of obligation share a common deficiency: they are somewhat too objective. This deficiency can be illustrated in connection with moral obligation. Suppose that S's believing a proposition, p, would probably, on his evidence, be more conducive to his moral goodness than his denying that p and his withholding that p, but that S lacks the conceptual sophistication needed to understand p. Lacking such conceptual sophistication, S will be incapable of understanding p, and so will not have a moral obligation to believe that p. For so long as S is incapable of understanding p, S will also be incapable of having a genuine belief that p. Genuine belief in a proposition requires an understanding of it. But since "ought" implies "can", an obligation (of any sort) to believe that p presupposes a capability to believe that p. Hence, if S is to have an obligation (of any sort) to believe that p, S must be capable of understanding p. Consequently, in the envisaged situation S does not have a moral obligation to believe that p.

The following principles, I find, capture the foregoing notions of obligation and provide the needed revision:

EO.   A person, S, has a *(prima facie)* epistemic obligation to believe that p if and only if: (i) p is likely to be true on S's total evidence; (ii) S's believing that p is not incompatible with S's believing a proposition, q, which is likely to be true on S's evidence, and which is epistemically more important than p; and (iii) S is capable of coming to recognize the truth of (i) from reflection on his evidence.

MO.   S has a *(prima facie)* moral obligation to believe that p if and only if: (i) S's believing that p is probably, on S's total evidence, more conducive to S's moral goodness than is S's denying that p and S's withholding that p; (ii) S's believing that p is not incompatible with S's believing a proposition, q, which is likely to be morally advantageous on S's evidence, and which is morally more important than p; and (iii) S is capable of coming to recognize the truth of (i) from reflection on his evidence.

PO.   S has a *(prima facie)* prudential obligation to believe that p if and only if: (i) the prudential advantages for S of S's believing that p probably, on S's total evidence, outweigh the prudential advantages for S of S's denying that p and of S's withholding that p; (ii) S's believing that p is not incompatible with S's believing a proposition, q, which is likely to be prudentially advantageous on S's evidence, and which is prudentially more important than p; and (iii) S is capable of coming to recognize the truth of (i) from reflection on his evidence.

These principles clearly avoid the forementioned problem facing the earlier notions of obligation; for given clause (iii) in each of these principles, they do not allow that a proposition not understandable by a person can be obligatory for that person to believe. But regarding clause (ii) we should note that there may be varying degrees of difficulty of a person's coming to recognize the truth of clause (i) in the above principles. And where the effort needed to recognize the truth of (i) is immense, we might be inclined to hold that the respective obligation is considerably weakened, if not overridden. But, of course, if the relevant obligation is very important, from a normative point of view, we should be less inclined to hold that the difficulty of coming to recognize the truth of (i) overrides that obligation. (Note, furthermore, that there are direct analogues to EO, MO, and PO concerning the denying and the withholding of a proposition; but the present principles merit special attention, since the focus of the following discussion is on rationally obligatory belief in a proposition.)

There are principles of what I have called "rational obligation" corresponding to the foregoing principles of nonrational obligation, EO, MO, and PO. They are:

ER.   S has a (*prima facie*) epistemically rational obligation to believe that p if and only if: (i) p is likely to be true on S's total evidence; (ii) S's believing that p is not incompatible with S's believing a proposition, q, which is likely to be true on S's evidence, and which is epistemically more important than p; (iii) S is capable of coming to recognize the truth of (i) from reflection on his evidence; and (iv) S has a preference for true belief whose satisfaction is evidently best provided for by his believing that p.

MR.   S has a (*prima facie*) morally rational obligation to believe that p if and only if: (i) S's believing that p is probably, on S's total evidence, more conducive to S's moral goodness than is S's denying that p and S's withholding that p; (ii) S's believing that p is not incompatible with S's believing a proposition, q, which is likely to be morally advantageous on S's evidence, and which is morally more important than p; (iii) S is capable of coming to recognize the truth of (i) from reflection on his evidence; and (iv) S has a preference for morally advantageous belief whose satisfaction is evidently best provided for by his believing that p.

PR.   S has a (*prima facie*) prudentially rational obligation to believe that p if and only if: (i) the prudential advantages for S

of S's believing that p probably, on S's total evidence, outweigh the prudential advantages for S of S's denying that p
and of S's withholding that p; (ii) S's believing that p is not
incompatible with S's believing a proposition, q, which is
likely to be prudentially advantageous on S's evidence, and
which is prudentially more important than p; (iii) S is capable
of coming to recognize the truth of (i) from reflection on his
evidence; and (iv) S has a preference for prudentially advantageous belief whose satisfaction is evidently best provided
for by his believing that p.

It should be stressed now that principles ER, MR, and PR require that S
has a preference whose satisfaction is evidently best provided for by his
fulfilling his relevant epistemic, moral, or prudential obligation. For it is
a preference of this sort that typically makes such obligations *rational*
obligations for S. Lacking such a preference, S might nonetheless be
anti-epistemic, immoral, and imprudent, but S would evidently not qualify as epistemically, morally, or prudentially *irrational*. (I shall elaborate
on the present point, and on the relevant notion of preference in the
following section.)

We often say that a person *should* believe a proposition, but now we
can see that such talk is ambiguous between at least three senses of
'should': the epistemic, the moral, and the prudential. Further, we now
can see that corresponding to principles ER, MR, and PR there are
three distinct senses of 'rational justification' and 'rational permissibility'.
Less obviously, there are also three distinct senses of 'reason' and 'evidence'. An *epistemic* reason for the belief that p is epistemic evidence
indicating that the belief that p is, to some extent, likely to be true. A
moral reason for the belief that p is moral evidence indicating that the
belief that p is, to some extent, probably conducive to moral goodness.
And a *prudential* reason for the belief that p is prudential evidence
indicating that the belief that p is, to some extent, probably conducive to
prudential well-being. A *justifying* reason for the belief that p, however,
is more than mere evidence for that belief; such a reason provides
(*prima facie*) justifying evidence for the belief that p in the sense that it
makes that belief (*prima facie*) rationally permissible. But we now can
see that insofar as rational obligation and justification come in at least
three distinct forms − the epistemic, the moral, and the prudential, so
also does rational evidence, including justifying reasons.

Despite their plausibility, the revised principles ER, MR, and PR still allow for conflicts of rational obligation. In the next section I aim to provide, among other things, a resolution of rational conflicts in terms of what may be called "all-things-considered" rationality.

3. ALL-THINGS-CONSIDERED RATIONALITY

In a typical rational dilemma we are forced to ask whether we should believe in accordance with our epistemic (justifying) evidence for the belief that p or in accordance with our moral (justifying) evidence for the belief that $-p$. Although a question of this sort motivates the usual disputes over the ethics of belief, I find such a question to be unintelligibly ambiguous. For the key term 'should' has been left quite unclear. Given some of the distinctions drawn above, we can clarify the present question in at least three ways:

(3)   In order to be *epistemically* rational, should we believe that p, or should we believe that $-p$?

(4)   In order to be *morally* rational, should we believe that p, or should we believe that $-p$?

(5)   In order to be *prudentially* rational, should we believe that p, or should we believe that $-p$?

These reformulations of our question are necessary insofar as they specify whether 'should' has an epistemic, moral, or prudential sense. Lacking such a specification, our initial question, 'What should we believe?', is at best perplexing. But once this question is disambiguated in terms of (3)–(5), it no longer perplexes. The obvious answer to (3) is that we epistemically should believe that p, rather than that $-p$, since, by hypothesis, the belief that p, and not the belief that $-p$, is epistemically justified. And the obvious answer to (4) is that we morally should believe that $-p$, rather than that p, since, by hypothesis, the belief that $-p$, and not the belief that p, is morally justified. As for question (5), a similarly natural answer is available: If the belief that p, rather than the belief that $-p$, is prudentially justified, then, in the present case, we prudentially should believe that p (assuming, of course, that the conditions set by PR are met). Consequently, when reformulated in terms of (3)–(5), our initial question is quite manageable.

However, the present strategy seems to be ultimately dissatisfying. For our initial question leads automatically to the question whether, in cases of rational conflict, we should be epistemically, morally, or prudentially rational. Yet here again, it should be noticed, we are faced with a gravely ambiguous use of 'should'. Thus, one might be tempted again to propose that once 'should' is disambiguated, the following obvious answers emerge: (i) if 'should' is epistemic, then epistemic rationality receives priority; (ii) if 'should' is moral, then moral rationality deserves priority; and (iii) if 'should' is prudential, then prudential rationality must be given priority.[6] So much seems true by virtue of the respective notions of 'should'.

Why, then, have philosophers, at least since the time of the celebrated Clifford—James exchange, found the question of what we should believe to be perplexing? Does this perplexity rest solely on an ambiguity? W. K. Clifford, among others, has suggested that we have a *moral* obligation to believe only what is likely to be true on our evidence.[7] But Clifford appears to have confused moral and epistemic obligation. In any case, he fails to account for cases where one's believing a proposition *un*likely to be true is morally advantageous, and one's believing a proposition likely to be true is morally *dis*advantageous. (The above example of Ed and Edna provides one such case.) Perhaps Clifford's view will be defended on the ground that one's believing what is unlikely to be true is always "self-deceptive". But it is doubtful that such a charge can be sustained. For in believing-true a proposition unlikely to be true, one can honestly and consistently acknowledge that the proposition is unlikely to be true, but still believe the proposition to be true on moral or prudential grounds.

Brand Blanshard, however, has claimed that in believing-true a proposition unlikely to be true, we would be self-deceptive at least insofar as we would be telling ourselves that "we might justifiably take [the proposition] as true, whereas on the evidence before us we could not".[8] But Blanshard's accusation hides the crucial distinctions between epistemic, moral, and prudential justification and evidence. If we properly qualify Blanshard's use of 'justifiably' with 'epistemically', his argument clearly fails; for a person believing an unlikely proposition on moral or prudential grounds need not misrepresent the nature of his reasons. On the other hand, if we modify 'justifiably' with 'morally' or 'prudentially', and continue to assume that 'evidence' means 'epistemic evidence', then Blanshard's accusation is similarly unfounded. For in that case there is not even the appearance of self-deception, if by 'self-deception' we mean one's concealing the truth from oneself. Admittedly, in the envisaged case, one would be believing against one's epistemic evidence, but it does not thereby follow that one is doing so self-deceptively. There seems, then, not to be anything inherently immoral about one's believing, on moral or prudential grounds, a proposition unlikely to be true on one's evidence.

In opposition to Clifford's view, H. H. Price has argued that there are no good grounds — I presume he means 'epistemic grounds' — for thinking that we sometimes have a *moral* obligation to believe certain things. (At the same time, however, Price holds that we prudentially should believe certain things.[9]) Price introduces (pp. 206–207) an important distinction which might undercut many of the apparent examples of morally obligatory belief: the distinction between one's having a moral obligation to believe that *p*, and one's having a moral obligation to *act as if* one believed that *p*. Perhaps in many cases where it appears that we have a moral obligation to believe that *p*, we simply have a moral obligation to act as if we believed that *p*. But it is doubtful that this is true of all cases. For, at least in some cases, a person's beliefs are linked with his actions in such a way that were the beliefs not held, the person would be guilty of moral irresponsibility. The forementioned example of Ed and Edna provides a realistic illustration of this point. Thus, insofar as a belief is essential to one's morally responsible conduct, we can plausibly regard that belief as morally obligatory.

Price's only objection to the moral obligatoriness of beliefs is as follows: "If we are to be allowed, or even encouraged, to blame [people] for the way they direct their thoughts, as well as for their actions, there will be a perfect orgy of moral indignation and condemnation" (pp. 214–215). But this objection altogether misses its target, since we can plausibly distinguish between a person's having morally obligatory beliefs and a person's having a right to blame others for their beliefs. Certainly the former does not require the latter. It might be, for instance, that one has morally obligatory beliefs, but that the morality of one's believing is not open to assessment by others, since it depends on considerations available only to the believer. In any event, since Price does not show that the morality of believing requires that others have a right to blame, his objection is at best inconclusive. Thus, we can plausibly persist in our talk of the morally rational obligation of believing.[10]

But what now remains of the ethics of belief? We have seen thus far that, contrary to common philosophical opinion, it is not intelligible to ask simply what one should believe, or simply whether one should be epistemically, morally, or prudentially rational in one's believing. The use of 'should' in such questions is unintelligibly ambiguous, and once the ambiguity is removed, as noted above, such questions cease to perplex. But this observation does not preclude the familiar questions whether it is prudentially rational to be epistemically or morally rational, and whether it is morally rational to be epistemically rational. Such questions are quite intelligible, given the above characterizations of epistemic, moral, and prudential rationality. But it is highly doubtful that such questions lend themselves to simple 'yes' answers. For the above example of Ed and Edna indicates that one's being epistemically rational can conflict with one's being morally and prudentially rational.

Let us ask then whether we can resolve conflicts of rational obligation by introducing a kind of rationality broader than epistemic, moral, and prudential rationality: "all-things-considered" rationality (or 'ATC rationality' for short). A natural proposal is that in cases of rational conflict, one should conduct one's believing in accordance with ATC rationality. But what exactly is such rationality? Or, to raise a more specific, two-pronged question: *What* are the things to be considered in cases of rational conflict, and *how* are they to be considered? Clearly, if ATC rationality is to resolve rational conflicts, it will have to prescribe how we are to consider, or weigh, the relevant conflicting evidence, whether it be epistemic, moral, or prudential. Further, it is clear that the principles of epistemic, moral, and prudential rationality, such as ER, MR, and PR, are unable, in and of themselves, to provide a resolution of rational conflicts. For the content of such principles provides no basis for the comparative assessment of conflicting kinds of evidence. The content of principles of ATC rationality, in contrast, must provide such a basis.

Note also that if ATC rationality is not to be equivalent to epistemic, moral, or prudential rationality in cases of rational conflict, then it must not require that epistemic, moral, or prudential evidence is necessarily overriding in such cases. For given such a requirement, ATC rationality would always prescribe, in cases of rational conflict, just what is prescribed by the less general sort of rationality that is necessarily overriding. Thus, ATC rationality would not really be a distinct sort of rationality in cases of rational conflict. If it is to be genuinely distinctive, then, ATC rationality must allow for the *possibility* of each less general sort of rationality being overridden in an instance of rational conflict. Furthermore, ATC rationality, if it is to be distinctive, must allow for a conflict of rational obligations which is not resolved just in virtue of the sorts of rational obligation in conflict. For in disallowing this, ATC rationality would again be equivalent, in cases of rational conflict, to the less general sort of rationality that withstands conflicts. Thus, if ATC rationality is to be a special sort of rationality, it must require the consideration of factors other than the particular rational obligations in conflict.

Note that it is not now very helpful to propose simply that in cases of rational conflict, ATC rationality requires one to decide in accordance with what is "best for one all things considered".[11] For the notion of "best" here is infected with the same three-way ambiguity that typically characterizes 'should', 'evidence', and 'rational'; in short, there is (at least) epistemic, moral, and prudential bestness.

Yet one might naturally propose that the notion of "best" be construed more broadly. On this proposal the talk of a belief that is "best for one all things considered" might be taken to refer to that belief which is conducive to the satisfaction of the greater number of one's preferences (regardless of whether the preferences are epistemic, moral, or prudential). But it is highly doubtful that such a purely quantitative account of bestness is acceptable. For some preferences are (justifiably) much more valuable to a person than are others; and one might (rationally) prefer the satisfaction of these more important preferences, even if this precludes the satisfaction of a greater number of less important preferences. Thus, on the present proposal, we are led to a qualitative ranking of one's preferences, and candidate preference-fulfilling beliefs, in terms of their relative importance.

It is quite plausible, I find, to let a person's own preferences determine the relative importance of his candidate preference-fulfilling beliefs. Thus, let us consider the following principle:

AR.   If a rational obligation of one sort — call it O_e — prescribes that S should believe that p, and a rational obligation of a different sort — call it O_m — prescribes that S should deny (withhold) that p (and S has no other particular rational obligations bearing on his believing, denying, or withholding that p), then S is ATC rationally obligated to fulfill O_e rather than O_m if and only if (i) the fulfillment of O_e is more likely than the fulfillment of O_m, on S's total evidence, to satisfy S's superior preference, (ii) the fulfillment of O_e is more likely than the fulfillment of neither O_e nor O_m, on S's total evidence, to satisfy S's superior preference, and (iii) S is capable of coming to recognize the truth of (i) and (ii) from reflection on his evidence.[12]

Let us understand a preference to be a desire related either to a goal or to a means to a goal. Thus, let us say that S prefers, for instance, to resolve a rational conflict by fulfilling O_e rather than O_m if and only if S desires to fulfill O_e rather than O_m. S's desiring to fulfill O_e rather than O_m, as I understand it, is just S's desiring to make true the proposition that he will fulfill O_e rather than O_m. Further, I take the desiring-to-make-true relation to involve at least a form of wanting to make true a proposition; thus preference in its present comparative sense should be taken to involve a pro-attitude of favoring the truth of one proposition over another. But I shall not digress here on the details concerning the objects of preference.[13]

With regard to S's individual preferences, the notion of a *superior* preference is to be understood roughly as follows: Preference P_1 is preferentially superior to preference P_2 for S if and only if when P_1 comes into conflict with P_2 for S, insofar as both cannot be satisfied for S, then S will prefer to fulfill P_1 rather than P_2. (This criterion of superiority will be refined somewhat below.) It might be the case, however, that although P_1 is preferentially superior to P_2 for S, S would prefer to satisfy P_2 & P_3 rather than P_1 in a case of conflict. In such a case, let us say that the conjunctive preference P_2 & P_3 is preferentially superior to P_1 for S. More generally, then, let us say roughly that one possibly conjunctive preference is preferentially superior for S to another possibly conjunctive preference if and only if in a case of conflict S would prefer the satisfaction of the former to the latter. (Note that since one's preferences are susceptible to change, these remarks on superiority are to be relativized to a time.) Given the present approach, S's own preferences determine preferential superiority for him, insofar as they will provide, in cases of conflict, a ranking of S's preferences in terms of relative importance to S. Thus, on the present construal of AR, we can avoid the inadequacies of a purely quantitative approach to preference-satisfaction.

Let us try to clarify AR further by anticipating some likely objections. It might be objected, first of all, that in a case of rational dilemma, one ATC rationally should fulfill neither of the conflicting rational obligations. More specifically, it might be proposed that when O_e prescribes that one should believe that p, and O_m prescribes that one should deny that p, then one ATC rationally should withhold p. This latter proposal, it should be noted, is only superficially analogous to the familiar epistemological view that when p and $-p$ are supported by epistemic evidence of equal strength, one epistemically should withhold that p. Further, such a proposal, like the general objection at hand, is seriously inadequate. For there are cases of rational conflict, as noted in connection with the example of Ed and Edna, where O_e prescribes that one should believe that p, and O_m prescribes that one should either withhold or deny that p.[14] In such cases one *must* choose between the conflicting rational obligations. Further, in conforming to the present objection, one would fail to fulfill at least two rational obligations in a case of rational conflict. But given AR, a person will typically fail to fulfill *at most* one rational obligation in a case of two-way conflict, since typically the fulfillment of one of the conflicting obligations is likely to satisfy one's superior preference. And, all things considered, it is typically rationally preferable for a person to fulfill one, rather than neither, of two conflicting rational obligations. For these reasons, AR is impervious to the objection at hand.

But the present objection does suggest a noteworthy case. Suppose that the fulfillment of O_e and the fulfillment of O_m are equally likely, on S's total evidence, to satisfy S's superior preference, that S's fulfilling neither O_e nor O_m is not likely to satisfy his superior preference, and that S recognizes this. What then is it ATC rational for S to do? I submit that in such a case S would be ATC rationally obligated to fulfill *either* O_e *or* O_m, even though S would be ATC rationally obligated neither to fulfill O_e nor to fulfill O_m. For in such a case it is false that the fulfillment of one of the obligations is more likely than the fulfillment of the other to satisfy S's superior preference; however, S's failure to fulfill O_e and to fulfill O_m would be less likely than the fulfillment of either O_e or O_m to satisfy S's superior preference.[15] Yet we can imagine a case where S's failing to fulfill O_e and to fulfill O_m is more likely, on S's total evidence, to satisfy his superior preference than is S's fulfilling either O_e or O_m, and where S recognizes as much. In such a case it is false that S is ATC rationally obligated to fulfill either O_e or O_m.

Note that AR does not imply that in a case of two-way conflict, a person ATC rationally should choose to fulfill *both* conflicting rational obligations. But the assumption here is not that necessarily one is ATC irrational if one chooses to believe contradictory propositions. Suppose, for instance, that O_e prescribes that one should believe that p, and O_m prescribes that one should believe that $-p$, and one's superior preference is, strangely enough, to believe contradictory propositions in cases of rational conflict. In such a case a person could very well be ATC rationally obligated to believe a contradictory proposition. This implication of AR suggests the question whether one can have a superior preference which is logically impossible to satisfy, but which nonetheless determines what is ATC rational for one. It seems plain enough that a superior preference determining what is ATC rational can be useless to society, morally outrageous, and highly unlikely to be satisfied given all available evidence. And I propose that such a preference might also be logically impossible to satisfy. For something that is logically impossible can be likely, on one's evidence, not to be logically impossible. The history of mathematics provides familiar cases of this. (Consider, for instance, a mathematician living during Hobbes' time whose superior preference is to square the circle.) It seems implausible, therefore, to place a logical possibility constraint on the satisfaction of one's superior preference.[16]

But I do not intend to suggest that by believing contradictory propositions, one might fulfill *both* of two conflicting rational obligations. On the contrary, I find that one cannot fulfill both of two such obligations. Consider again the case where O_e prescribes that one believe that p, while O_m prescribes that one believe that $-p$. Were one to believe that p *and* that $-p$, one would only violate both rational obligations in one obvious way. Assuming that obligation O_e is epistemic, it requires, at least implicitly, that one *not* believe that $-p$; this seems clear once we acknowledge that O_e is just a particular instance of one's general epistemic obligation to believe those *and only those* propositions likely to be true on one's evidence (assuming of course that the forementioned condition concerning relative epistemic significance has been met). And directly analogous points hold for the fulfillment of morally and prudentially rational obligations in cases of conflict. Thus, if ATC rationality required the fulfillment of both of two conflicting rational obligations, it would require the violation of both such obligations. Although, as noted above, ATC rationality allows for such violation, it is implausible to suppose that it always requires it.

Anticipating another objection to AR, we can imagine someone proposing that in cases of rational conflict, one ATC rationally should decide between the conflicting obligations on the basis of the preferences of all those concerned, rather than on the basis of simply one's own superior preference. On this proposal, what is ATC rational is determined by the preferences of all those affected by one's cognitive decision.[17]

I believe two considerations show the present general view to be inferior to AR. First, it is unrealistic to require a person to base his cognitive decisions on the preferences of all those affected by those decisions. For typically a person is quite unable to determine who exactly will be affected by his decisions. This is due to one's typical inability to determine all the consequences of one's decisions. And a similar point holds even if we revise the requirement to concern the majority of those affected. It seems implausible, then, to hold that ATC rationality requires one to base one's cognitive decisions on the preferences of all or even the majority of those affected.

It might be proposed, in reply, that ATC rationality requires one to base one's cognitive decisions, in cases of rational conflict, on the preferences of all those whom one *knows* to be affected. This, I grant, is an improvement, but it nonetheless faces the second problem anticipated above. Aside from the complicated issue of just *how* one should base one's cognitive decisions on known preferences, there is the problem that it is not rational in any obvious way always to fulfill the preferences of everyone, or even the majority, known to be affected by one's cognitive decision. Sometimes those known to be affected have blatantly inconsistent preferences, and ordinarily in such cases it would hardly be rational in any straightforward sense to choose to fulfill those preferences. Consequently, one might be led to revise the present view to concern only the *consistent* preferences of those known to be affected. This, again, is an improvement, but as before it does not go far enough. For, aside from the question of which consistent set of preferences should be fulfilled, it is still quite unclear that it would be more rational for one to fulfill the consistent preferences of others than to fulfill one's own superior preference. In fact, it is not clear that it would be rational *at all*, at least in some cases, to fulfill the consistent preferences of others. Consider the person whose superior preference is inconsistent with the consistent preferences of those known to be affected by his cognitive decision. If such a person were ATC rationally required to fulfill the consistent preferences of those known to be affected, then such a person would be required to make a cognitive decision inconsistent with his superior preference. ATC rationality would thus require inconsistency. Insofar as this is an implausible requirement, AR is to be preferred to the proposal under consideration.

Yet one might elaborate on the present objection by proposing further that in many instances a person's superior preference *should* be changed. This apparently is a common assumption, even though it seems quite unclear. Note, however, that if 'should' has an epistemic, moral, or prudential sense, then there is little reason to question the objection. For in that case the objection, in connection with the moral 'should' for example, amounts to the relatively uncontroversial claim that, in conflicts involving moral obligation, one *morally* should decide in accordance with one's moral obligation − even if one has a superior preference to fulfill one's conflicting prudential obligation. I readily grant this latter claim, but deny that it threatens AR; for this claim does not imply that one ATC rationally should decide in accordance with one's moral obligation. Moreover, there appears to be no sound argument showing that moral obligations − or epistemic or prudential obligations, for that matter − are always, all things considered, overriding in cases of rational conflict. And if ATC rationality is, as I have proposed in effect, a matter basically of one's doing the best one can relative to the satisfaction of one's superior preference given one's evidence, then it is doubtful that there can be such an argument.

Another, more forceful objection to AR stems from the following possible case. S decides to resolve a conflict between O_e and O_m by fulfilling O_m rather than O_e, since he recognizes that the fulfillment of O_m is more likely than not only the fulfillment of O_e, but also the fulfillment of neither O_m nor O_e to satisfy his superior preference, P. Now, S has P, as it turns out, only because of an epistemically *un*justified belief that (the satisfaction of) P is required by the achievement of his more general end E. The satisfaction of P is actually in no logical or epistemic way linked to the achievement of E, and, what's more, S's own evidence indicates as much. The question, then, is whether what is ATC rational for S can rest on such an epistemically unjustified belief. It seems not. For in a case involving such epistemically unjustified belief, we can plausibly say that S ATC should not have had P; after all, P is obviously inappropriately related to the desired end E. We need, then, to revise AR by requiring that S's superior preference not depend for its existence on an epistemically unjustified belief of S's.[18]

Although one can clearly be ATC irrational because of a decision based on an epistemically unjustified belief, it might be wondered whether, given AR, there is any other way in which one might be ATC irrational. Consider, in this connection, the following case. S prefers to fulfill O_m rather than O_e in a case of conflict, since he recognizes that the fulfillment of O_m is more likely than the fulfillment of O_e, as well as the fulfillment of neither O_m nor O_e, to satisfy his ultimate superior preference. But actually S decides to fulfill O_e rather than O_m because of, say, his weakness of will. Such a case of weakness of will can be developed in at least two ways. Either S might decide to fulfill O_e rather than O_m without any preference to do so, or S might prefer to fulfill O_e rather than O_m while preferring at the same time to fulfill O_m rather than O_e. In the former case S would clearly be ATC irrational, given AR, to decide to fulfill O_e rather than O_m; for the fulfillment of O_e, by hypothesis, is not appropriately related, in the way specified by AR, to the satisfaction of S's superior preference. But in the latter case S will have apparently contrary preferences; he will prefer to fulfill O_m rather than O_e, *and* he will prefer to fulfill O_e rather than O_m. I say '*apparently* contrary preferences', since it seems that typically in such a case of weakness of will, two different kinds of preference are involved: *evaluative* and *motivational*.[19] Evaluatively S, we may say, prefers to fulfill O_m rather than O_e, but due to weakness of will he motivationally prefers to fulfill O_e rather than O_m. S's preference to fulfill O_m rather than O_e qualifies as evaluative for S insofar as it arises from his evaluative ranking of his possibly conflicting objectives, or, more specifically, from his related belief (or at least his disposition to believe in the case of unconscious preference) that he ATC ought to prefer to fulfill O_m rather than O_e in the present case of conflict (where such a ranking and belief do not depend on any epistemically unjustified belief of S's). And S's preference to fulfill O_e rather than O_m qualifies as motivational for S in the envisaged circumstances insofar as it is the preference that generates his actual cognitive decision.

In the imagined case it is clearly ATC irrational for S to decide to fulfill O_e rather than O_m. For such a decision is inconsistent with S's superior evaluative preference, and thus with his evaluative ranking of rational obligations on the basis of his ordered objectives. More specifically, on the basis of AR we can say that S's preference to fulfill O_e rather than O_m is ATC irrational because it is not appropriately linked, in the manner specified by AR, to S's superior evaluative preference.

Given the latter preference, S ATC rationally should motivationally prefer, and should decide, to fulfill O_m rather than O_e.

S's superior evaluative preference, then, is not necessarily motivational; that is, it does not necessarily move S to act in accordance with it. For, while determining what is ATC rational for S, such a preference does not preclude S's having weakness of will. Thus, such a preference does not preclude S's being ATC irrational. It follows further that AR does not imply that just any cognitive decision will qualify as ATC rational for a person.

But none of the present considerations implies that evaluative preferences have no motivational force. Indeed, it is plausible to assume that, barring weakness of will, a rational agent will typically be motivated to fulfill his superior evaluative preference. (I cannot digress though on the various accounts of motivation that can explain this assumption.) But insofar as weakness of will is a real possibility, we should construe a superior preference as an evaluative pro-attitude that might not engender an ATC rational decision. In short, we should distinguish one preference's being *evaluatively superior* to another from the former's being *motivationally stronger* than the latter. An alternative view states that a preference, P_1, is evaluatively superior to another preference, P_2, if and only if P_1 is motivationally stronger than P_2. But this view is wrong on both its necessary and its sufficient condition. Its necessary condition implausibly rules out the possibility of irrational weakness of will, and its sufficient condition makes many obviously irrational impulsive preferences ATC rational. By maintaining a clear distinction between evaluative superiority and motivational strength, we can happily avoid such implausible consequences. (Hereafter, then, my talk of preferences will concern evaluative preferences unless otherwise indicated.)

A final objection to AR is that it fails to account for cases where there is a three-way rational dilemma: a rational trilemma. In one such trilemma, a person has an epistemic obligation to withhold that p, a moral obligation to deny that p, and a prudential obligation to believe that p. It is clear that AR fails explicitly to account not only for such cases, but also for cases where two or more rational obligations prescribe that one believe that p, while a smaller number of such obligations prescribe that one deny or withhold that p. (Clearly it is implausible to hold that in cases of the latter sort, one ATC rationally should decide to fulfill the greater number of obligations; for obviously the fulfillment of the majority of obligations might be quite insignificant and so preferentially inferior to the fulfillment of the minority.) I believe that AR suggests a natural way to accommodate such cases. Consider this generalization of AR, which incorporates the needed revision discussed above:

AR*   In a case of rational conflict of any sort, S has an ATC rational obligation to fulfill a particular obligation, O_i, if and only if (i) the fulfillment of O_i is likely (*i.e.*, more likely than not), on S's total evidence, to satisfy his superior evaluative preference, which does not depend on an epistemically unjustified belief of S's, and (ii) S is capable of coming to recognize the truth of (i) from reflection on his evidence.

Note that AR* is similar in form to ER, MR, and PR. AR* also resembles those particular principles insofar as it is not purely subjective; it does not base ATC rationality for S on what S merely believes about his superior preference's satisfaction. In addition, AR* is sufficiently general to apply to rational conflicts more complicated than two-way dilemmas. The upshot of AR*, roughly, is that ATC rationality is determined by what is likely to provide superior-preference satisfaction, in the sense that the fulfillment of a particular rational obligation is ATC rationally obligatory for one when and only when it is likely to satisfy one's superior preference, and one can come to know this on the basis of one's evidence. Further, AR* allows for the possibility that the fulfillment of O_i is ATC rationally obligatory for a person in one context, but not in another, due perhaps to a change of superior preference or to the relevance of additional conflicting rational obligations.

Several questions about AR* must be anticipated. First, it should be asked whether one must prefer to fulfill an ATC rational obligation if one is to be ATC rational or irrational with respect to its fulfillment or violation. Let us approach this question by means of an example. Suppose S is faced with a rational dilemma involving a morally rational obligation, O_m, and an epistemically rational obligation, O_e. Since O_m and O_e are rational obligations for S, S has either general or specific preferences whose satisfaction is evidently provided for by the fulfillment of O_m and O_e. The relevant general preferences might simply be S's preference to fulfill all his moral obligations, and his preference to fulfill all his epistemic obligations (where these preferences do not depend on any epistemically unjustified belief of S's). Note that S might fail to prefer to fulfill the particular obligations O_m and O_e, perhaps because of an epis-

234 CHAPTER VI

temically unjustified belief about them; but given the forementioned
general preferences of S's, it would still be proper to say that O_m and O_e
are (*prima facie*) rational obligations for S. If we suppose, however, that
S has no such general preferences, then it will be in virtue of specific
preferences of S's that O_m and O_e are (*prima facie*) rational obligations
for S. These specific preferences might be simply S's preferences to
fulfill O_m and to fulfill O_e, or some other specific preferences whose
satisfaction is evidently provided for by the fulfillment of O_m and O_e
(where, again, the relevant preferences do not rest on any epistemically
unjustified belief of S's).

Now let us suppose that S's fulfilling O_m is more likely than not to
fulfill his superior preference, P, which does not rest on any epistemically unjustified belief, and S recognizes as much. In such a case, given
AR*, S will be ATC rationally obligated to fulfill O_m rather than O_e. For
assuming that the fulfillment of O_m and the fulfillment of O_e are incompatible, as is typical in a case of rational dilemma, the fact that the fulfillment of O_m is likely to satisfy P entails that the fulfillment of O_e is not
likely to satisfy P; it also entails that the fulfillment of neither O_m nor O_e
is not likely to satisfy P, for the fulfillment of neither O_m nor O_e is
incompatible with the fulfillment of O_m. But of course S's only options
in a case of rational dilemma involving O_m and O_e are (i) to fulfill O_m
rather than O_e; (ii) to fulfill O_e rather than O_m; and (iii) to fulfill neither
O_m nor O_e. And if option (i)'s being more likely than not to satisfy P
entails (i)'s being more likely than (ii) and (iii) to satisfy P, then (i), in
virtue of being more likely than not to satisfy P, will be the *most* likely of
all of S's possible options to satisfy P in the envisaged situation. And in
requiring (i) of S, AR* requires that S do what is most likely of all his
possible options to satisfy p in the envisaged situation. More generally,
then, we can understand AR* as requiring that in cases of rational
dilemma S should do the best he can, given his evidence, to satisfy his
superior evaluative preference.

Returning, then, to the question whether S must prefer to fulfill the
obligation O_m if he is to be ATC rationally required to fulfill O_m, we can
now see that the answer is 'no'. It is sufficient for S's being ATC rationally required to fulfill O_m that the fulfillment of O_m be more likely than
not to satisfy S's superior preference, P, which does not rest on any epistemically unjustified belief, and that S be capable of coming to recognize
this from reflection on his evidence. Yet it is worth stressing that given
the above account of superior preference, one *will* evaluatively prefer to

satisfy one's superior preference. And it is one's superior preference (when it does not rest on any epistemically unjustified belief) that determines, in the manner specified by AR*, what is ATC rational for a person.

The next question is whether one of two conflicting rational obligations is overridden, or defeated, when the fulfillment of the other is ATC rationally obligatory. The most plausible answer is that the first of the two obligations would be overridden as a *rational* obligation, by an ATC rational obligation, even though it would not be overridden as a binding nonrational obligation. Suppose, for instance, that I find myself in a rational dilemma where a morally rational obligation conflicts with an epistemically rational obligation, and, in accordance with what is ATC rational for me, I decide to fulfill my epistemically rational obligation rather than my morally rational obligation. In such a situation, I could not properly be called *irrational,* even though I would qualify as immoral. For ATC rationality overrides my moral obligation as a *rational* obligation, even though not as a *moral* obligation. More generally, once we distinguish obligations as rationally binding and obligations as morally, epistemically, or prudentially binding, the question at hand admits of a straightforward answer.

A final question is whether ATC rationality as presented by AR* can be said to be commendatory or normative. It seems plain enough that it can. Admittedly, ATC rationality does not provide us with a system of categorical imperatives. But it does provide one with a system of hypothetical imperatives relative to one's ordered system of evaluative preferences, or more specifically, relative to one's possibly conjunctive superior evaluative preference. On the basis of AR*, we can properly say of a rational agent, S, that given his superior evaluative preference, P, and his evidence concerning P, S ATC rationally should fulfill O_i (assuming of course that O_i meets the requirements set by AR*). Or, more schematically, on the basis of AR* we can regard ATC rational cognitive decisions as being supported by sound reasoning of the following form:

1.   S has a superior evaluative preference to satisfy P.
2.   S's believing that *p* is likely, given S's evidence, to satisfy P.
3.   Hence, S ATC rationally should believe that *p.*

This form of reasoning is somewhat oversimplified, but in light of the above qualifications it provides a straightforward pattern displaying the logical structure of ATC rational cognitive decisions. One obvious lesson of this pattern is that a person's cognitive decisions are ATC rational or irrational relative to his evidence and his superior evaluative preference. This point underlies the earlier observation that ATC rationality provides one with a system of hypothetical rational imperatives. And insofar as ATC rationality does so, it can be said to be hypothetically normative and commendatory.

In conclusion, then, I recommend AR* on the ground that it provides a straightforward, intuitively plausible account of all-things-considered rationality as one's doing the best one can given one's evidence and one's superior evaluative preference. In the end, it is quite difficult to see what else such rationality could plausibly require of one; and this consideration itself speaks in favor of AR*. Without much difficulty, it seems clear, AR* could be generalized to resolve practical rational dilemmas, dilemmas of so-called practical reasoning, in addition to cognitive rational dilemmas of varying complexity. But that of course is a task for another occasion. Perhaps the most important lesson of the present discussion, however, is that it is erroneous to assume that an account of epistemic justification, by itself, can provide a full explanation of rational belief.

NOTES

[1] I assume that a person can exercise indirect control over various beliefs by many means, including his choosing to undergo hypnosis and his bringing about or his refusing to consider some state of affairs. Thus, with respect to the case of Ed and Edna, we might imagine Ed refusing to consider the evidence indicating that Edna is disloyal. For useful discussion of the voluntary basis of belief see R. M. Chisholm, 'Lewis' Ethics of Belief', in *The Philosophy of C. I. Lewis*, ed. Paul Schilpp (Open Court, La Salle, Illinois, 1968), pp. 223–227, and H. H. Price, 'Belief and Will', in R. F. Dearden *et al.* (eds.) *Reason* (Routledge & Kegan Paul, London, 1975), pp. 208–213; cf. John Heil, 'Believing What One Ought', *Journal of Philosophy* **80** (1983), 752–764. It should be noted, however, that rational dilemmas need not be belief-oriented. We could easily modify the above example of Ed and Edna in such a way that Ed has an epistemically rational obligation to pursue further evidence relevant to the proposition that Edna is disloyal, but also has a morally rational obligation not to pursue such evidence. For those opposed to doxastic voluntarism of any sort, I recommend such a modification; yet if only for ease of expression I shall speak as though belief is at least indirectly voluntary. In addition, I shall assume with respect to rational obligation that "ought" implies "can".

[2] For discussion of this normative approach to epistemic permissibility, see Hilary Kornblith, 'Justified Belief and Epistemically Responsible Action', *Philosophical Review* **92** (1983), 33–48, and my paper 'Pure Enquirers and Epistemic Values' (forthcoming).

Cf. R. M. Chisholm, *Theory of Knowledge, 2d ed.*(Prentice-Hall, Englewood Cliffs, New Jersey, 1977), p. 14, and Chapter IV above.

[3] To avoid problems from lottery-style paradoxes, let us restrict the present remarks about probability to individual propositions, thus excluding sets of propositions. Note further that my talk of likelihood and chance does not commit one to giving quantitative probability assignments to propositions; nonnumerical comparative probability assignments may be all one needs. Thus, when I say that a proposition, p, is likely, I typically mean that p is more likely to be true than is $-p$. For some of the details concerning the general kind of probability relevant to the present remarks see Henry Kyburg, 'Epistemological Probability', in *Epistemology and Inference* (University of Minnesota Press, Minneapolis, 1983), pp. 204–216. And see the second section of Chapter I above for elaboration on the relation of justification to probability.

[4] A full account of moral obligation would require of course an explanation of the quantitative individuation and qualitative ranking of moral advantages. Obviously I cannot take up such an explanation here.

[5] It should be noticed that the analogue of note 4 regarding prudential obligation applies here.

[6] Note that analogous answers might be given to the analogous question, 'How are we rationally to resolve conflicts of rational obligation?' Once we disambiguate 'rationally' as above, the answers seem obvious.

[7] See Clifford, 'The Ethics of Belief', in L. Stephen and F. Pollock (eds.), *Lectures and Essays* (Macmillan, London, 1879), reprinted in B. Brody (ed.), *Readings in the Philosophy of Religion*, (Prentice-Hall, Englewood Cliffs, New Jersey, 1974), pp. 241–247.

[8] Blanshard, *Reason and Belief* (Allen & Unwin, London, 1974), p. 424.

[9] See Price, 'Belief and Will', in *Reason*, pp. 213–217. In effect, therefore, Price aims to replace the *ethics* of belief with the *economics* of belief.

[10] For additional arguments supporting this claim see Alex Michalos, 'The Morality of Cognitive Decision-Making', in M. Brand and D. Walton (eds.), *Action Theory*, (D. Reidel, Dordrecht, 1976), pp. 325–340, and Jack Meiland, 'What Ought We to Believe?, or The Ethics of Belief Revisited', *American Philosophical Quarterly* **17** (1980), 15–24.

[11] This notion has been invoked, for instance, by Donald Davidson, 'Paradoxes of Irrationality', in R. Wollheim and J. Hopkins (eds.), *Philosophical Essays on Freud* (Cambridge University Press, Cambridge, 1982), p. 297.

[12] There is of course a noteworthy complication due to the possibility of varying degrees of satisfaction of a preference. But I shall not bother with this complication here, since it can be easily accommodated by the following approach to preferential superiority, once we replace the unqualified talk of preference-satisfaction with talk of preference-satisfaction *to a certain degree*.

[13] For some useful discussion of the objects of preference see Richard Jeffrey, 'Preference Among Preferences', *Journal of Philosophy* **71** (1974), 377–391, reprinted in *The Logic of Decision, 2d ed.* (University of Chicago Press, Chicago, 1983), Appendix. See also David Braybrooke, 'Variety Among Hierarchies of Preference', in C. A. Hooker *et al.* (eds.), *Foundations and Applications of Decision Theory*, Vol. I. (D. Reidel, Dordrecht, 1978), pp. 55–65.

[14] Also, there are cases of three-way conflict between rational obligations, where believing, denying, and withholding that p are each required by some rational obligation

of a certain sort. In such cases the choice between rational obligations is unavoidable. I shall return to such cases below.

[15] Note that a similar consideration may be applied to cases where S has a couple of equally superior preferences, one of which is satisfied by the fulfillment of O_e, the other of which is satisfied by the fulfillment of O_m. For simplicity, however, I shall continue to focus on cases where a person has a single (possibly conjunctive) superior preference, while assuming that cases involving a plurality of such preferences can be handled in the way suggested above.

[16] Note, however, that we can still maintain, with respect to ATC rational obligations to believe a proposition, that "ought" implies "can". Clearly one's having a superior preference that is logically impossible to satisfy does not entail that one cannot believe any propositions the believing of which is likely, on one's evidence, to satisfy that preference; thus it does not entail that one cannot fulfill a rational obligation whose fulfillment is likely to satisfy that preference. Yet I do want to grant that in a case where a person is psychologically unable to believe against, say, his epistemic evidence and in accordance with his moral evidence, he will not have an ATC rational obligation to believe in accordance with his moral evidence. For support for my above assumption that one can believe contradictory propositions see John Williams, 'Believing the Self-Contradictory', *American Philosophical Quarterly* 19 (1982), 279–285.

[17] Such a view has definite affinities with so-called "preference utilitarianism" in ethics, according to which the moral rightness of an action is determined by the preferences of all those affected. See, for example, Peter Singer, *Practical Ethics* (Cambridge University Press, Cambridge, 1979), Chapters 1 and 2.

[18] Richard Brandt has also seen the importance of requiring that rational preferences not depend on unjustified beliefs; see *A Theory of the Good and the Right* (Clarendon Press, Oxford, 1979), Chapter 6. But Brandt's full requirement is excessively demanding, since it demands that a rational preference be unextinguishable in the face of repeated representation of all relevant scientifically available information. The problem of course is that rational agents rarely, if ever, can make use of all such information, since it is not typically part of their evidence base. For related criticisms of Brandt's account see Allan Gibbard, 'A Noncognitivistic Analysis of Rationality in Action', *Social Theory & Practice* 9 (1983), 203–206. The upshot of such criticisms of Brandt's account of rational decision-making is that it is excessively idealized. I believe a similar point applies to standard Bayesian decision-theoretic accounts of rationality. Cf. in this connection, Lanning Sowden, 'The Inadequacy of Bayesian Decision Theory', *Philosophical Studies* 45 (1984), 293–313.

[19] Such a distinction has been suggested by, among others, Gary Watson, 'Skepticism About Weakness of Will', *The Philosophical Review* 86 (1977), 316–339, especially 320–321; Cf. Alfred Mele, 'Akrasia, Reasons, and Causes', *Philosophical Studies* 44 (1983), 345–368. My present reliance on this distinction will lead to a resolution of rational dilemmas in terms of a rational agent's *evaluative* preferential hierarchy, rather than his motivational hierarchy. A suggested resolution in terms of one's motivational hierarchy can be found in H. -N. Castañeda, *Thinking and Doing* (D. Reidel, Dordrecht, 1975), Chapter 11, especially pp. 303–305. I object to such a resolution below.

JUSTIFICATION, RELIABILISM AND EXTERNALISM

According to Alvin Goldman and like-minded proponents of a reliability theory of epistemic justification, "the justificational status of a belief is a function of the reliability of the process or processes that cause it, where [roughly] reliability consists in the tendency of a process to produce beliefs that are true rather than false."[1] Let us call such a general view *epistemic reliabilism*, and its proponents *reliabilists*. Nowadays epistemic reliabilism comes in many different forms, due mainly to the ways the details of the theory are developed. But, in what follows, I shall isolate a thesis common to many, if not all, of the prominent versions of epistemic reliabilism, and I shall argue that this thesis is untenable. In effect, my argument will falsify a necessary condition for epistemic justification proposed by reliabilism. But, in addition, I shall argue that since the prominent versions of reliabilism are almost invariably conjoined with a view called *epistemic externalism*, those versions typically fail to accommodate an important necessary condition of epistemically justified belief. However, my argument in this connection aims to undercut *any* version of epistemic externalism. I turn first to the deficiencies germane to epistemic reliabilism.

1. A COUNTEREXAMPLE TO RELIABILISM

According to the prominent versions of epistemic reliabilism, beliefs which are epistemically justified must satisfy what we may call a *reliability requirement*.[2] Roughly speaking, the requirement is that a belief of a certain type (a 'P-belief' for short), such as a perceptual belief, is epistemically justified only if that belief is due (causally) to a reliable belief-producing source, process, or mechanism. (Hereafter, I use the term 'mechanism' broadly to refer also to belief-producing sources and processes.) A reliable belief-producing mechanism, again roughly speaking, is a causal basis of beliefs, such as perception, memory, sensation, etc., whose resultant beliefs would "generally be true" in normal circumstances.[3] A major task for the reliabilist is to characterize exactly what count as *normal* circumstances, specifically what count as

239

relevant counterfactual, or alternative, situations. And there is not at present a uniformly accepted resolution of this task. Yet, however the relevant notion of normal circumstances is characterized, the central requirement of epistemic reliabilism, as here defined, is that an epistemically justified belief must be produced by a reliable mechanism.

Now there is, it seems, a fairly straightforward complication facing epistemic reliabilism, however its details are developed. Consider the following logical possibility: There is a deceiving super-neuroscientist who sees to it that the overwhelming majority of our P-beliefs due to a mechanism, M, are, contrary to our best evidence, actually false.[4] Furthermore, this deceiver effects similar deceptive ploys in *all* the relevant counterfactual situations. Consequently, it is false that P-beliefs due to M would generally be true in normal circumstances. For the deceiver and its deceptive ploys are sufficiently prevalent, across the range of relevant possible situations, to merit the status of being normal. In fact, on the present scenario, the deceiver deceives with law-like regularity in the actual world and the relevant counterfactual situations. Such an unhappy scenario, it seems clear, is coherently conceivable and thus logically possible, even if improbable.

Now this question arises: Should the *mere existence* of the above-described deceiver (in the actual world and the relevant counterfactual situations) be taken as sufficient to preclude epistemic justification for the P-beliefs due to M? Contrary to the implication of the reliability requirement, it seems not. For even if the deceiver is successful in his deceptive ploys, we have, by hypothesis, no reason whatsoever to believe he is. In fact, the deceiver's deceptions, and even his existence for that matter, are a mere conceptual possibility relative to the evidence in the actual world. Thus, even if our P-beliefs due to M are generally false (in the actual world *and* the relevant counterfactual situations), because of the deceiver's law-like ploys, we lack any reason to endorse their unreliability. For, by hypothesis, from the standpoint of our actual evidence, the P-beliefs due to M *seem* to be reliable, at least insofar as they seem not to be generally false. After all, the deceiver is very clever and effective. (On the relevant notion of evidence see pages 200–203 above.)

Now under the imagined circumstances, we could, it seems, be nonetheless justified in holding P-beliefs due to M. For, first, in the imagined case, none of our evidence provides reason to believe that our P-beliefs are generally false. Second, we may assume that in the imagined case our P-beliefs have a central role in our most comprehensive and coherent explanatory account of the perceptual world. Our P-beliefs, to use Quine's metaphor, are at the center of our "web of explanatory beliefs." And, third, we might suppose that our current P-beliefs are sanctioned by our epistemic objective of trying our best to believe a proposition if and only if it is true. In light of these considerations, the epistemic justification of our P-beliefs evidently does *not* require that those beliefs be actually true or generally true, or even generally true in normal circumstances. Such forms of reliability seem quite unnecessary, given that even in the above-described case we could nonetheless have epistemic justification for our P-beliefs. But if this is so, we should reject what I have called the 'reliability requirement' for epistemically justified belief. And in doing so, we shall reject epistemic reliabilism as standardly conceived.

2. RELIABILISM REVISED

One easy but drastic way to alter the reliability requirement is suggested by Goldman's claim that "the reason we *count* beliefs as justified is that they are formed by what we *believe* to be reliable belief-forming processes".[5] The requirement suggested here applies not to beliefs which simply *are* justified, but rather to beliefs which we *take* to be justified. Thus, according to the suggested requirement, we *claim* a belief to be epistemically justified only if we *believe* it to be actually reliable, *i.e.*, produced by a reliable belief-producing mechanism. It should be obvious that this alternative to the above-discussed reliability requirement would severely change the face of epistemic reliabilism. Given this alternative requirement, epistemic reliabilism would be a view simply about beliefs which we *take to be justified*; it would have no bearing on beliefs which *merely are justified*.

But even the suggested alternative requirement appears to be too stringent. For consider a person, S, who takes his perceptual beliefs to be epistemically justified, but who worries about the epistemic implications of the (possible) existence of a deceiver of the sort described above. Now, S takes his perceptual beliefs to be justified on the ground that (i) none of his evidence counts against their being true, (ii) those beliefs are central to his most comprehensive and coherent explanatory account of the perceptual world, and (iii) those beliefs are sanctioned by his epistemic objective of trying his best to believe a proposition if and only if it is true. But, being cautious about the status of the above-described deceiver case, S takes his perceptual beliefs not to be reliable (in the sense of being produced by a reliable mechanism which generally produces ture beliefs in normal circumstances), but only fo be *probably* reliable. That is, S believes simply that his perceptual beliefs are *probably* due to a reliable belief-producing mechanism.

Of course S takes his perceptual beliefs *to be true*; for, generally, one believes that *p* if and only if one believes that *p is true*. But this is not the issue under dispute. The issue is whether, in taking his perceptual beliefs to be justified, S must conceive of those beliefs as being produced by a mechanism which *generally* produces true beliefs in normal circumstances (in the actual world and in the relevant counterfactual situations). I have suggested that S might take his perceptual beliefs to be epistemically justified, because of their satisfying conditions (i)—(iii) above, but conceive of those beliefs not as being actually reliable (in the relevant sense), but simply as being *probably* reliable. For while S holds his justified perceptual beliefs to be true in the actual world, he might be so cautious as to refrain from believing that those beliefs are due to a mechanism which generally produces true beliefs in the actual world and the relevant counterfactual situations. In such a case, S could simply be a non-reliabilist holding that epistemic justification consists mainly in the satisfaction of conditions (i)—(iii), and not in the reliability of belief-producing mechanisms.

Or, alternatively, we might take S to be in the position of the celebrated grandmother who believes on the basis of her "aching bones" that it will rain. The grandmother explains the origin of her belief that it will rain simply by remarking, 'I feel it in my bones.' So, let us assume that the grandmother's belief is due to the circumstances of her swollen joints, and thus that the relevant belief-producing mechanism is broadly sensory insofar as it is neuro-skeletal. And let us suppose that the grandmother recognizes as much, since she is in the old-fashioned habit of believing on the basis of her neuro-skeletal aches, at least when it comes to forecasting precipitation. However, the grandmother has come to recognize the faultiness of her neuro-skeletal belief-mechanism as of late, and so does *not* take her belief about forthcoming rain to be justified because of its being produced by a reliable belief-producing mechanism. Yet, the grandmother nonetheless takes her belief to be justified, perhaps because she heard it being corroborated by the local TV meteorologist, and because she is inclined to believe that what is corroborated by the local meteorologist is true and justified (since she has no reason to believe his reports are false or unjustified).

Now, since the present case, as well as the previous one, seem quite possible, we should be most reluctant to endorse the alternative reliability requirement, suggested by Goldman, that one claims a belief to be epistemically justified only if one conceives it to be actually reliable (in the sense defined earlier). This alternative requirement, like the first-mentioned reliability requirement, is ultimately too stringent.

3. THE CIRCULARITY OF RELIABILISM

I want next to consider another problem which challenges epistemic reliabilism, but which has been widely neglected by reliabilists. The lesson of the above-described deceiver case is that there is not a *conceptual* connection between epistemic justification and reliable belief-producing mechanisms. Perhaps, then, the reliabilist will propose that the relevant connection with reliable mechanisms is not conceptual but *empirical*; that epistemically justified beliefs are simply *in fact* due to reliable belief-producing mechanisms. If so, the reliabilist must face a threatening problem of circularity emphasized recently by Roderick Firth.[6] The problem is basically that if the reliabilist is to avoid circularity in establishing (perhaps inductively) the empirical connection between justified beliefs and mechanisms which generally produce true beliefs (in the relevant circumstances), he must find a way to identify true beliefs independently of his justified beliefs and justification-conferring rules. But the reliabilist is hard put to do this, since, of course, our beliefs do not come specially labeled 'true' and 'false.' How, then, can the vitiating circularity be avoided?

I know of only one attempt to defend reliabilism against the present charge of circularity. John Heil has provided the following concise defense:

The task of picking out reliable cognitive mechanisms is indeed an empirical one, but one that affords no special threat of circularity. To the extent that it is empirical, it is no more circular then [sic] are procedures for measuring visual acuity that themselves depend on the vision of those that design and administer them.[7]

More generally, Heil finds that the present worry about epistemic reliabilism is a "red herring."[8]

Aside from whether the hunting dogs have been distracted, it is not at all clear how the present charge of the circularity of reliabilism is undercut by noting that similar circularity characterizes procedures for measuring visual acuity. It will be instructive, in this connection, to recall the general clinical procedure for measuring visual acuity, in order to assess the suggested analogy. The procedure uses a familiar Snellen chart to test the function of the fovea, the most sensitive part of the retina. The use of such a chart rests on the assumption that the component letters, 'E', 'F', 'P', 'T', etc., which (in the ophthalmologist's jargon) subtend an angle of five minutes of arc at the eye's nodal point, can be identified "appropriately" by the "normal eye." (It turns out, interestingly, that many and perhaps most people can resolve letters subtending a smaller visual angle, and consequently the letters on some Snellen charts are designed to subtend an angle of only four minutes. Isn't the use of the latter charts potentially unfair?) As is well-known, the typical visual test is given at a distance of 6 meters, or 20 feet, because at this distance the light rays from the chart's letters are roughly parallel, and the perceiver does (or at least should) not have to expend effort on focusing. Now if a perceiver seated 6 meters from the chart reads the line of letters subtending a visual angle of five minutes at 6 meters, we say that his vision is 6/6 or, if in the traditional (foot-oriented) USA, 20/20. The numerator of the fraction indicates the distance at which the test is given, while the denominator denotes the distance at which the smallest letters read subtend a visual angle of five minutes.

Having recalled the basics of the test for visual acuity, let us now return to the suggested analogy between such testing and the testing for the reliability of a belief-producing mechanism. Presumably, the analogy must presuppose that 6/6 vision qualifies as "reliable vision" in some objective, truth-relevant sense of 'reliable.' For if the analogy is to succeed, in the defense of reliabilism, it must provide an instance of successful testing for such objective reliability. (To see why recall the characterization of the reliability requirement in Part 1 above.) But the foregoing considerations suggest that the analogy will not fill the order. For, as noted, testing for visual acuity relies on a standard of "normal vision" determined by reference to how the "typical eye" (leniently construed) actually operates in characterizing the Snellen letters. The standard set by the subtending of a visual angle of five minutes is due, at bottom, to what is (liberally speaking) visually typical among the community of visual perceivers. Since the typical perceiver, broadly speaking, sees clearly, or at least would see clearly, (*i.e.*, without blurring, fuzziness or duplication) three bars of an inverted 'E', for instance, when he is standing 6 meters from the Snellen chart, such visual experience is taken as the standard for "normal vision." But, of course, this is not to say that such vision is optimal, truth-producing, or objectively reliable in any relevant sense. For the relevant notion of normal vision is based loosely on an assumed statistical average, and not on considerations purporting to indicate reliability in a relevant truth-producing sense. Consequently, upon inspection, the suggested analogy between visual-acuity testing and testing for reliable belief-producing mechanisms breaks down.

The main problem here, of course, is that the reliabilist needs more than the sort of standard central to visual-acuity testing: an assumed statistical normalcy, broadly construed. What the reliabilist needs is a non-circular means of linking justified beliefs to reliable belief-producing mechanisms, which generally produce true beliefs (in the relevant circumstances). But at present there evidently is no way to identify true beliefs apart from assumed justified beliefs and perhaps corresponding justification-conferring rules. Consequently, it appears that the reliabilist, in attempting to draw the needed empirical connection, is faced with a serious form of circularity. If this is so, the reliability requirement central to reliabilism has neither a conceptual basis (given Part 1 above) nor an empirical basis (given the upshot of the present section).

4. RELIABILISM AND EXTERNALISM

For the most part I have been arguing against the central necessary condition for justified belief set by epistemic reliabilism. But now I want to argue against a sufficient condition of epistemic justification typically proposed by reliabilists. This sufficient condition is objectionable, I shall argue, because it commits one to a version of *epistemic externalism*, the view that a person does not have to *possess* any evidence to be justified in believing a proposition.

For purposes of illustration, let us consider the following justificatory schema:

(1)   If a belief, *B*, is produced by a reliable belief-producing mechanism, *M*, under appropriate conditions, *C*, then *B* is likely to be true.

(2)   S's belief that p is produced by M under C.

(3)   Hence, S's belief that p is likely to be true.

The externalist of a reliabilist persuasion typically holds that for S's belief that p to be epistemically justified, the conditions 1 and 2 need only obtain; S need not have any sort of cognitive possession of 1 and 2. Thus, the truth of 1 and 2, according to such an externalist, can be quite external to anything S is aware of, has been aware of, or has had access to. In this sense externalism permits that S's belief that p is justified, while S possesses no evidence whatsoever for that belief. Such externalism is endorsed by virtually all reliabilists, including those mentioned above in note 1 (with the possible exception of Swain).

But I submit that the present sort of externalism is incompatible with the primary sense of 'justified belief.' For purposes of contrast, let us recall in this connection Jaakko Hintikka's widely discussed characterization of the primary sense of *knowledge*. According to Hintikka, 'S knows that p' "implies that the person in question is in a position to defend a statement to the effect that he knows that p is the case."[9] Hintikka goes on to argue, as is well-known, that "in the primary sense of *know*, if one knows, one *ipso facto* knows that one knows" (p. 28). Such is Hintikka's notorious "KK thesis." Now one might propose that analogues of Hintikka's claims hold for epistemically justified belief. The relevant analogues would be: (i) 'S is justified in believing that p' implies that S is in a position to defend the claim that he is justified in believing that p is the case, and (ii) S is justified in believing that p only if S is justified in believing that he is justified in believing that p. Analogue (ii) is an explicit statement of what may be called the "JJ thesis."

The main problem with analogues (i) and (ii) is twofold. First, they commit us to holding that one is epistemically justified in holding a belief only if one has the concept of epistemic justification. For one will be in a position to defend a claim about justified belief, and one will have a justified belief concerning a justified belief, only if one has the concept of justified belief. Thus, the present requirement precludes justified belief on the part of all those lacking the concept of epistemically justified belief. Such a requirement, needless to say, is excessively stringent. Second, analogue (ii) will commit us to an endless regress of required justified beliefs. For if one is justified in believing some proposition, p_1, only if one is justified in believing another proposition of a higher epistemic order, p_2, (concerning the epistemic status of p_1), the present general requirement will also apply to the belief that p_2, and thus demand justified belief in a further proposition, p_3, of a still higher epistemic order. And a similar requirement applies to the belief that p_3, as well as to each member of the ensuing endless regress of required justified beliefs. Obviously, the threatening sort of regress is sufficiently complex to make it highly doubtful that some such regress always accompanies justified belief. Further, once such a regress is begun, it would be perfectly arbitrary to terminate it at one level rather than another. Thus, any alternative to externalism which generates such a regress will be ultimately unacceptable. (Incidentally, the well-known objections to epistemic externalism set forth by Laurence Bonjour, as noted above in Chapter IV, evidently rest on an alternative which generates such endless regresses of required justified beliefs; to that extent, at least, Bonjour's alternative is unsatisfactory.[10])

The primary sense of 'justified belief' which I have in mind does not commit us to any infinite regress of required justified beliefs. According to this sense, a person, S, is justified *in holding* a belief that p only if S is *capable* of calling to attention evidence which in fact justifies *the proposition* that p (by making that proposition more likely to be true than its available contrary competitors).[11] But, clearly, S's being thus capable does not entail that S is justified in believing that he is justified in believing that p. For the latter, higher order justified belief entails that S believes that he is justified in believing that p, but the forementioned capability clearly does not. Also, that higher order justified belief requires that S have the concept of justified belief, but the capability in question does not. S's being capable of calling to attention evidence, e, which justifies the proposition that p minimally requires that S have, or have had, some sort of awareness of e, for instance, a belief with respect to e that it obtains (in the case of non-propositional evidence) or is true (in the case of propositional evidence). But S need not therefore be justified in believing that e justifies p. Thus, the present characterization of the primary sense of justified belief does not entail the controversial "JJ thesis."

My basic contention is that epistemic externalism goes awry in allowing situations where S is justified in believing that p at a time, t, on the basis of evidence, e, even though S is completely unaware at t, and has never been aware before t, of e. For in allowing such situations, externalism permits cases where S is justified in believing that p at *t*, even though S is *in*capable of calling to attention evidence which justifies the proposition that *p*. This incapability is due of course to the fact that S is, by hypothesis, completely unaware at *t*, and has never been aware before *t*, of the relevant evidence justifying the proposition that *p*. By failing to provide for the needed capability, epistemic externalism falls short of capturing the primary sense of 'justified belief.' In fact, given its denial, by implication, of the relevant capability condition, externalism turns out to be incompatible with that sense.

Of course some users of the English language do sometimes use the terms 'justified belief' and 'knowledge' with an externalist sense, where the appropriate capability condition is not satisfied. But it appears that such use is just a loose and derivative *façon de parler*, rather like our familiar talk of the vacationing five-month-old child's *knowing* that she is not in her own crib. The motivation for such talk is perhaps due to the fact that in the derivative cases full-fledged knowledge or justified belief would be present *if only* the quasi-knower were to meet certain obviously unfulfilled conditions (such as the forementioned capability condition). At any rate, significant support for my claim about the primary sense of 'justified belief' comes from the intrinsic oddness of one's claiming 'I am justified in believing that *p*, but I am incapable of calling to attention any evidence which justifies the proposition that *p*.'

My diagnosis of the central defect of epistemic externalism is actually quite straightforward. Externalism, as I see it, gives inadequate attention to the distinction between what is justifiedly believed (or known) relative to the (first-person) position of a given epistemic agent, S, and what is justifiedly believed (or known) relative to the (third-person) position of the epistemologist theorizing about S's epistemic situation. Since the theorizing epistemologist is typically well aware of the evidence which can be called to attention in favor of S's perceptual beliefs, for instance, he (the epistemologist) is typically justified in believing the perceptual propositions believed by S. Further, given his awareness of the relevant justifying evidence, it is dangerously easy for the epistemologist to assume automatically that *S himself* is also justified in holding his perceptual beliefs. But such an automatic assumption leads to the basic mistake of externalism. For such an assumption leads to the neglect of the fact that S's evidential situation might lack a crucial feature of the epistemologist's evidential situation relative to the perceptual propositions believed by S. Specifically, such an assumption gives inadequate consideration to the fact that S, unlike the theorizing epistemologist, might be incapable of calling to attention evidence which justifies the perceptual propositions he believes. Given the present diagnosis, we can provide a fairly plausible explanation of the failure of epistemic externalism to capture the primary sense of 'justified belief.'

However, it is commonly suggested by proponents of externalism that their critics confuse either levels of justification (*i.e.*, one's being justified in believing that one is justified in believing that *p*), or the *having* of justified belief with the *showing* of justified belief.[12] I have already spoken to the charge of a level-confusion; it seems quite clear that my objection to externalism, based on the primary sense of 'justified belief,' does not trade on any such level-confusion. Similarly, it seems clear that my objection does not assume that one's having justified belief that *p* requires one's showing that the belief that *p* is justified. The objection assumes only, in light of the primary sense of 'justified belief,' that one's being justified in believing that *p* requires one's being *capable* of calling to attention evidence which justifies the proposition that *p*. (For if S lacks such a capability, it will be only a derivative and loose sense, if any, in which *S's belief* that *p* is justified.) The present objection to externalism, consequently, safely escapes the snares into which many alternatives to externalism have fallen.

5. CONCLUSION

In conclusion, then, the lesson of the above arguments is basically twofold. First, epistemic reliabilism, as defined earlier, fails to state an acceptable conceptual connection between epistemically justified belief and reliable belief-producing mechanisms. Also, if that connection is purported to be empirical rather than conceptual, reliabilism falls prey to a vicious form of circularity. Second, the short of externalism typically conjoined with reliabilism is ultimately unacceptable, insofar as it fails to accommodate a certain evidence-adducing capability required by the primary sense of 'justified belief.' However, the present failure is not peculiar to externalist versions of reliabilism, but is germane to all versions of epistemic externalism. Given this twofold lesson, our concluding moral is that we should look for superior alternatives to epistemic externalism and reliabilism, alternatives which avoid the problems raised above. I hope the position of this book is one such alternative.

NOTES

1 Goldman, 'What is Justified Belief?', in G. S. Pappas (ed.), *Justification and Knowledge* (D. Reidel, Dordrecht, 1979), p. 10; cf. Goldman, 'The Internalist Conception of Justification', in P. French *et al.* (eds.), *Midwest Studies in Philosophy, Vol. V: Studies in Epistemology* (University of Minnesota Press, Minneapolis, 1980), p. 47. Like-minded philosophers are legion. Here is a partial list: W. P. Alston, 'Self-Warrant: A Neglected Form of Privileged Access', *American Philosophical Quarterly* **13** (1976), 268−70; *idem*, 'The Epistemic Status of Epistemic Principles', (forthcoming), section 1; John Heil, 'Foundationalism and Epistemic Rationality', *Philosophical Studies* **42** (1982), 182; *idem*, 'Reliability and Epistemic Merit', *Australasian Journal of Philosophy* **62** (1984), 327−38; Hilary Kornblith, 'Beyond Foundationalism and the Coherence Theory', *Journal of Philosophy* **77** (1980), 608−12; G. S. Pappas, 'Non-Inferential Knowledge', *Philosophia* **12** (1982), 81−98; F. Schmitt, 'Justification as Reliable Indication or Reliable Process', *Philosophical Studies* **40** (1981), 409−17; *idem*, 'Reliability, Objectivity, and the Background of Justification', *Australasian Journal of Philosophy* **62** (1984), 1−15; and Marshall Swain, *Reasons and Knowledge* (Cornell University Press, Ithaca, 1981), Chapter 4; *idem*, 'Justification, Reasons, and Reliability', *Synthese* **64** (1985), 69−92. The views of Swain and Alston are discussed above in Chapter IV. For some comments on Pappas' reliabilism see my paper 'Knowledge Without Evidence', *Philosophia* **15** (1985).
2 Such a requirement is clearly endorsed by the papers by Alston and Goldman cited in Note 1; and some such requirement is at least implicit in the other papers cited above.
3 The present reference to beliefs which "would generally be true in normal circumstances" is intended to guarantee reliability in the relevant counterfactual situations. On the motivation for this intention, see Kornblith, 'Beyond Foundationalism and the Coherence Theory', *Journal of Philosophy* **77** (1980), 609−10.
4 Recall, in this connection, the observation of Chapter II above that we cannot plausibly construe the deceiver hypothesis as entailing that *all* our perceptual beliefs, for instance, are false. See page 58 on this issue.
5 Goldman, 'What is Justified Belief?', in *Justification and Knowledge*, p. 18. Cf. Heil, 'Reliability and Epistemic Merit', *Australasian Journal of Philosophy* **62** (1984), 337−38.
6 Firth, 'Epistemic Merit, Intrinsic and Instrumental', *Proceedings and Addresses of the American Philosophical Association* **55** (1981), 18−19.
7 Heil, 'Reliability and Epistemic Merit', *Australasian Journal of Philosophy* **62** (1984), 336.
8 Perhaps it would be polite here to remind certain readers of the use of red herring to distract hunting dogs from the pursued scent.
9 Hintikka, *Knowledge and Belief* (Cornell University Press, Ithaca, 1962), p. 21.
10 For Bonjour's objections see Bonjour, 'Can Empirical Knowledge Have a Foundation?', *American Philosophical Quarterly* **15** (1978), 5−7; *idem*, 'Externalist Theories of Empirical Knowledge', in *Midwest Studies in Philosophy, Vol. V: Studies in Epistemology*, p. 55.
11 Here I am presupposing the earlier-mentioned distinction between *doxastic* and *propositional* justification. For a characterization of the distinction see page 3 above, and Firth, 'Are Epistemic Concepts Reducible to Ethical Concepts?', in A. I. Goldman and J. Kim (eds.), *Values and Morals* (D. Reidel, Dordrecht, 1978), pp. 217−18. Below I point out some significant support for my present claim about the primary sense of 'justified belief'.
12 See, for instance, Alston, 'What's Wrong With Immediate Knowledge?', *Synthese* **55** (1983), 73−95; and Heil, 'Foundationalism and Epistemic Rationality', *Philosophical Studies* **42** (1982), 181, 184−85.

SELECT BIBLIOGRAPHY

JUSTIFICATION AND PROBABILITY

Carnap, Rudolf, 'Inductive Logic and Rational Decisions', in R. Carnap and R. C. Jeffrey (eds.), *Studies in Inductive Logic and Probability* (University of California Press, Berkeley, 1971), pp. 5—32.

Hanen, Marsha, 'Confirmation, Explanation, and Acceptance', in Keith Lehrer (ed.), *Analysis and Metaphysics: Essays in Honor of R. M. Chisholm* (D. Reidel, Dordrecht, 1975), pp. 93—128.

Harman, Gilbert, 'Induction', in Marshall Swain (ed.), *Induction, Acceptance, and Rational Belief* (D. Reidel, Dordrecht, 1970), pp. 83—99.

Hilpinen, Risto, 'Rules of Acceptance and Inductive Logic', *Acta Philosophica Fennica* **22** (1968), 3—134.

Jeffrey, Richard, *The Logic of Decision*, 2d ed. (University of Chicago, Chicago, 1983).

Kaplan, Mark, 'A Bayesian Theory of Rational Acceptance', *Journal of Philosophy* **78** (1981), 305—330.

————, 'Rational Acceptance', *Philosophical Studies* **40** (1981), 129—145.

Kyburg, Henry, 'Conjunctivitis', in M. Swain (ed.), *Induction, Acceptance,˙ and Rational Belief* (D. Reidel, Dordrecht, 1970), pp. 55—82.

————, *Epistemology and Inference* (University of Minnesota Press, Minneapolis, 1983).

————, *Probability and Inductive Logic* (Macmillan, New York, 1970).

————, *Probability and the Logic of Rational Belief* (Wesleyan University Press, Middletown, Connecticut, 1961).

Lehrer, Keith, 'Coherence and the Racehorse Paradox', in P. French *et al.* (eds.), *Midwest Studies in Philosophy, Vol. V: Studies in Epistemology* (University of Minnesota Press, Minneapolis, 1980), pp. 183—192.

Pappas, George, 'Lehrer on Evidence, Induction, and Acceptance', in R. J. Bogdan (ed.), *Keith Lehrer* (D. Reidel, Dordrecht, 1981), pp. 129—163.

Pollock, John, 'Epistemology and Probability', *Synthese* **55** (1983), 231—252.

Swinburne, Richard G., *An Introduction to Confirmation Theory* (Methuen & Co., Ltd., London, 1973).

————, 'Probability, Credibility, and Acceptability', *American Philosophical Quarterly* **9** (1971), 275—283.

EPISTEMIC CONTEXTUALISM

Annis, David, 'A Contextualist Theory of Epistemic Justification', *American Philosophical Quarterly* **15** (1978), 213—219.

251

Brown, Harold, *Perception, Theory, and Commitment: The New Philosophy of Science* (University of Chicago Press, Chicago, 1977).

Kuhn, Thomas, 'Objectivity, Value Judgment, and Theory Choice', in Kuhn, *The Essential Tension* (University of Chicago Press, Chicago, 1977), pp. 320–329.

———, 'Reflections on My Critics', in I. Lakatos and A. Musgrave (eds.), *Criticism and the Growth of Knowledge* (Cambridge University Press, Cambridge, 1970), pp. 231–278.

———, *The Structure of Scientific Revolutions, 2d ed.* (University of Chicago Press, Chicago, 1970).

Laudan, Larry, *Progress and Its Problems: Towards a Theory of Scientific Growth* (University of California Press, Berkeley, 1977).

———, 'Two Dogmas of Methodology', *Philosophy of Science* **43** (1976), 585–597.

Morawetz, Thomas, *Wittgenstein and Knowledge* (University of Massachusetts Press, Amherst, 1978).

Rorty, Richard, *Philosophy and the Mirror of Nature* (Princeton University Press, Princeton, 1979).

Shiner, Roger, 'Wittgenstein and the Foundations of Knowledge', *Proceedings of the Aristotelian Society* **78** (1977–78), 102–124.

Siegel, Harvey, 'Justification, Discovery, and the Naturalizing of Epistemology', *Philosophy of Science* **47** (1980), 297–321.

Toulmin, Stephen, *Human Understanding, Vol. I: The Collective Use and Evolution of Concepts* (Princeton University Press, Princeton, 1972).

Williams, Michael, 'Coherence, Justification, and Truth', *Review of Metaphysics* **34** (1980), 243–272.

———, *Groundless Belief* (Basil Blackwell, Oxford, 1977).

Wittgenstein, Ludwig, *On Certainty*, G. E. M. Anscombe and G. H. von Wright (eds.) (Basil Blackwell, Oxford, 1969).

———, *Philosophical Investigations* (Basil Blackwell, Oxford, 1953).

EPISTEMIC COHERENTISM

Blanshard, Brand, *The Nature of Thought*, 2 vols. (Allen & Unwin, London, 1939).

Bonjour, Laurence, 'The Coherence Theory of Empirical Knowledge', *Philosophical Studies* **30** (1976), 281–312.

Firth, Roderick, 'Coherence, Certainty, and Epistemic Priority', *Journal of Philosophy* **61** (1964), 545–557.

Harman, Gilbert, *Thought* (Princeton University Press, Princeton, 1973).

Lehrer, Keith, *Knowledge* (Clarendon Press, Oxford, 1974).

———, 'The Knowledge Cycle', *Noûs* **11** (1977), 17–26.

———, 'Self-Profile', in R. J. Bogdan (ed.), *Keith Lehrer* (D. Reidel, Dordrecht, 1981), pp. 3–104.

Pastin, Mark, 'Social and Anti-Social Justification: A Study of Lehrer's Epistemology', in *Keith Lehrer* (D. Reidel, Dordrecht, 1981), pp. 205–222.

Rescher, Nicholas, 'Blanshard and the Coherence Theory of Truth', in Paul Schilpp (ed.), *The Philosophy of Brand Blanshard* (Open Court, La Salle, Illinois, 1980), pp. 574–588.

————, *Cognitive Systematization* (Basil Blackwell, Oxford, 1979).

————, *The Coherence Theory of Truth* (Clarendon Press, Oxford, 1973).

Sellars, Wilfrid, 'Epistemic Principles', in H.-N. Castañeda (ed.), *Action, Knowledge, and Reality: Critical Studies in Honor of Wilfrid Sellars* (Bobbs-Merrill, Indianapolis, 1975), pp. 332—348.

————, 'Givenness and Explanatory Coherence', *Journal of Philosophy* **70** (1973), 612—624.

————, 'More on Givenness and Explanatory Coherence', in G. S. Pappas (ed.), *Justification and Knowledge* (D. Reidel, Dordrecht, 1979), pp. 169—181.

————, *Science, Perception, and Reality* (Routledge & Kegan Paul, London, 1963).

Tibbetts, Paul, 'The Weighted Coherence Theory of Rationality and Justification', *Philosophy of the Social Sciences* **10** (1980), 259—272.

EPISTEMIC FOUNDATIONALISM

Alston, William, 'Has Foundationalism Been Refuted?' *Philosophical Studies* **29** (1976), 287—305.

————, 'Self-Warrant: A Neglected Form of Privileged Access', *American Philosophical Quarterly* **13** (1976), 257—272.

————, 'Two Types of Foundationalism', *Journal of Philosophy* **73** (1976), 165—185.

————, 'Varieties of Privileged Access', *American Philosophical Quarterly* **8** (1971), 223—241.

————, 'What's Wrong With Immediate Knowledge?' *Synthese* **55** (1983), 73—96.

Annis, David, 'Epistemic Foundationalism', *Philosophical Studies* **31** (1977), 345—352.

Armstrong, David, *Belief, Truth, and Knowledge* (Cambridge University Press, Cambridge, 1973).

Bonjour, Laurence, 'Can Empirical Knowledge Have a Foundation?' *American Philosophical Quarterly* **15** (1978), 1—13.

————, 'Externalist Theories of Empirical Knowledge', in P. French *et al.* (eds.), *Midwest Studies in Philosophy, Vol. V: Studies in Epistemology* (University of Minnesota Press, Minneapolis, 1980), pp. 53—74.

Chisholm, Roderick, 'The Directly Evident', in G. S. Pappas (ed.), *Justification and Knowledge* (D. Reidel, Dordrecht, 1979), pp. 115—127.

————, 'On the Nature of Empirical Evidence', in G. S. Pappas and M. Swain (eds.), *Essays on Knowledge and Justification* (Cornell University Press, Ithaca, 1978), pp. 253—278.

————, *Theory of Knowledge, 1st ed.* (Prentice-Hall, Englewood Cliffs, New Jersey, 1966).

————, *Theory of Knowledge, 2d ed.* (Prentice-Hall, Englewood Cliffs, New Jersey, 1977).

————, 'Theory of Knowledge in America', in Chisholm, *The Foundations of Knowing* (University of Minnesota Press, Minneapolis, 1982), pp. 109—196.

————, 'A Version of Foundationalism', in Chisholm, *The Foundations of Knowing*, pp. 3—32.

Cornman, James, 'On the Certainty of Reports about What is Given', *Noûs* **12** (1978), 93—118.

——, 'On Justifying Non-Basic Statements by Basic-Reports', in G. S. Pappas (ed.), *Justification and Knowledge* (D. Reidel, Dordrecht, 1979), pp. 129—149.

——, *Skepticism, Justification, and Explanation* (D. Reidel, Dordrecht, 1980).

Goldman, Alan H., 'Appearing Statements and Epistemological Foundations', *Metaphilosophy* **10** (1979), 227—246.

——, 'Epistemic Foundationalism and the Replaceability of Ordinary Language', *Journal of Philosophy* **79** (1982), 136—154.

Heidelberger, Herbert, 'Chisholm's Epistemic Principles', *Noûs* **3** (1969), 73—82.

Lewis, C. I., *An Analysis of Knowledge and Valuation* (Open Court, La Salle, Illinois, 1946).

——, 'The Given Element in Empirical Knowledge', *Philosophical Review* **61** (1952), 168—175.

——, *Mind and the World Order* (Scribner's Sons, New York, 1929).

Meyers, Robert G., 'Sellars' Rejection of Foundations', *Philosophical Studies* **39** (1981), 61—78.

Moser, Paul K., 'A Defense of Epistemic Intuitionism', *Metaphilosophy* **15** (1984), 196—209.

Pastin, Mark, 'Lewis' Radical Foundationalism', *Noûs* **9** (1975), 407—420.

——, 'Modest Foundationalism and Self-Warrant', in Nicholas Rescher (ed.), *American Philosophical Quarterly Monograph Series, No. 9: Studies in Epistemology* (Basil Blackwell, Oxford, 1975), pp. 141—149.

Pollock, John, *Knowledge and Justification* (Princeton University Press, Princeton, 1974).

Quinton, Anthony, 'The Foundations of Knowledge', in Bernard Williams and Alan Montefiore (eds.), *British Analytical Philosophy* (Routledge & Kegan Paul, London, 1966), pp. 55—86.

——, *The Nature of Things* (Routledge & Kegan Paul, London, 1973).

Russell, Bertrand, *Human Knowledge: Its Scope and Limits* (Simon & Schuster, New York, 1948).

——, *An Inquiry into Meaning and Truth* (Norton, New York, 1940).

——, 'On Verification', *Proceedings of the Aristotelian Society* **38** (1937—38), 1—15.

Scheffler, Israel, *Science and Subjectivity* (Bobbs-Merrill, Indianapolis, 1967).

Sosa, Ernest, 'The Foundations of Foundationalism', *Noûs* **14** (1980), 547—564.

——, 'The Raft and the Pyramid: Coherence versus Foundations in the Theory of Knowledge', in P. French *et al.* (eds.), *Midwest Studies in Philosophy, Vol. V: Studies in Epistemology* (University of Minnesota Press, Minneapolis, 1980), pp. 3—25.

Van Cleve, James, 'Foundationalism, Epistemic Principles, and the Cartesian Circle', *Philosophical Review* **88** (1979), 55—91.

GENERAL WORKS

Alston, William, 'Concepts of Epistemic Justification', *The Monist* **68** (1985), 57—89.

——, 'Level-Confusions in Epistemology', in P. French *et al.* (eds.), *Midwest Studies in Philosophy, Vol. V: Studies in Epistemology* (University of Minnesota Press, Minneapolis, 1980), pp. 135—150.

————, 'Meta-Ethics and Meta-Epistemology', in A. I. Goldman and J. Kim (eds.), *Values and Morals: Essays in Honor of William Frankena, Charles Stevenson, and Richard Brandt* (D. Reidel, Dordrecht, 1978), pp. 275–297.

Aune, Bruce, 'Epistemic Justification', *Philosophical Studies* **40** (1981), 419–429.

————, *Knowledge, Mind, and Nature* (Random House, New York, 1967).

Butchvarov, Panayot, *The Concept of Knowledge* (Northwestern University Press, Evanston, Illinois, 1970).

Chisholm, Roderick, *Perceiving: A Philosophical Study* (Cornell University Press, Ithaca, 1957).

Cornman, James, 'Foundational versus Nonfoundational Theories of Empirical Justification', *American Philosophical Quarterly* **14** (1977), 287–297. Reprinted as Chapter 6 of Cornman, *Skepticism, Justification, and Explanation* (D. Reidel, Dordrecht, 1980).

————, *Perception, Common Sense, and Science* (Yale University Press, New Haven, 1975).

Dicker, Georges, *Perceptual Knowledge* (D. Reidel, Dordrecht, 1980).

Ginet, Carl, *Knowledge, Perception, and Memory* (D. Reidel, Dordrecht, 1975).

Goldman, Alvin I., 'The Internalist Conception of Justification', in P. French *et al.* (eds.), *Midwest Studies in Philosophy, Vol. V: Studies in Epistemology* (University of Minnesota Press, Minneapolis, 1980), pp. 27–51.

————, 'What is Justified Belief?', in G. S. Pappas (ed.), *Justification and Knowledge* (D. Reidel, Dordrecht, 1979), pp. 1–23.

Klein, Peter, *Certainty: A Refutation of Scepticism* (University of Minnesota Press, Minneapolis, 1981).

Levi, Isaac, *Gambling with Truth* (MIT Press, Cambridge, 1967).

Oakley, I. T., 'An Argument for Scepticism Concerning Justified Belief', *American Philosophical Quarterly* **13** (1976), 221–228.

Pollock, John, 'A Plethora of Epistemological Theories', in G. S. Pappas (ed.), *Justification and Knowledge* (D. Reidel, Dordrecht, 1979), pp. 93–113.

————, 'Reliability and Justified Belief', *Canadian Journal of Philosophy* **14** (1984), 103–114.

Shope, Robert, *The Analysis of Knowing* (Princeton University Press, Princeton, 1983).

Swain, Marshall, *Reasons and Knowledge* (Cornell University Press, Ithaca, 1981).

Thagard, Paul, 'The Best Explanation: Criteria for Theory Choice', *Journal of Philosophy* **75** (1978), 76–92.

INDEX OF NAMES

(excluding Appendix and Bibliography)

257

INDEX OF SUBJECTS

PALLAS PAPERBACKS